99

.P. SAUCE

Published by in association with

Pedigree Books Limited, The Old Rectory, Matford Lane, Exeter, Devon EX2 4PS
books@pedigreegroup.co.uk

YOURS is a monthly magazine for the young at heart. Look out for it in your local newsagent.
YOURS, Bushfield House, Orton Centre, Peterborough PE2 5UW. Tel: 01733 237 111

Compiled by Helen Henry, designed by Sharon Reid and David Reid.
Heart-felt thanks to all the readers who contributed to this annual
by sending in their letters, tips, stories, recipes and photos.

With thanks to all who helped to compile this annual: •Flower of the Month: Words by Geoff Stebbings • Flower of the Month: Photos by Geoff Stebbings (P7, P35, P63, P90, P105, P133) and Emap Gardening Picture Library (P23, P49, P79, P119, P149, P163) • Short story illustrations (P18, P44, P74, P100, P128, P158) by Antonia Enthoven • A Charitable Cause illustration (P32) by Alan Hunt • Illustration for Horoscopes, Health Check, Recipe Corner, This Week In Your Garden: Jill Sheppard • This Week Through The Years: Words by Maya Isaaks (who also contributed to Health Check) • Housewife's Choice: Words and photos by Robert Opie • Additional photos: Topham (Elvis Presley, P7; Elizabeth Taylor, P23; Brigitte Bardot, P118), Hulton Archive (Michael Caine and Joan Crawford, P34; Doris Day and Gregory Peck, P49; Audrey Hepburn, P63; Tony Curtis and Judy Garland, P78; Roger Moore, P133; Grace Kelly and Richard Burton, P148; Ava Gardner, P162), Mirror Syndication (Nelson Mandela and Diana, Princess of Wales, P90)

Hello!

The warmest of welcomes to a brand new year – and a brand new book from YOURS to keep you company over the next 12 months.

We are sure that this first edition of A Year With YOURS will bring interest, amusement and comfort to your daily life, whatever the season (we've built in a touch of humour to see you through even the gloomiest of days).

May the fondness and friendship that went into making this book be multiplied many times in your daily life as the year unfolds, and may the calendar pages be filled with lots of pleasurable events and happy anniversaries.

We are sure this book will bring the warm pleasure of happy days rediscovered and give useful tips and advice to help you enjoy the whole year to the full.

Do have a wonderful Year with YOURS!

Very best wishes,

Neil

Neil Patrick
Editor-in-chief

£5.99

January 2002

MONDAY	TUESDAY	WEDNESDAY	THURSDAY
	1 New Year's Day	2 Bank Holiday (Scotland)	3
7	8	9	10
14	15	16	17
21	22	23	24
28	29	30 February YOURS on sale	31

RIDAY	SATURDAY	SUNDAY
	5	*6* Epiphany
	12	*13*
	19	*20*
	26	*27*

Flower of the month
WITCH HAZELS
(Hamamelis)

Just as the first cuppa in the morning is the best of the day, the spidery flowers of witch hazels *(Hamamelis)* are especially welcome because they are among the first flowers of the year. Making snowdrops look like slouches in comparison, they are undamaged by frost and can brave the harshest weather – their yellow, orange or reddish spidery blooms cower in the bitter cold but open as soon as the temperatures rise. This singles them out from other winter blossoms, such as viburnums and honeysuckles, which are browned by frost but open more buds as the weather warms.

Witch hazels not only provide a feast for the eyes, their flowers exude a sweet, spicy perfume that scents the January air.

Their habit is elegance itself, most growing into a wide, spreading bush, and the foliage that appears, only when the flowers have dropped their last petal, is broad and velvety when young, turning to fiery shades of yellow, gold and scarlet in autumn before falling.

Witch hazels, named after the North American *H. virginiana* that was used for water divining and looks like hazel, are slow-growing and need a sheltered site with moist soil. They are difficult to propagate, so costly to buy. But a sniff of that perfume on a sunny winter's day is enough to make you part with £20.

Born this month...
- Louis Braille *(4 January, 1809)*
- Rowan Atkinson *(6 January, 1955)*
- **Elvis Presley** *(8 January, 1935)*
- Faye Dunaway *(14 January, 1941)*
- Cary Grant *(18 January, 1904)*
- Michael Crawford *(19 January, 1942)*
- Benny Hill *(21 January, 1925)*
- Oprah Winfrey *(29 January, 1954)*
- Vanessa Redgrave *(30 January, 1937)*
- Jean Simmons *(31 January, 1929)*

THOUGHT FOR THE WEEK

He who breaks a resolution is a weakling; he who makes one is a fool.

F M Knowles

THIS WEEK IN YOUR GARDEN

The landscape may be bleak and bare, the days short and dark, but there are still gardening jobs to be done…

- Order summer-flowering bulbs and seeds from mail-order catalogues if you haven't already done so.
- Clean pots and seed trays with household bleach and hot water ready for spring.
- Lawn mowers and tools should be checked and sent for servicing.
- Plant new roses but stay off the soil if it's sticky. Start pruning bush and standard roses.

TIP TIME

Pictures from large calendars make pretty notelets if they are plain on the reverse side. Trim the picture, then fold over to form a notelet.
Mrs J Bagshaw, Heaton Moor, Stockport

FROM ME TO YOU

A year in verse
Marguerite Howarth, from Skipton in North Yorkshire writes:
"I wonder how many people recall this rhyme about the seasons. I have known this verse since I was a little girl and I'm now 92.

January brings the snow,
Makes our feet and fingers glow.
February brings the rain,
Thaws the frozen lakes again.
March brings breezes, loud and shrill,
Stills the dancing daffodil.
April brings the primrose sweet,
Scatters daisies at our feet.
May brings flocks of pretty lambs,
Skipping by their fleecy dams.
June brings tulips, lilies, roses,
Fills the children's hands with posies.
Hot July brings cooling showers,
Apricots and gilly flowers.
August brings the sheaves of corn,
Then the harvest home is borne.
Warm September brings the fruit,
Sportsmen then begin to shoot.
Fresh October brings the pheasant,
Then to gather nuts is pleasant.
Dull November brings the blast,
Then the leaves are falling fast.
Chill December brings the sleet,
Blazing fires and Christmas treat.

TIP TIME

To machine-wash a sunray pleated skirt, hold skirt lengthwise and pull three rubber bands over the skirt – top, middle and bottom. Wash as usual, remove bands and dry on a coat hanger. The skirt will retain its shape and pleats.
Gloria Knight, Fishermead, Milton Keynes

GO ON, SMILE!

Good morning to you, too!
One bitterly cold winter morning I met an elderly gentleman walking away from the town and carrying a bulging shopping bag. As he passed me, he politely raised his hat and said: "Good morning, Madam. Could you possibly tell me who it was who invented shopping? Whoever it was ought to be shot!"

With that, he replaced his hat and went on his way.
Mary Calcraft, Bexhill-on-Sea, East Sussex

FASCINATING PHOTOS

This snapshot of a local football team has special significance for Ruby Hickmott from Hailsham, East Sussex...

"Here's a picture of the South Suburban Gas Company football team, who were the winners of the Bromley and District Charity Cup in the season 1923-24.

"It was taken a year before I was born and it has a special meaning for me because both my father and future husband are pictured in it. The gentleman in the light suit is my father, and the little boy mascot is my husband.

"I went to many company sporting events and Christmas parties but it wasn't until 1945 that my husband and I met properly and then we got married in 1946."

HEALTH CHECK

Supplementary advice

It seems everyone is taking vitamin supplements these days. But do we really need them? The first thing to remember is that taking a vitamin supplement will not turn a poor diet into a healthy one. The best way to promote good health is to eat a balanced, varied diet. Having said that, there are times when taking a supplement might be beneficial. Because the body's ability to absorb calcium declines with age, many doctors recommend a calcium supplement as a protection against osteoporosis. Also, if you are sick, recuperating from an illness or have found that your appetite has decreased with the advancing years, then taking a daily multi-vitamin supplement will give your nutrition levels a top-up.

RECIPE CORNER

Fragrant Potato and Red Onion Soup

After the excesses of Christmas, it's good to get back to more simple pleasures. And what could be more satisfying than a bowl of steaming soup to keep out winter chills?
Serves 4-6

2 red onions, peeled, halved and thinly sliced
2 tablespoons olive oil
1 lb/455 g potatoes peeled and sliced
1 celery stalk, trimmed and sliced
Sprigs of herbs such as parsley, basil, tarragon, coriander and rosemary
2 pints/1.15 litres vegetable stock
3-4 spring onions, trimmed and chopped
Salt
Black pepper

1 In a large pan, sweat the onions in the olive oil. Add the potatoes and celery.
2 Strip the herb leaves and set aside. Tie the stalks together and add to the pan along with the stock and spring onions. Bring to the boil and simmer until the celery and potatoes are soft.
3 Chop enough herb leaves to give 2-3 tablespoonfuls, then stir half of them into the soup. Pureé the soup and return to the pan. Bring back to the boil, add the remaining herbs and season to taste.

THIS WEEK THROUGH THE YEARS

- **1 January, 1951** Radio drama The Archers was broadcast to the whole of the UK for the first time.
- **1 January, 1960** Cliff Richard's hit single Living Doll entered the pop charts for the third time.
- **1 January, 1973** Britain became a member of the EEC.
- **4 January, 1967** Donald Campbell, the British water-speed hero, was killed on Lake Coniston while attempting to break his own world record.

THOUGHT FOR THE WEEK

Live for today as yesterday is already a dream and tomorrow is only a vision. But today well-lived makes every yesterday a new dream of happiness and every tomorrow a vision of hope.

Gladys Kell, Cleckheaton, West Yorkshire

THIS WEEK IN YOUR GARDEN

If weather permits, don your warmest clothes and go out into your garden, even it it's just for an hour...

- Dig out annual and perennial weeds; chickweed and groundsel continue to seed even in winter.
- Plant sweet peas in peat-free compost and keep at room temperature. Once they have germinated put them outside in a cold frame but watch out for frost.
- Clean greenhouse panes to let in as much light as possible.
- Shake or knock heavy snow off shrubs and conifers before the weight breaks the branches.

TIP TIME
To clean a furred kettle: use a mixture of equal parts salt and vinegar mixed with warm water. Pour into an empty kettle and leave overnight. Drain and wash thoroughly before use.
Gloria Knight, Milton Keynes, Bucks

FASCINATING PHOTOS

Mary Reed from Nottingham is fascinated by this photo of her late mother and her workmates, who were involved in 'top secret' war work...

"This is a favourite photograph of my mother with her workmates. My mother, whose name was Edith Lavington (later Martinson) is sitting at the front on the left. She worked for Fosters Engineering in Lincoln during the First World War. The girls were on secret war work. They were told they were 'making water tanks for Afghanistan'. The truth was revealed when the first 'tank' was finished. Photos of all the staff were taken with it, and they were also given a bumpy ride through the streets of Lincoln to the testing fields.

"I always like to think of my gentle mother in her early teens, helping to make these huge machines that would play such an important part in the war effort. She had small white burn marks on her neck for the rest of her life from particles of hot metal from her lathe."

GO ON, SMILE!

Flower power

I went into a fruit shop to pay for some flowers and as the assistant handed them to me, she said: "There you are, flower." We both had a good laugh at that.

Mrs T Hall, North Anston, Sheffield

FROM ME TO YOU

Fun in the sun

I raised my hands in horror when my son announced: "Mother, for your birthday, we are taking you to Spain." I was flabbergasted. Leave my house, my dogs and my hens in the middle of winter?

My son said: "Shiver in the snow in Scotland or bask in the sunshine in Spain? It's up to you, Mother."

At my age chances don't come twice so I quickly packed my case and, once up in the air, the thought of frozen pipes, livestock missing me or attempted burglaries faded to the back of my mind. The picture shows my Spanish birthday dinner. Six days of great weather before returning to Scotland and the snow.

I will start making arrangements now for next winter, in the hope I will be asked again.

Isabella Morrison, Willisdale, Linlithgow

TIP TIME
When I get letters I cut my address off the envelope and add my phone number. I keep these in my coat pocket, handbag and glasses case so they can be returned if I lose them.
Edith Abraham, Pennington, Hants

HEALTH CHECK

A bone to pick

Osteoporosis affects one in three women. In a nutshell, this is when the bones become porous and brittle, fracturing easily. Causes include a lack of the hormone oestrogen after menopause, and immobility, which weakens the bones. To help protect yourself, eat a diet rich in calcium, found in dairy products, green leafy vegetables and fish – sardines and pilchards especially. Weight-bearing exercises such as swimming and walking are also beneficial. You might also want to ask your doctor about hormone replacement therapy (HRT). **Call the National Osteoporosis Society helpline on 01761 472 721 for more help and advice.**

THIS WEEK THROUGH THE YEARS

- **7 January, 1925** Gerald Durrell, conservationist and writer, was born.
- **10 January, 1929** Belgian cartoonist Hergé introduced his new cartoon character, a boy detective called Tintin.
- **10 January, 1985** Sir Clive Sinclair brought out the C5, a battery-powered tricycle designed to be the answer to traffic problems in Britain.
- **11 January, 1974** The TV series Happy Days was first shown in the US. It starred Henry Winkler as the Fonz and became a big hit on both sides of the Atlantic.

RECIPE CORNER

Real hot chocolate with marshmallows

Once you've tried the real thing, you'll never use the powdered hot chocolate again! This recipe is perfect central heating for a chilly winter's night. Makes 2 big mugs or 4 cups.

3 oz/75 g good-quality chocolate (dark or milk)
4 fl oz/110 ml single cream
1 pint (600 ml) milk
4 marshmallows (optional)

1 Break the chocolate into pieces and place it in a saucepan with the cream. Gently heat it until all the chocolate has melted.

2 In a separate pan, heat the milk until boiling, then pour it on to the melted chocolate. Stir to combine and pour into mugs or cups. Float a marshmallow or two on top and stand back to enjoy the fireworks.

THOUGHT FOR THE WEEK

My neighbour says he has found the three-word answer to a happy marriage: "I'm going out!"

C Joseph, Lelant, Cornwall

THIS WEEK IN YOUR GARDEN

The temperature is still low and a really cold snap will help clear the garden of any prevailing pests…

- Protect fruit buds, particularly plums, gooseberries and pears, from attack by birds. Bullfinches can be responsible for much of the damage.
- Continue to harvest vegetables. It's thought a frost on Brussels sprouts, leeks and parsnips improves their flavour.
- Make sure bird-feeders are regularly refilled and there is clean (unfrozen) water for birds to drink.
- Plant potatoes in frames and pots.
- Prune wisteria now to encourage winter flowering. Shorten the sideshoots back to 2-3 buds.

TIP TIME

Hang an old envelope next to your wall calendar to put appointment cards in for the coming month.
Margaret Gott, Ripon, North Yorkshire

FASCINATING PHOTOS

Amy Price from Hay-On-Wye in Herefordshire, remembers working in the telephone exchange…

"In 1960 my husband had an accident and was unable to work, so I had to find a job in order to look after our three small children.

"I managed to find employment in Hay-On-Wye's telephone exchange and, after six gruelling weeks of training, I was ready to start on the telephones. Every call had to be recorded on a ticket, with the destination and the times the call started and ended.

"During the day the telephone exchange was very busy and needed three operators and a supervisor. I opted to do night duty, which meant I could sleep between phone calls in the flat upstairs. When a call came in I was wakened by a buzzer and had to run down two flights of stairs to answer the call. I didn't even have time to put on a dressing gown. Then I had to sit shivering until the call ended to 'unplug'.

"Despite everything, I loved my job and was very sad when the manual exchange went over to automatic and we were all made redundant."

THIS WEEK THROUGH THE YEARS

- **15 January, 1992** Slovenia and Croatia, having declared independence from Yugoslavia, both won recognition from the European Community.
- **17 January, 1995** Thousands of people died after a massive earthquake hit the port of Kobe in western Japan.
- **19 January, 1937** 18-year-old ballerina Margot Fonteyn made her debut in Giselle at Saddler's Wells theatre in London.
- **19 January, 1966** Indira Ghandi became the new prime minister of India following the death of her father, Lal Bahadur Shastri, from a heart attack.

HEALTH CHECK

Feeling SAD?
Many people are affected by SAD (Seasonal Affective Disorder), where they feel lethargic, sleepy and depressed and generally out of sorts during the winter months. This is thought to be because sufferers are sensitive to the reduction in natural light during this time of the year. There are several ways to help:

- Use a light box (which emits a high intensity of light) for one to two hours each day. The bright light stimulates your hormones and can relieve the symptoms.
- Try to get out even if it's not sunny – you'll feel better for the fresh air.
- Keep active – regular exercise increases your sense of wellbeing.
- Contact **The SAD Association at PO Box 989, Steyning, BN44 3HG** or visit its website at **www.sada.org.uk** for more information.

GO ON, SMILE!
**No thanks,
Suddenly I'm not hungry**
I was walking with a friend past a pub advertising 'three-coarse bar meals'.

"I'd heard the food was rough in there, but that's ridiculous!" he said.
*Mr F Butler,
Glazebury, Warrington*

FROM ME TO YOU
Has anyone else noticed that the more sophisticated children's playtime becomes, the earlier they mature. Computers are used from such an early age and the types of games we played when we were young never seem to hold their attention for long.

Board games are just a bore to them, a game of hide and seek is looked at with scorn and a second-hand bike is never good enough when high-tech scooters are the 'in' machines.

Sadly, children today lose their childhood so quickly and with it a lot of fun has gone, too. Our young days were so carefree and we were much more satisfied with basic toys. And, as far as I can tell, we grew up pretty intelligently.
*Sylvia Monk,
Attleborough, Norfolk*

RECIPE CORNER
Drunken Beef
A hearty casserole with a satisfyingly rich and glossy sauce. Serves 4-6.

1 tablespoon olive oil
2 lb/900 g chuck steak, cut into 2 in/5 cm squares
8-10 shallots, peeled
1 tablespoon plain flour
15 fl oz/425 ml light ale
12 button mushrooms
1 sprig fresh thyme or
1/2 teaspoon dried thyme
1 bay leaf
1 clove garlic, crushed
Salt and pepper

1 Preheat oven to 140°C/275°F/gas mark 1. Heat oil in flameproof casserole and brown meat in batches. Remove to a plate and keep warm. Add shallots and toss on a high heat until browned. Return the meat to the casserole.

2 Turn the heat down, add the flour and cook, stirring constantly, to 'cook off' the flour. Gradually stir in the light ale, and add the button mushrooms, thyme, bay leaf and garlic. Season. Bring to the simmer, cover and transfer to the middle shelf of the oven for 2 1/2 hours.

January 21-27

My favourite saying is: "Worry is rust upon the brain".

Dorothy McCrory, London

THIS WEEK IN YOUR GARDEN

Take advantage of the occasional mild days…

- Continue to plant dormant, deciduous shrubs and hedges.
- Check that spring biennials, such as wallflowers, sweet williams and polyanthus haven't lifted during the cold weather.
- Finish laying manure and compost mulches on flower borders as soon as possible. The job becomes more difficult once spring growth pushes through.
- Clean moss and algae from slippery paths, using a stiff brush and paving cleaner.
- If your lawn is squelchy underfoot, aerate it with a garden fork to improve its drainage.

HEALTH CHECK

Cope with pain – naturally

If you bump your head, you instinctively rub it to ease the pain – with good reason. Research has shown that rubbing is a natural pain reliever, and this is why massage is so effective at easing daily aches and pains. It works by stimulating touch receptors in your skin to send impulses to your brain that intercept pain information, so blocking the pain.

If you have backache, this can be relieved by massage, but it's important to go to a qualified practitioner, as the wrong massage strokes can make matters worse.

FROM ME TO YOU

Age accident

A friend of mine was most upset when she was involved in a road accident. It wasn't so much the damage to her car that caused her so much distress, as the fact that her age was published in the local newspaper report for all to see.

Barbara Butler, Warrington, Cheshire

GO ON, SMILE!

While I was out shopping with a portly friend, she plucked a packet from the shelf, saying it was 90 per cent fat-free. "That means it's 10 per cent pure fat," I reasoned. She stared at me for a moment and then put the packet into her trolley. "In that case," she assured me, "I'll only eat 90 per cent of it."

Mr T Parr, Windsor, Berkshire

TIP TIME

To clean artificial flowers, put a good handful of salt into a paper carrier bag. Holding the flowers upside down by their stems, place the flower head in the bag. Tighten the bag around the stems and shake several times. They'll come up as good as new.

Peggy Owen, Gwynedd

THIS WEEK THROUGH THE YEARS

- **21 January, 1924** Soviet leader Lenin, 'father of the Russian Revolution', died aged 54, seven years after he led the Bolshevik party in the coup that marked the beginning of communism in Russia.
- **26 January, 1972** Yugoslavian air hostess Vesna Vulovic, survived a fall from 33,330 feet when the aeroplane in which she was travelling blew up.
- **26 January, 1988** Australia celebrated its bicentenary, the 200th anniversary of the arrival of the first British settlers to the continent.
- **27 January, 1926** Television was first introduced at the Royal Society by Scottish inventor John Logie Baird.

TIP TIME

When freezing cooked vegetables, rice or pasta, pour a little cooking oil over and mix to coat each piece. This makes it easier to take out a small portion when required.

Mrs E Walmsley, Thornton-Cleveleys

FASCINATING PHOTOS

May Oldrey from Harold Hill, Essex, remembers the day when her Uncle Bill met actor Michael Rennie…

"Here's a picture of my Uncle Bill, aged 14, after a boxing tournament at Barking Baths in 1950.

"Because he had won his match, Uncle Bill got to meet Michael Rennie and he was also given a solid silver cup, which he still treasures to this day.

"Uncle Bill often used to box for the Dagenham and District Boxing Club and I remember all the fighters used to wear green shorts with a red flash on the side and white singlets.

"My grandfather, Richard Smith, is the one wearing glasses and standing next to Uncle Bill. I was just ten at the time but I was very proud that Uncle Bill had won and got to meet Michael Rennie."

TIP TIME
Cut the tops off clear plastic fizzy drinks bottles. Put them over seedlings to protect them from frost.
Mrs Y Jackson, Thirsk, North Yorkshire

RECIPE CORNER

Fruity Pork Casserole
Pop this in the oven and leave to cook slowly while you get on with other things. The result is wonderfully tender meat, sweetened by apricots and prunes. Serves 3-4

2 tablespoons sunflower oil
1 onion, finely chopped
1½ lb/700 g shoulder of pork trimmed and cut into
1½ in/3.5 cm cubes
1 oz/25 g plain flour
½ pint/275 ml chicken stock
2 tablespoons white wine vinegar
2 tablespoons clear honey
1 tablespoons soy sauce
Salt and pepper
4 oz/110 g large mushrooms, quartered
2 oz/50 g each ready-to-eat stoned prunes and apricots
Chopped parsley to garnish

1 Preheat the oven to 170°C/325°F/gas mark 3. Heat oil in a flameproof casserole and fry onion until tender. Add the pork in batches and cook for 5 minutes or until golden brown. Return all the meat to the casserole, sprinkle with flour and cook for 1 minute, stirring constantly. Stir in the chicken stock, white wine vinegar, honey and soy sauce. Season and bring to the boil.
2 Cover and cook in oven for 2 hours. Add the mushrooms, prunes and apricots and cook for a further 1 hour or until the pork is tender. Check seasoning and garnish with parsley.

January 28-February 3

THOUGHT FOR THE WEEK

M Cunliffe from Farsley, Pudsey, likes these words of wisdom:
It's not getting what you want that makes you happy, but wanting what you've got.

THIS WEEK IN YOUR GARDEN

February can be an unpredictable month, with rain, gales and snow – so keep a close watch on the weather…

● Protect vulnerable plants from sudden cold spells by covering them with horticultural fleece.

● Keep a close watch on seedlings as they emerge – they need all the light they can get.

● Cut back dead stems of herbaceous perennials to ground level.

● Check your gardening supplies. Stock up on pots, compost, twine, labels and non-fade pens.

● Plant up window-boxes and pots with spring bulbs and primulas.

TIP TIME
Cake lovers on a diet should replace the cream filling in a sponge cake with thick yoghurt.
Mrs B Franklin, Lawford, Essex

FASCINATING PHOTOS

Mrs K Dunford from Redcar in Cleveland, shares her memories of her sister's hospital stay in the '30s…
"My sister, Muriel, had hip problems as a child and spent almost three years in the Children's Orthopaedic Hospital in Kirbymoorside.

"Here she is pictured at the age of seven. Her bed is the one nearest the camera and, as you can see, she was a very shy child.

"She was only allowed visitors on the first Saturday of each month. My parents had to take it in turns to visit, as times were very hard and there were five other children to take care of.

"Mother saved sixpence a week to pay her fare and dad used his bicycle to travel the many miles from our small village of Yearby. Muriel left the hospital the day after her ninth birthday and our whole village turned out to welcome her back home."

HEALTH CHECK
Diabetes
Insulin is a hormone, produced by the pancreas, which stimulates cells to absorb and store sugar. When your pancreas does not produce enough insulin, too much sugar is left in the bloodstream, causing diabetes – which can give rise to lots of health problems. Symptoms include: Passing large quantities of urine, excessive thirst and fatigue. As food affects blood sugar and insulin, it is a major factor in both triggering and controlling diabetes.

The best way to combat diabetes with food is to eat a high-carbohydrate (50-60 per cent of your daily calories), high-fibre, low-fat (less than 30 per cent of your daily calories) diet. Good sources of high-fibre carbohydrate are wholegrain bread, pasta, rice, peas and beans. Fish is also recommended, as are plenty of fresh fruits and vegetables.

THIS WEEK THROUGH THE YEARS
● **28 January, 1986** The space shuttle Challenger exploded immediately after take-off, killing all seven astronauts on board.
● **29 January, 1942** Desert Island Discs was first broadcast on Radio 4.
● **1 February, 1973** Women were allowed on the Stock Exchange floor for the first time.
● **3 February, 1942** Maximum clothes prices were laid down by the Government – a suit was not allowed to cost more than £4 18s 8d (£4.93).

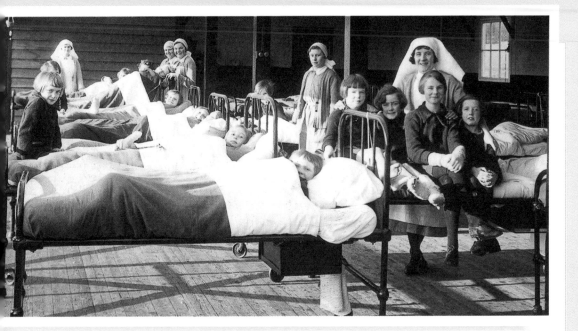

Go on, smile!

My mum and dad were Londoners and knew nothing about the country. When they got married and moved into their first home in 1920, dad brought a rabbit back from the butchers. Coming in from work, he expected a fine stew, but couldn't understand why he couldn't smell cooking. My mum said: "I'm sorry dear – I've spent all morning plucking it and it's still not finished."

Mrs O Wiseman, Kings Langley, Hertfordshire

Recipe corner

Creamy Sausage Pasta
The herbs in Lincolnshire sausages work well in this substantial pasta dish, but you can use your own choice of sausage. Serves 2.

12 oz/350 g pasta shapes
Salt and pepper
6 Lincolnshire sausages
2 tablespoons olive oil
1 onion, finely chopped
1 garlic clove, crushed
14 oz/400 g can chopped tomatoes
1 teaspoon dried oregano
1 tablespoon fresh basil, chopped
1 teaspoon Dijon mustard
1 tablespoon red or green pesto
2 tablespoons crème fraîche

1 Cook pasta in large pan of salted, boiling water for 10-12 minutes, until just tender. Drain and return to pan.
2 While the pasta cooks, grill sausages until cooked and well browned all over. Cut into thick slices. Heat oil in pan and fry onion and garlic for 5 minutes. Add tomatoes with their liquid, the sausage, oregano and basil. Stir in the mustard. Cover, reduce the heat and simmer for 10 minutes. When the sauce has thickened, stir in the pesto and crème fraîche.
3 Stir the sauce into the drained pasta and serve immediately.

Tip time

If you have a faulty zip on your trousers, cover each half with a piece of Velcro and you'll have a perfect repair in a matter of minutes.
Mrs E Wooster, Birchington, Kent

From me to you

Dinner's ready
For the first meal I ever cooked as a newlywed I set the kitchen table with my best gingham cloth and lit the candles, then served up a roasted duck and waited for my husband's reaction. With a scratch of his head he said: "Lovely dear, but who's going to eat the beak?"
Freda Miller, Enfield, Middlesex

THAT OLD THING!

By Jill Butcher

"That old thing!" reacted Susie. "I wouldn't want that old thing."

The words were like daggers in Linda's heart. She'd put a lot of thought into making the offer. The 'old thing' to which her daughter was referring was the very first item that she and Brian had bought for their marital home.

They had been young then, with stars in their eyes and hope in their hearts but not very much money in their pockets. They had responded to a postcard in the window of the sub post office down the road. That was in the days when there were sub post offices down almost every road.

"Dining table and four chairs," the postcard had said. Thirty shillings or nearest offer was the price that had been suggested. Brian had knocked the old lady down to twenty-five shillings and paid her by cheque. It had taken them two journeys to walk the purchases the three-quarters of a mile up the hill, over the zebra crossing and round the corner to the basement flat that had become their love-nest. On the first journey they had carried the table, Brian walking backwards, Linda forwards, directing him past lamp-posts and post-boxes and stopping every hundred yards or so to rest.

"It's a good, solid table," she protested to Susie. That's what she'd said to Brian each time she paused to get her breath back ready for the next leg of the journey. And so it had been, heavy too – it still was. "It was good enough for your Dad and me."

The second journey had been for the four chairs. They'd balanced them in pairs, one upside down and one the right way up, and had carried a pair each. This time, when they stopped to rest, they each split the pair and put the chairs down on the pavement, so they could sit down and put their feet up. They'd got a few funny looks and some even funnier remarks from passers-by but they didn't care. They were in love and they wanted the whole world to know.

The table was finished in a dark, ugly varnish that was peeling in places. "I'll paint it," Linda had said. Those were the heady days of psychedelia, when yellow submarines and blue daffodils were everyday experiences.

What Linda hadn't realised was that, however creative your ideas, you need a good foundation. It never occurred to her to rub down the old varnish with sandpaper, to prepare the surface with primer and put on two layers of undercoat with a quality paintbrush. A year later, when the green rabbits and the pink mushrooms she had painted were peeling off she had no idea what had gone wrong.

The marriage wasn't going too well either. They had discovered that living together had involved rather more than nights of romantic passion. There were blocked sinks and dirty socks and bank statements to deal with too.

But Brian got another job and they moved upmarket to a flat with a balcony, a lounge-diner and a fitted kitchen.

"That old thing! We don't want that old thing," said Brian when they were loading the table into the self-drive removal van.

"It'll do for a while," said Linda.

This time she was older and wiser. She'd learned you had to work at the things that mattered to you. As had Brian. They'd learned to compromise, to take less for granted and to listen to each other.

The postcard read, 'Dining table and four chairs: Thirty shillings or nearest offer'

This time Linda did the job properly. Paint stripper, sandpaper and woodfiller. Beneath the peeling paint she rediscovered the peeling varnish, but beneath was the natural pattern of a light oak veneer. It took days of sanding and stripping to get the varnish off the spiral carved legs. Then, after she had finished, she gave the whole thing a coat of varnish. It looked beautiful.

They were in love and they wanted the whole world to know

Brian got another promotion and Linda became pregnant. The next move was to a detached house and the table was demoted to the kitchen while the dining room was honoured with a mahogany dining suite with eight chairs and matching side-board.

"That old thing!" said Linda's mother when she saw the table. "It doesn't go." The cupboards were pine. "You can't put oak with pine," she said.

'I can!' said Linda.

The table had two leaves you could draw out, and, at a push, you could get 12 children around it. It served for the next ten years' worth of children's birthday parties.

Linda went back to work and decided that the time had come to treat herself to a new kitchen. She decided on light oak doors, with matching panels for the fridge and dishwasher. When the kitchen designer measured up he looked

rather doubtfully at the old table. "Are you keeping that?" he asked doubtfully. He was too polite to say 'That old thing!' but Linda knew he was thinking it.

"It's oak," said Linda defensively. "It should fit in very well."

"You're the boss," he shrugged.

The new kitchen was a dream and Linda treated the table to some more rubbing down and new coat of varnish, She felt sad that Mum wasn't around to see it any more. That was just about the time when Susie and her boyfriend were going through a phase of making popcorn. They put the oven on as high as it would go, put the corn in a pan and heated it until it exploded – the corn, not the pan! That would have been fine if they hadn't put the red-hot pan on the kitchen table. The heat burned through the varnish, to leave a blackened ring burned deeply into the wood.

"I'm sorry, Mum," said Susie when Linda's explosion matched that of the popcorn.

"Honestly, we didn't mean to do it," added the boyfriend, sheepishly.

Linda was in floods of tears as she tried to sand down the burn. "That old thing," said Brian, putting a comforting hand on her shoulder. "Lucky it wasn't the new work surface. It's only an old table."

"No, it's not," she sobbed. It was much more.

She got out most of the burn, filled the dent with woodfiller, and re-varnished the top. After a couple of years she stopped noticing the mark.

And now Brian was settling down to his retirement while Susie was settling down to married life. Setting up home, planning for the future. So many changes, thought Linda.

It was Brian who suggested they give Susie the table. "We never meant it to last a lifetime," he said. "We don't need it just for the two of us. We could have a breakfast bar fitted."

"I suppose so," said Linda sadly. It did make sense. And it would fit well in Susie's home. So she offered. "It's a good, solid table," she said.

Susie curled her lip in distaste: "That old thing! It's only fit for the dump," was her response.

Linda smiled with relief at the rejection. She couldn't expect Susie to understand. She couldn't expect anyone to understand. She ran a hand over the battered surface that had survived as many ups and downs as a good solid marriage.

"Maybe I'll give the old thing another coat of varnish," she said.

IT'S IN THE STARS

Patrick Arundell looks to the heavens to predict what's in store for you this month

CAPRICORN (22 December – 20 January)
You are the most stoic zodiac sign. Your steadfastness and sense of humour can be relied upon, even in the most testing of situations. Money matters will benefit from a more imaginative approach this month.

AQUARIUS (21 January – 19 February)
Your energy levels will be low, but in the second half of the month you'll come back to life.

PISCES (20 February – 20 March)
After a lively start, you may want to spend time quietly. Avoid those who grate on you.

ARIES (21 March – 20 April)
Children – even grandchildren – might need your support but you're pleased to help.

TAURUS (21 April – 21 May)
A hobby, or charitable pursuit, could be the source of pleasure for Taureans this month.

GEMINI (22 May – 21 June)
Your New Year's resolution might have centred on travel or learning. Now is the time to explore pastures new.

CANCER (22 June – 23 July)
Lucky Jupiter continues in your own sign. Combine your Cancerian ingenuity and imagination and you can't fail.

LEO (24 July – 23 August)
An acquaintance with whom you've never had anything in common could be a good companion. Don't pre-judge people or you could miss out.

VIRGO (24 August – 23 September)
Your attention to detail helps you to identify unique ways to reorganise your life. A New Year health regime can work wonders, too.

LIBRA (24 September – 23 October)
Life's pleasure zone is brightly lit. Your busy social life and new creative pursuits will benefit.

SCORPIO (24 October – 22 November)
Interaction with neighbours and close family members is emphasised, so enjoy being sociable.

SAGITTARIUS (23 November – 21 December)
Enjoying the good things in life may be important but mental stimulation is also needed.

HOUSEWIFE'S CHOICE

Robert Opie takes a nostalgic peek at shopping-basket bygones

FORCE TOASTED WHEAT FLAKES

Force Toasted Wheat Flakes were introduced to America in 1901 and the following year they came to Britain, the first breakfast cereal to be imported. The character initially used to promote Force was Miss Prim, but she was quickly replaced by Sunny Jim, who from 1903 used the ditty: 'High o'er the fence leaps Sunny Jim, Force is the food that raises him!' Ever since there have been many ways that Sunny Jim promoted Force. A rag doll has been the most popular, but also jigsaw puzzles, masks and painting booklets. In the 1930s a booklet of Force recipes suggested such delights as Force Cheese pie and Force Potato Rissoles.

CAMP COFFEE

Since 1849, R Paterson & Sons of Glasgow had preserved pickles and chutney. In 1885 they produced a liquid coffee essence for use by the Gordon Highlanders who were serving in India at the time. It was called Camp Coffee and the label showed a Gordon Highlander drinking a cup of coffee while his Indian servant stood by with a tray (in 1957 this label was altered and the tray was removed). During the 1930s, Camp dominated the liquid coffee market with a 50 per cent share even though there were many other brands such as Symingtons, Chivers, Ivel, Brooke Bond, Shieldhall and Lyons.

Cryptic crosswords and tea-time teasers to keep your brain busy

Alphabet ends

Every word in this puzzle ENDS in a different letter of the alphabet, and the letter next to each clue refers to the LAST letter of the answer. You must decide where the answers fit, but the final letters A and Z have been fitted in to give you a start. Numbers in brackets indicate letters in each word.

A is a biscuit of almond flavour (7)
B means at leisure, spontaneously
   to savour (2-3)
C is something with plenty of spring (7)
D shapes a jelly fit for a king! (5)
E is a taste, which might be free (6)
F is to snub reprovingly (6)
G is a pet upon one's knee (6)
H is afloat, perhaps at sea (5)
I is a spicy sausage meat (6)
J is an Indian prince elite (3)
K is for writing on a blackboard (5)
L describes land which faces
   seaward (7)
M is simply an empty space (6)
N helps climbers grip safely in place (7)
O is to cap, or better perform (5)
P is striped and stings in a swarm! (4)
Q is a measure of one's brain-power
   (1,1)
R means coming at a future hour (5)
S are old instruments with strings (5)
T is to scurry, with speed of wings (5)
U means lost in France, it can (5)
V is an East European man (4)
W comes from the vegetable bed (6)
X is a tribe that Sitting Bull led (5)

Y is the state of events which are rare (11)
Z is the hat on Tommy Cooper's hair! (3)

Splashing out

Mrs North, Mrs Bouquet and Mrs Church each treated themselves on a different day last week between Wednesday and Friday. One of the three, whose name is Shirley, told the others it was the most fun she'd had for ages. From the clues given, can you identify the three? What form did their treat take and on which day did they enjoy it?

Clues

1   It was Mrs Bouquet who treated herself to a meal in an expensive restaurant.
2   Judy enjoyed her treat the day after the woman who bought a new dress.
3   It was on Wednesday that one friend treated herself to an expensive new hairdo.
4   Mae is not Mrs Church, who treated herself earlier in the week.

First name	Surname	Treat	Day

For solutions turn to Page 161

February 2002

MONDAY	TUESDAY	WEDNESDAY	THURSDAY
4	5	6 Queen Elizabeth II's Golden Jubilee	7
11	12 Shrove Tuesday	13 Ash Wednesday	14 St Valentine's Day
18	19	20	21
25	26	27	28 March YOURS on sale

IDAY	SATURDAY	SUNDAY
	2	3
	9	10
g ceremony, Winter Games lt Lake City	16	17
	23	24

Flower of the month
MIMOSA
(Acacia dealbata)

Tasmania is most famous for a ferocious cartoon animal, but it has had a considerable effect on our gardens, too. Being one of the coldest parts of Australasia, its plants have a good chance of being hardy in the UK and one of its eucalyptus, *E. gunii*, has proved to be the most enduring species in our gardens, whether as a large tree with beautiful bark or as a silvery bush.

Garden centres are chock-a-block with tree ferns, another Tasmanian import, though one that may have less of an impact in the long term. But the most beautiful and romantic of Tasmanian shrubs must be the mimosa *(Acacia dealbata)*.

A fast-growing tree with finely divided foliage covered with tiny scales to give a silvery sheen, it can reach 100ft (30m) in the wild, and has reached 70ft (22m) in this country. It is evergreen and is loved for its flowers of mounds of tiny, yellow pompons, as soft as down and with a beautiful, flowery perfume. It blooms as early as February in mild gardens and into March. Unfortunately, this beautiful tree is not reliably hardy. In five years a young specimen will become a superb sight in spring so it is worth the risk, especially if you live by the coast. If your garden is cold, try it in a pot. Its main requirement is sun; it will grow in any soil except those over chalk.

Born this month...

- Clark Gable *(1 February, 1901)*
- David Jason *(2 February, 1940)*
- Ronald Reagan *(6 February, 1911)*
- Zsa Zsa Gabor *(6 February, 1919)*
- Charles Dickens *(7 February, 1812)*
- Lana Turner *(8 February, 1921)*
- Charles Darwin *(12 February, 1809)*
- John Travolta *(18 February, 1954)*
- Cindy Crawford *(20 February, 1966)*
- **Elizabeth Taylor** *(27 February, 1932)*

February 4-10

THOUGHT FOR THE WEEK

Everybody talks about the weather, but nobody does anything about it.

Charles Dudley Warner (1829-1900) American writer

THIS WEEK IN YOUR GARDEN

This month the sap begins to rise; snowdrops and crocuses start to push through to remind you that spring is just round the corner...

- Prune winter-flowering shrubs (including winter heathers) and late summer-flowering clematis. Stems made last year should be cut back to within one or two joints of the older wood.
- Put out slug-bait to prevent damage to early-flowering herbaceous plants.
- Tuberous begonias, gloxinias and achimenes can be started off in the greenhouse or warm windowsill.

FROM ME TO YOU

Wonderful weather

We all spend our time moaning about the British weather – in fact it is a primary source of conversation. We constantly talk about the snow, wind, mist, fog and let's not forget all the wonderful rain, especially in Scotland.

But do we ever stop to think that our friends living in the sunshine spots would love a shower of rain and many have never seen snow or ice? How they would enjoy such diversity, particularly if their climate was too hot to enjoy doing anything. Maybe, though, a good moan does us all good, even if it doesn't improve our wonderful weather!

Gretchen King, Huddersfield, West Yorkshire

FASCINATING PHOTOS

John Stavordale, from Stockpot in Cheshire, reminisces about the golden days at the Palace in Blackpool...

"I wonder if any readers can remember the Palace cinema/variety theatre/ballroom in Blackpool. It fell to the bulldozers many moons ago but in its heyday, it was a magical place. When I was a young lad in the late '30s, I can recall being taken to the pictures there and then going up the stairs to the magnificent Palace Ballroom, where Will Hurst and his Syncopators would be playing for the multitude of dancers. This was a special occasion as my father, Kenneth Stavordale, was a member of the orchestra. To me the Palace was a wonderland. I can remember the sunken lights in the dance floor which were illuminated when the main lights were dimmed – it was truly magical.

"The photograph shows the palace orchestra with my father in the middle playing the banjo. It was taken in 1927. In those days, people came from all over to visit the Palace. For the price of a ticket to the pictures, you could catch a couple of acts at the varieties and then finish off the evening with a quick turn around the dance floor."

GO ON, SMILE!

Hitting a brick wall

When my nephew, Joshua, was little, he came home from school to find his father demolishing the outside wall of the kitchen (to build an extension). Joshua asked: "Did you forget your key, Daddy?"

Jan Savage, Colchester, Essex

> ### TIP TIME
> In the garden or greenhouse, place yoghurt pots on top of canes to prevent nasty eye injuries when you bend down.
> *Jean Bradley, Rugby*

HEALTH CHECK

Eat to beat arthritis

When YOURS magazine cookery writer Marguerite Patten developed arthritis, she turned to her own knowledge of food and nutrition to beat the debilitating condition.

"Arthritis makes you feel as if you're locked in a prison," she explains. "It bars you from living the life you want to lead."

Marguerite experimented with many 'cures' such as acupuncture but in the end she was faced with the prospect of surgery. Preferring not to go down that road, she developed her special diet.

"The results have been outstanding," she claims. The regime involves 'detoxifying' the body by eliminating from the diet certain foods which can cause joint pain and swelling, such as processed foods, sugar, citrus foods, tomatoes,

aubergines and red meat. Then slowly over the following weeks, 'problem' foods are reintroduced to identify which ones have an adverse effect on the arthritis.

Find out more from: Eat to Beat Arthritis by Marguerite Patten and Jeanette Ewin (Thorsons, £14.99)

RECIPE CORNER
Roasted Tomato, Red Pepper and Lentil Soup
Roasting the tomatoes gives this soup a real flavour boost.

1 red pepper
20 ripe tomatoes, chopped
1 red onion, peeled and sliced
2 cloves garlic, peeled and crushed (optional)
2 tablespoons sugar
Handful basil leaves (optional)
3 fl oz/75 ml olive oil
3oz/75 g green or brown lentils
3½ pints/2 litres stock or water
1 bay leaf
3 tablespoons tomato purée

1   Preheat grill to 'high'. Cut the pepper in half, place on a baking tray (cut side down) and grill until skin blackens. When cool, remove skin and roughly chop flesh. Preheat the oven to 200°C/400°F/gas mark 6
2   Place the chopped pepper, tomatoes, onions, garlic and sugar in a roasting tin. Add basil leaves and drizzle with oil. Roast for 45 minutes until the tomatoes are very soft.
3   Meanwhile, place the lentils in a large pan with the stock/water and bay leaf. Boil for 45 minutes till tender.
4   Add the roaseted tomato and onion mix, purée and seasoning (to taste) to the lentils and heat through.

THIS WEEK THROUGH THE YEARS
- **4 February, 1975** Margaret Thatcher became the first woman leader of a British political party, beating four male rivals to succeed Edward Heath as leader of the Conservatives.
- **6 February, 1921** Charlie Chaplin's first feature film, The Kid, opened in the US. The film also featured five-year-old child actor Jackie Coogan.
- **6 February, 1925** The original film version of Ben Hur, starring Roman Navarro, was released.
- **6 February, 1981** Jayne Torvill and Christopher Dean won the European ice dancing title for Britain – the first time in 12 years – with their innovative free dance performance.

THOUGHT FOR THE WEEK

Let no one who loves be called altogether unhappy. Even love unreturned has its rainbow.

J M Barrie (1860-1937)
Scottish novelist and dramatist

HEALTH CHECK

Are heart attacks catching?
Scientists think they have discovered that a common bacteria might cause heart attacks. Research headed by consultant cardiologist Dr Sandeep Gupta, of St Bartholomew's Hospital in London, suggests the bacteria could be spread by a simple cough or sneeze. The resulting infection causes plaques to form, which block arteries, leading to heart attack. Currently, 20,000 people worldwide are in clinical trials to see if antibiotics could treat it. "We're close to an answer," says Dr Gupta.

THIS WEEK IN YOUR GARDEN

The occasional sunny day may mean you want to get on with jobs such as seed sowing but don't be in too much of a hurry – there can still be bad weather to come...

- Cut back overgrown shrubs and hedges before the nesting season begins.
- Complete winter pruning of apple and pear trees.
- Force spring bulbs for early colour, indoors and out.
- Re-shape conifers after frost and snow damage.
- Remove lawn weeds by digging out with an old knife, or use a weedkiller if the weather is mild and dry.

GO ON, SMILE!

Music maestro!
One of the men at our afternoon club said that his grandfather played the piano by ear. Jim, who was a bit of a wag, replied: "That's nothing. Mine used to fiddle with his moustache!"

Name and address supplied

TIP TIME

In bad weather, place a dishcloth or towel over the outlets in the sink and bath – it'll prevent a draught coming up through them.
Miss P Allen, Luton, Beds

FROM ME TO YOU

Ode to the good life
Mrs L Baker, from Chislehurst in Kent, wrote this little ditty to celebrate how lucky she is:

Free bus pass
Free foot clinic
Free walking stick – from family
Free winter fuel cheque
Who wants to be young again?

THIS WEEK THROUGH THE YEARS

- **11 February, 1990** In South Africa, black leader Nelson Mandela was finally released from prison after 27 years, to huge celebrations worldwide.
- **12 February, 1993** British explorers Sir Ranulph Fiennes and Dr Michael Stroud completed the first unsupported crossing of the Antarctic ice shelf.
- **14 February, 1975** The creator of Jeeves and Wooster, PG Wodehouse, died, aged 93.
- **16 February, 1923** French fashion designer Coco Chanel, creator of Chanel perfume, decreed that even sweaters could be chic as part of her move towards a new freedom in women's clothes.

EXAMINE THE GIFTS

TIP TIME
Dried orange peel makes fantastic firelighters!
Mrs Y Jackson, Thirsk, North Yorkshire

FASCINATING PHOTOS

Dorothy Cloynes, from Knaresborough, West Yorkshire, remembers happy days serving behind the counter…

"This is a photo of me, when I was then Dorothy Machin, manning the Gift Shop, Market Street, Bolton, Lancashire in 1932. I am sure many readers will remember Perfection Soap and Pinkabolic Soap by Crosfields. It was one of the first companies to offer coupons on its products. I also gave pep talks on Persil, made by Lever Bros, which was just coming on to the market. They were happy days."

TIP TIME
Before slicing corned beef, place it in a polythene bag in your freezer for five minutes. You'll find it slices easily.
Mary Franks, Gedling, Nottingham

RECIPE CORNER

Pumpkin and Carrot Soup
Hearty and comforting, with just a hint of more exotic climes to see you through a chilly winter day! Serves 4.
2 tablespoons olive oil
1 onion, peeled and chopped
1 tablespoon brown sugar
2 cloves garlic, peeled and crushed
2 lb/900 g pumpkin, deseeded, peeled and chopped
$^1/_2$ lb/225 g carrots, peeled and diced

2 cups water
14 oz/400 g can coconut milk
1 red chilli (optional), deseeded and finely chopped
Salt and pepper
Handful chopped parsley

1 Heat oil in a large pan and cook onion with sugar and garlic until softened. Add all other ingredients, except parsley, cook until pumpkin is tender – about 20 minutes.
2 Mash ingredients and serve piping hot, sprinkled with chopped parsley.

27

THOUGHT FOR THE WEEK

We all know it's the early bird who catches the worm, but it's the second mouse that gets the cheese.

Doris Gibbs,
Barnstaple, Devon

THIS WEEK IN YOUR GARDEN

Even though buds are beginning to break and insects are stirring, food is still scarce for garden birds, so don't forget them...

- Put up bird boxes so they can get used to them before selecting which one to nest in.
- When snowdrops and aconites finish flowering, large clumps can be divided and planted.
- Test your soil for lime and dress if necessary – especially on vegetable plots.
- Begin forcing dahlia tubers and other tender perennials such as fuchsias, into early growth for cuttings.
- Turf can be laid on prepared ground provided it's not frozen or too wet.

TIP TIME

Rub soap along the inside of trouser and shirt creases before ironing – it will give your creases a sharper finish.
Thurza Blurton,
Orpington, Kent

FASCINATING PHOTOS

For Phyllis Barnes, from Addlestone in Surrey, this photograph brings back memories of the factory where she worked during the war...

"In the '40s, I worked in a factory called Eldart where we made darts for the troops. It was the only dart factory in Britain and our darts were sent all over the world.

"They were made with wooden shanks and lead bands and had four feathers to help them fly. You can see me on the left working on the table at the front of the photograph, packing the darts into boxes.

"The conditions in which we worked would never be allowed these days but we were very happy. All the workers were teenagers and we listened to the wireless as we worked. We also had visits from officers in the forces to give us talks on how important our work was for the morale of the men.

"As soon as the war ended, the market for our darts was frozen out by cheaper foreign dart manufacturers and so ended our teenage war effort."

TIP TIME

Wrap your notepaper and envelopes in a handkerchief and place into a lidded box along with a good sprinkling of pot pourri – you'll get fragrant stationery.
Emma White, Crook,
County Durham

HEALTH CHECK

Ease fluid retention
There are several things you can do to help ease the discomfort of fluid retention:
- Keep up your fluid intake, making sure you drink at least two and a half litres of water a day.

- Cut down on caffeine – coffee, tea, chocolate and cola – and have fruit and herbal teas or fruit juice instead.
- Eat lots of fresh fruits and vegetables, as they contain vitamins and minerals that will help your body get rid of the unwanted fluid.
- Keep your salt intake down – try using herbs and spices in cooking to give food extra flavour.
- Exercise regularly.

THIS WEEK THROUGH THE YEARS

- **18 February, 1930** A new planet was sighted in our solar system, which was named Pluto after the Greek god of the underworld.
- **19 February, 1985** The first episode of the soap opera EastEnders was screened on British TV.
- **23 February, 1997** Dolly the sheep made history when researchers in Scotland announced that she was the first clone to be made of an adult animal.
- **24 February, 1988** Italian tenor Luciano Pavarotti received 165 curtain calls after his performance in the opera L'Elisir d'Amore in Berlin.

RECIPE CORNER

Smoked Fish Cakes

The ultimate comfort food for a dreary February day. Serve with lots of ketchup! Enough for 4 people.

1 lb/450 g cooked potatoes, peeled and chopped into quarters
Salt and pepper
1 lb/450 g smoked haddock
½ pint/300 ml milk
1 bay leaf
8 black peppercorns
2 oz/60 g butter
Handful frozen peas, cooked
4 tablespoons chopped parsley

6 oz/175 g fresh breadcrumbs
1 egg, beaten
Oil for frying

1 Boil the potatoes in salted water until tender (about 20 minutes), then drain.
2 Meanwhile, place the fish in a pan with the milk, bay leaf and peppercorns. Bring to the boil slowly and simmer for 10 minutes.

Drain the fish and leave to cool, reserving the liquid. Remove the skin and bone and flake the flesh.

3 Place the potatoes in a large bowl. Add the butter and 3 tablespoons of the fish cooking liquid and mash until smooth. Add the flaked fish, peas and parsley and mix well. Season to taste.
4 Put the breadcrumbs in a shallow dish. Shape the fish and potato mixture into 8 flat cakes. Dip each fish cake into the beaten egg then coat with breadcrumbs. Fry in a little oil for 5 minutes on each side until golden brown.

FROM ME TO YOU

It's good to talk

Once I attempted to phone a friend in British Columbia, Canada, but dialled a wrong digit in the international code. Imagine my surprise when a young man answered from Penang, Malaysia. I said I had the wrong number but he was excited to be speaking to someone in England and kept me talking. He wanted to know all about me. When I got a word in I asked what the weather was like there. "Hot," he replied. As it was a cold February, I told him I'd love to feel sunshine. He said: "Please come, you would be welcome."

When we'd finished talking, I finally got through to my friend in and she roared with laughter when I told her what had happened.

Emily Soper, Gosport, Hampshire

GO ON, SMILE!

Bare necessities

I couldn't stop laughing when I saw this notice in a launderette: "Please remove all your clothes when the light goes out."

James McDonald, Croydon, Surrey

February 25-March 3

THOUGHT FOR THE WEEK

Do what is easy as if it were difficult, and what is difficult as if it were easy.

Baltasar Gracian (1601-58)
Spanish writer and
Jesuit priest

THIS WEEK IN YOUR GARDEN

The weather is still unpredictable, with sunshine one day and hard frost the next, but spring's on its way…

- Continue to prune bush and standard roses.
- Prepare seed beds for vegetables.
- If it's too cold to work outside, prick out or pot up seedlings in the greenhouse.
- This is a good time to sow some early vegetables for planting out under cloches next month.
- Make a small sowing of parsley in a warm, sheltered spot.
- Finish digging and start the breaking down of soil, if you haven't done so already.

TIP TIME
Tape your television licence to the side of the TV – you'll be able to find it instantly when required.
Daisy-Anne Borge,
Whitestone, Hereford

FROM ME TO YOU

Best-loved award

My friend, who is a well-known writer of children's stories, was delighted to be asked to judge the dolls' dressmaking competition at our church fete.

Then came the final entry – a battered wooden doll that had clearly seen better days. Her 'mama' was a little girl with anxious eyes who had obviously dressed her protégée with loving care.

"I award the final prize," my friend said firmly, "to the best-loved doll of all."

Miss S Betts, Kingsbury, London

THIS WEEK THROUGH THE YEARS

- **25 February, 1964** Boxer Cassius Clay (who later changed his name to Mohammed Ali) beat Sonny Liston to win the world heavyweight title.
- **27 February, 1900** The British Labour Party was founded, with Ramsay MacDonald as secretary.
- **27 February, 1935** Child star Shirley Temple was awarded an Oscar for her outstanding contribution to the movies.
- **28 February, 1983** The last episode of the comedy M*A*S*H was transmitted in the US and an estimated 125 million people tuned in to watch.

FASCINATING PHOTOS

Ellen Bonner from Sutton Coldfield in the West Midlands, remembers when Queen Mary paid a visit to her local church...

"This photograph was taken in 1930 in Barking Road, London. I am the girl on the left, behind the children waving flags. I was 16 at the time.

"The West Ham Central Mission had built a new church for adults and the old church was altered to accommodate young people and teenagers.

"Queen Mary came to open the new church. She wore a thick coat and a hat, as it was a chilly day. The lady standing next to the Queen is the minister's wife, Mrs Rowntree Clifford.

"There were hordes of people pressing to see the Queen. As I was very active in the church I had the honour of meeting her. I was thrilled and it is a memory I treasure to this day."

1 tablespoon French mustard
1 egg yolk
Salt and pepper
2 mackerel, cleaned, boned and heads removed
1 tablespoon flour

RECIPE CORNER

Stuffed Mackerel
A tangy mustard stuffing complements the flavour of this delicious oily fish. It only takes minutes to prepare. Serves 2.

½ onion, finely chopped
1½ oz/40 g butter
3 oz/75 g fresh breadcrumbs
1 tablespoon freshly
Chopped parsley
Grated rind and juice 1 lemon

1 Preheat oven to 190°C/375°F/gas mark 5. Cook onion in 1/3 butter until softened. Remove from heat and stir in breadcrumbs, parsley, lemon rind, mustard and egg yolk. Season.
2 Press mixture into cavity of the fish. Place on a baking tray and make deep cuts in the skin. Dust with flour, drizzle over lemon juice and dot with remaining butter. Bake in oven for 30 minutes, basting frequently.

HEALTH CHECK

Wise eyes
Did you know you can exercise your eyes, just like any other part of your body? Here's how...

● Hold a pen (or similar object) in front of you and focus on it. Without moving your head, move the pen slowly down as far as you can while keeping it in focus. Repeat the exercise, moving the pen as high as you can, then to the left and the right.

● Try Trayner exercise glasses. These look like ordinary sunglasses, but they have lots of pin-sized holes drilled in them. Wearing them for 15 minutes a day is said to exercise the eye muscles and help your eyes focus better on their own. You can find out more by calling freefone 0800 071 2020 or visiting the website at www.trayner.co.uk/info

GO ON, SMILE!

It never rains, it pours
While sheltering in a doorway from a heavy shower, a friend of mine put his hand out to see if it had stopped raining. An elderly lady who was passing by dug into her pocket and brought out a 50p piece, which she pressed into my friend's hand.
Mrs M Benn, Bedford

It's in the stars

Patrick Arundell looks to the heavens to predict what's in store for you this month

AQUARIUS (21 January – 19 February)
Loyal and kind, you're surrounded by staunch friends and, from the 14th, things really start to go your way. This boosts your confidence – and cash-flow!

PISCES (20 February – 20 March)
Low energy and a touch of despondency after the New Year celebrations will be swept away by the 19th.

ARIES (21 March – 20 April)
Friendships are highlighted, but watch out for fair weather friends later in the month.

TAURUS (21 April – 21 May)
A financial matter might cause an initial blip this month, so sort this out right away.

GEMINI (22 May – 21 June)
Even if you want to throw caution to the wind and do your own thing, responsibilities can mount as the month ends.

CANCER (22 June – 23 July)
You're feeling lucky this month, so a small flutter could pay off.

LEO (24 July – 23 August)
Relationships are in focus this month and you might need extra freedom. No one should doubt your wisdom on long-term finances.

VIRGO (24 August – 23 September)
If your obligations and responsibilities to others have stifled you in the past, this is the perfect time to assert your independence.

LIBRA (24 September – 23 October)
A playful, even artistic time continues until the last week of the month, when getting down to practicalities might be necessary.

SCORPIO (24 October – 22 November)
Initially you could feel restless, especially within the family. You need your own space but also the comfort of security.

SAGITTARIUS (23 November – 21 December)
An up-beat start with new skills, but personal issues emerge later that will occupy your time.

CAPRICORN (22 December – 20 January)
Although financial affairs continue to be blessed, expect delays until the second half of the month.

Housewife's choice

Robert Opie takes a nostalgic peek at shopping-basket bygones

Woodbine

During Queen Victoria's reign most men who smoked found a pipe the most economic, although the more affluent could afford to buy hand-made cigarettes or cigars. But it was the arrival of efficient mechanisation in the form of the Bonsack machine from the

WOODBINE - the great little cigarette

USA that made cheap cigarettes possible. Wills launched Wild Woodbine cigarettes in 1888 at the low cost of five for a penny. By 1893 more than 150 million Woodbine cigarettes were being sold annually, and they remained as Britain's leading cigarette until 1960.

Lifebuoy Toilet Soap

Lifebuoy Soap, 'for saving life and for preservation of health', was launched by Lever in 1894. This household soap contained carbolic for disinfectant properties – and a distinctive smell. At this time there was a growing awareness that many diseases were caused

"Good looks are not enough! I'm making sure of personal freshness with Lifebuoy Toilet Soap!"

by unsanitary conditions. Lifebuoy Toilet Soap was launched in Britain in 1933, although an earlier launch around 1905 had been unsuccessful. During the early 1930s a price war in toilet soap reduced the cost of a bar to 3d (it had been three times that only a few years earlier), thus many more people could afford to use soap. Lifebuoy advertising talked about personal freshness and later on body odour, referred to as BO.

A CHARITABLE CAUSE

'I thought you might find a use for this' are words that strike terror into Margaret Hollis's heart...

Some people are born targets. For most of my life I've been the object of other people's mistaken benevolence with a talent for making them feel I need their unwanted possessions. Do I have a car boot or garage sale aura about me?

We started our married life with a table that sloped at one end, passed on from a friend. We were glad of it on an income of £5 a week, but it was disconcerting to field my food every few moments as it accelerated towards my lap.

After our children were born an elderly neighbour arrived with a tarnished three-tiered metal cake-stand and a frayed tablecloth.

"I was going to send these to the jumble sale," she said, "but I'm sure you can use them."

The crunch usually comes when friends are moving house – not the close friends who know you don't need 60 back numbers of Farmers Weekly – but acquaintances who see you as an amiable and needy alternative to a skip.

One of the more useless presents we were given was an electric blanket that didn't work. The giver started to say: "I'm sure you can…" then tailed off. Unfortunately, she left the blanket.

A bag of ladies' hats arrived when I was eight months' pregnant and moving like a crippled tank. The hats – which resembled old felt tea cosies – came in dusty maroon, dark green and

I've been trying to find an outlet for a 5kg tin of chick peas for years

sinister black and smelled of mothballs. Not the height of fashion, so I spent half the week's housekeeping money on a new one.

And what do you say to: "I thought you'd like 'this' for the baby but I'm not sure it's safe"?

'This' proved to be the most unstable-looking high chair I'd seen – a tiny, red plastic seat with long, tubular chrome legs, like an overgrown spider.

We all have the urge to offload surplus belongings occasionally. I've been trying to find an outlet for a 5kg tin of chick peas for years. It's when people moving house give you cups without saucers that you realise their desperation.

One neighbour gave us an ancient, very earthy duffel coat with a positively penitential look about it. My husband liked his clothes to

blend in with the vegetable beds, so wore the coat for years, with binder twine for a belt.

I still find it hard to bond with the second-hand clothes some people give me. At 60 and three stones overweight, it did my morale no good to receive a shocking pink T-shirt labelled Naughty Sport. I felt like an huge overripe fruit in it.

Years ago, when I helped at a charity sorting office, I found the art of inappropriate giving raised to new heights. It made past things given to me positively useful by comparison!

The charity appeal was for clothes for earthquake victims. Sackfuls of good clothing had been given. The star performers were an enormous corset which looked as if it had come from the whalebone era, with grubby pink laces and flesh-coloured armour plating, and a mauve see-through nightie. I couldn't imagine picking over rubble in see-through nylon, though the corset might have qualified as protective clothing.

When I receive the next consignment of weird articles, I shall hand the donor one of Osbert Lancaster's wartime cartoons and let it speak for me. In it a dowager is handing a huge cavalry sabre to a horrified young woman in 1939 Army uniform, with the caption: 'Your grandfather wore it at Rorke's Drift. Gird it on and never let it leave your side.'

Even at 70, I'm still a pushover – I would certainly have ended up wearing it.

March 2002

MONDAY	TUESDAY	WEDNESDAY	THURSDAY
4	5	6	7
11 YOURS Spring Special on sale	12	13	14
18	19	20	21
25	26	27	28

Born this month...

- David Niven *(1 March, 1910)*
- Glenn Miller *(1 March, 1904)*
- Liza Minnelli *(12 March, 1946)*
- **Michael Caine** *(14 March, 1933)*
- Ursula Andress *(19 March, 1936)*
- **Joan Crawford** *(23 March, 1908)*
- Harry Houdini *(24 March, 1874)*
- Diana Ross *(26 March, 1944)*
- Vincent Van Gogh *(30 March, 1853)*

DAY	SATURDAY	SUNDAY
	2	*3*
David's Day		
	9	*10*
		Mother's Day
	16	*17*
		St Patrick's Day
	23	*24*
	30	*31*
Good Friday Public Holiday	April YOURS on sale	Easter Sunday British Summer Time begins

Flower of the month

EUPHORBIAS
(Euphorbia characias subsp wulfenii)

Green may not be a popular flower colour but it has not prevented euphorbias from becoming some of the most fashionable plants in the garden. Yet, with hundreds of species, coming from all over the world, euphorbias have a rather Jekyll and Hyde personality. Euphorbias all have irritant sap and most have tiny flowers. They include a number of annual weeds (spurges), good herbaceous plants, exotic leafless succulents and the popular poinsettia *(E. pulcherrima)*.

Although the flowers are tiny, in most cases showy bracts surround them. While few have the poinsettia's 'wow' factor, most are attractive.

The Mediterranean area is home to many good plants, such as *Viburnum tinus* and Chamaerops palms, but it is also the origin of *Euphorbia characias,* a wonderful evergreen shrub. The upright stems are covered in narrow, grey leaves. Then, in autumn, the tips of the shoots start to curl over to find protection from the cold, and in spring they unfurl again to produce a thick column of flowers with lime green bracts. These have black eyes, giving it the name of frogspawn bush, but in the variety *wulfenii* these are yellow, giving a brighter effect. Given sun and a well-drained soil it is easy to grow. Cut out the flowered stems in late spring to give room for new shoots to grow.

35

March 4-10

THOUGHT FOR THE WEEK
Wise words for Mother's Day:
God could not be everywhere and therefore he made mothers.

Hebrew proverb

THIS WEEK IN YOUR GARDEN
The first month of spring at last, the freshness of the air is noticeable but sometimes so sharp that it's good to retreat to the greenhouse...

- Damping-off fungus can attack greenhouse seedlings and cuttings. Adequate air flow will help prevent it.
- Slugs attack new shoots, especially delphiniums and hostas. Surround the crown of each plant with a layer of sharp grit.
- Lay growing bags out in the greenhouse to let the compost warm through before planting.
- Bed out wallflowers and forget-me-nots.

GO ON, SMILE!
Darling, you were wonderful!
I was making small talk with an acquaintance I was visiting in hospital. Knowing she had been in films, I asked her what roles she had played. In her 'actressy' voice, which reverberated around the ward, she replied: "My dear, I was once a French prostitute!"

Mrs B Fenton, Hove, Sussex

FROM ME TO YOU
Hello, little Josh
The news came in a phone call just as I was feeling down because my painful wrist was playing up again. I was a grandma at last!

You can keep your painkillers! Within a minute of hearing the news I had been waiting for, for more than ten long years, I felt like a spring chicken and went tearing off to the hospital like a young whippet (well, youngish... I am 67 after all).

When I got to the ward I spotted my daughter grinning like a Cheshire cat, and beside her in the cot baby Josh was asleep. He looked like a cherub. He had his granddad's snub nose and his mum's long, piano-playing fingers.

Late that night, my husband turned to me in bed and said: "How's the wrist?"

"What wrist?" I replied.

Mary Pennington, Liverpool

HEALTH CHECK
Fancy a cuppa?
Everyone knows that tea flows through the veins of the average Englishman! But now doctors and scientists are getting excited about the health-promoting properties of the humble cuppa. This is because of the discovery of substances found in tea called 'polyphenols'. These are antioxidants which destroy damaging molecules, called 'free radicals', thought to cause

cancer. Research has also shown they play a part in preventing heart and liver disease. For a boost of polyphenols, scientists recommend drinking green tea, popular in Japan and China. It's on sale at most big supermarkets or health-food stores.

FASCINATING PHOTOS

Dee Pascoe, from Kircudbright, waited for 70 years to see her dream come true…

"All my life, I had longed to walk on the Great Wall of China. I finally achieved it in March 1999 – I was 79! As a schoolgirl, I had read all about this magical place, but all I had was a bicycle and no money so I couldn't get there. I grew up, got married and raised a son but I never let go of my dream of visiting the Great Wall.

"When my husband passed away and my son married, I moved to a smaller house. Suddenly, money wasn't the problem, but I didn't feel I could take the trip on my own at 79 years young!

"When my dear friend Peggy, who is a sprightly 83, heard of my ambition, she said straightaway, 'I'll come!' So I finally made it – that's Peggy and me standing on the Great Wall (I'm in the yellow coat). There were 39 of us on the trip, and we made lots of new friends. The holiday lasted for three weeks. We arrived home exhausted but happy. It was wonderful – truly the trip of a lifetime."

TIP TIME
Put some sugar or lemonade in the water with fresh flowers to make them last longer.
Mrs M Clarke, Motherwell, Lanarkshire

RECIPE CORNER

Slow-cooked Lamb Shanks
Cooked long and slow, the lamb almost melts in your mouth. For a wintry treat, serve with creamy mashed potato. Makes enough for 2-4 people.

4 lamb shanks
Oil to fry
½ onion, finely chopped
1-2 cloves garlic, crushed (optional)
8 fl oz/225 ml each beef stock and red wine
4 oz/100 g canned chopped

tomatoes
1 tablespoon fresh herbs (optional)
Salt and pepper

1 Preheat your oven to 170°C/325°F/gas 4. Heat a little oil in a frying pan, add lamb shanks and brown for a couple of minutes. Place them in a roasting tin.

2 Add onion and garlic, is using, to frying pan and cook until soft. Add stock, wine (or extra stock) and tomatoes and bring to boil. Pour over lamb the, sprinkle with fresh herbs and season. Cover roasting tin with foil and bake for 2-2½ hours, turning once, until the lamb is very tender.

TIP TIME
Before heading to the bank to withdraw cash, make a note of how you would like your money. For example, if you are withdrawing £25, you might ask for 1 x £10, 2 x £5, 5 x £1 – and hand this to the cashier. It saves a lot of misunderstanding and means that you don't have to broadcast your conversation to everyone in the queue.
Frances Bunyan, Stanmore, Middlesex

THIS WEEK THROUGH THE YEARS

- **4 March, 1982** The British Government gave the go-ahead for the introduction of satellite television.
- **8 March, 1971** In London, The Daily Sketch closed down after 62 years of publication.
- **9 March, 1923** Thirty New York policemen were revealed as members of the Klu Klux Klan.
- **9 March, 1964** British forces became involved in the fighting between Greeks and Turks in Cyprus.

THOUGHT FOR THE WEEK

Anne White from Birmingham offers these words of wisdom from Anthony Trollope, about one of her favourite hobbies:
Book love, my friends, is your pass to the greatest, the purest, the most perfect pleasure available to man. It lasts when all other pleasures fade. It will support you when all other recreations are gone. It will last until your death.

THIS WEEK IN YOUR GARDEN

By the end of this month, all kinds of hardy vegetables can go in and it's time to sew annual flower seeds…
- Prepare the soil for sowing by breaking it down into fine crumbs, then rake level.
- If your garden is small, plant vegetables in among flowers – they can grow together very successfully.
- Sew herbs outside – chervil, fennel, dill, marjoram and coriander. Lift, divide and replant clumps of chives in a sunny position.
- As you walk round the garden, pull out a few weeds. Keep ahead of them as they soon become a problem!

TIP TIME
Use baby oil on squeaky hinges and talcum powder in cracks of squeaky floorboards.
Mrs M Clarke, Motherwell, Lanarkshire

FASCINATING PHOTOS

Audrey Phillips describes a very special day off school…
"In March 1942, my late father Joesph Henry Beagley received the Distinguished Service Medal from King George VI. My mother was unable to be there for the ceremony, as she was heavily pregnant with my younger sister, Gillian. My brother, Ron, then 19, was given a 48-hour pass to attend the service. He was posted to India very soon after and we didn't see him again until 1946.

"My father had been badly wounded in 1940 when his ship HMS Amethyst hit a mine. He wasn't able to go back to sea and spent the rest of the war on shore.

"I was 13 when he received his medal at Buckingham Palace. I was given special permission to take the day off school, on the understanding that I write an account of the day and read it out to the whole school. You can imagine how proud I was when I stood up to speak."

GO ON, SMILE!

Imaginary friends
My little niece had an imaginary dog and pony which went everywhere with her. Walking along with her one day, she said: "Auntie, my dog is tired now." So, joining in the game, I 'picked up' the imaginary dog, carried it for a while and then put it down again. Later on, my niece told me that her pony was also tired, so I obligingly picked him up too. "Don't be silly!" my niece responded, crossly. "He's too heavy for you to carry." And like a fool, I put him down again.
A Lucas, Moreton-in-Marsh, Gloucestershire

HEALTH CHECK

Cheers!
More and more doctors and researchers are convinced that red wine is good for you. In a recent study, ten beneficial ingredients were found and doctors announced that middle-aged and older people would benefit from a moderate daily intake. But the key word is 'moderate'. More than two glasses a day are likely to do more harm than good.

THIS WEEK THROUGH THE YEARS

- **13 March, 1996** Sixteen school children and their teacher were killed by a gunman, Thomas Hamilton, at Dunblane Primary School in Dunblane, Scotland.
- **15 March, 1990** The Observer journalist Farzad Bazoft, found guilty of spying, was hanged in Baghdad.
- **16 March, 1967** Singer Sandie Shaw entered the UK singles charts with Puppet on a String.
- **17 March, 1921** The UK's first birth control clinic, founded by Marie Stopes, opened in London.

RECIPE CORNER

Pasta bake with tuna, haricot beans and tomato

This quick supper dish is a real godsend as it's made entirely from your storecupboard ingredients. Fresh herbs give it a lift, but don't make a special trip out to get some, as the dish works perfectly well without them. Serves 4.

12 oz/350 g pasta shapes
2 tablespoons olive oil
1 onion, peeled and sliced
1-2 cloves garlic, chopped (optional)
1 fresh red chilli pepper, deseeded and chopped (optional)

1 x 14 oz/400 g tin plum tomatoes, chopped
1 x 14 oz/400g tin haricot beans, drained and rinsed
1 x 8 oz/225 g tin tuna, drained and flaked
2 tablespoons fresh herbs (eg, basil, thyme), chopped (optional)
Salt and pepper
Handful of mozzarella or your favourite melting cheese, roughly sliced

1 Cook pasta according to packet instructions, then drain thoroughly.
2 While pasta cooks, prepare the sauce. Heat the oil in a large pan. Add the onion and cook until soft and golden. Add garlic and chilli and cook a further 5 minutes. Add the tomatoes (including juice), beans, tuna and herbs. Cook until beans are heated through. Season to taste with salt and pepper.
3 Add drained pasta to tomato sauce. Stir to combine and tip into baking dish. Top with the cheese and bake in oven until cheese begins to bubble and melt.

FROM ME TO YOU

A valued visitor

During a telephone conversation with my 96-year-old aunt, she told me that her friend hadn't visited for some time.

I diplomatically explained that her friend had a long journey, with two buses and quite a walk. I also reminded her that her friend was getting on in years.

I received a swift reply, telling me not to be so silly as her friend was only 83. Guess who was left speechless!

Audrey Watson, Laceby, Lincs

THOUGHT FOR THE WEEK

The only thing to do with good advice is to pass it on. It is never of any use to oneself.
Oscar Wilde (1854-1900)

THIS WEEK IN YOUR GARDEN

Generally, temperatures should now be rising, but don't put your tender plants out yet…

- It's time to start mowing the lawn again but set the mower blades to high.
- Carry out lawn repairs and reseed bare patches, covering with clear polythene until germination.
- Wild flowers make a glorious show. Try poppy, larkspur and cornflower.
- Sets of outdoor tomatoes can be sown now. Sow indoors, for planting out when the risk of frost has passed.

FASCINATING PHOTOS

This photograph brings back memories of living in India more than 50 years ago for Marjorie Dent from Sutton in Surrey…

"I was born and lived for many years in India where my father was working in the Indian Civil Service. This photograph was taken at Simla, just after the First World War when I was a baby.

"It shows life as it was then. You can see a typical Indian bungalow in the background. The horse and groom nearby were the only means of transport in the hill stations where families spent the hot months of the summer.

"In the foreground my mother, Violet, is standing with my aunt and uncle, and my two cousins are sitting in front of them. My brother, Denzil, is in a carriage attended by two house servants, called 'bearers' and a nurse known as 'Ayah' is sitting on the floor holding me.

HEALTH CHECK

Feel-good foods

It's official! Food can affect your mood. Chemicals in the brain, called neurotransmitters, help to pass messages from one cell to another. Two of these, serotonin and noradrenaline, both endorphins, appear to affect mood and they are made by your body when it breaks down the food you eat. It's possible, therefore, to raise your levels of these by eating particular foods.

Unfortunately, endorphins are mostly derived from sugary foods such as chocolate, biscuits and jam, which give you a quick boost – followed by a sudden slump in endorphin levels. This can make you crave more sugary foods, leading to mood swings and unhealthy eating habits. However, you can enjoy the effects of this feel-good food in two ways:

1 By eating them with a meal.
2 By choosing a slowly-released carbohydrate such as a flapjack, a slice of wholemeal bread or some fresh or dried fruit.

TIP TIME
Wrap fresh carrots in foil. They keep for much longer that way.
Mrs Danning, Honiton, Devon

THIS WEEK THROUGH THE YEARS

- **20 March, 1999** The Breitling Orbiter 3, piloted by Brian Jones of the UK and Bertrand Piccard of Switzerland, became the first balloon ever to go around the world non-stop.
- **21 March, 1990** The Republic of Namibia became an independent state.
- **23 March, 1983** US President Ronald Reagan proposed a new defence system, to be based on earth and in space. It was called 'Star Wars'.
- **24 March, 1957** Singer Elvis Presley was drafted into the US Army for two years of national service.

GO ON, SMILE!

Shirt sale

As I was looking around in a men's clothes department recently, I spotted a notice near some shirts, which made me smile. It read, 'Plenty of bargains in shirts, for men with 16 or 17 necks'.
Mrs A Grimes, Bridlington, East Yorkshire

From me to you

Second time around

I was browsing around a charity shop recently when a young woman came in loaded with bags of clothing. Dumping them on the floor, she said to the assistant: "Here you are, my annual clear-out. Anything I haven't worn for a year has to go."

Bemused, I stood there in a dress I'd had for three years and a coat that I'd had for six – both bought from the very shop and still going strong.

Irene Burton, Ossett, West Yorkshire

Recipe corner

Cheese and Bacon Pudding
This delicious savoury pudding is just the thing for a delicious light lunch. Serves 4

½ pint/300 ml milk
2 oz/50 g fresh breadcrumbs
2 eggs, separated
1½ oz/40 g Cheddar cheese, grated
2 oz/50 g Parmesan cheese, grated
4 rashers bacon, grilled and chopped
1 tablespoon butter or margarine, softened
Salt and pepper

1 Preheat the oven to 180C/350F/gas mark 4 and grease a pie dish. Bring the milk to the boil and pour it over the breadcrumbs in a bowl. Leave to stand for 10 minutes.
2 Beat in the egg yolks, then the cheeses, bacon and butter. Whisk the egg whites until they are just stiff, stir in a spoonful into the cheese mixture, then fold in the rest.
3 Turn the mixture into the prepared pie dish and bake for 30 minutes until golden brown on top.

THOUGHT FOR THE WEEK

Get the advice of everybody whose advice is worth having – they are very few – and then do what you think best yourself.

Charles Parnell, Irish nationalist leader, (1846-91)

THIS WEEK IN YOUR GARDEN

The clocks go forward at the end of this week, lengthening daylight hours, so you can use the extra time in the garden…

- Pinch out the top of sweet peas when they're 4 in (10 cm) high.
- Pot up chrysanthemums for late colour.
- Dig out and divide large clumps of hostas before the leaves begin to expand too much.
- Pull out weeds from around fruit trees, soft-fruit bushes and strawberry plants to prevent them competing for nutrients.
- Unless your garden is very cold, it should now be safe to make a first sowing of lettuces outdoors.

FROM ME TO YOU

Young love

While I was out walking the other day, I saw a young couple holding hands. But what amused me was that they were listening to a Walkman and he had one earphone and she had the other. Is this a new way of demonstrating 'togetherness'?

Evelyn Cundall, Prestwich, Manchester

FASCINATING PHOTOS

Les Allington from Cheltenham in Gloucestershire, fondly remembers his grandparents…

"Here's a picture of my father's parents, Charles and Elizabeth Allington, taken in 1924 when they were on a day trip to the seaside resort of Hastings. They are pictured on a 1921 600cc Blackburn, which was the beach photographer's prop.

"My grandmother is wearing a warm hat and tippet, which she seemed to wear every winter. And my grandfather looks rather smart in his three-piece suit and flat cap.

"I remember my Grandma Allington as a formidable woman. Whenever I visited her, she'd take me straight to the sink and wash my neck!"

HEALTH CHECK

Keep your heart healthy by:
- Eating oily fish such as sardines and mackerel.
- Reducing your intake of saturated fat, found in full-fat dairy products, fatty meat and hard margarines made from hydrogenated oils.
- Lowering your salt intake.
- Eating more fresh fruits and vegetables.
- Eating seeds and fresh, unsalted nuts.
- Giving up smoking.
- Taking regular exercise.
- Trying to keep your weight under control.
- Avoiding stress as much as possible.

TIP TIME

To stop your cooking-oil bottle getting messy, wrap a sheet of folded kitchen paper around it and secure with an elastic band.

Margaret Gray, Tavistock, Devon

GO ON, SMILE!

Back-seat driver

At a social gathering, I was making small talk with another man. He was complaining about back-seat drivers. "I never have that trouble," I remarked. "I drive a hearse."

David Eakin, Belfast

TIP TIME

To prevent your telephone cable from tangling, thread a plastic-covered curtain wire through the coils.

Margaret Tapp, West End, Southampton

RECIPE CORNER

Handmade Chocolate and Rum Truffles

Impress friends and family by giving home-made chocolates this Easter. They'll never guess how easy they are to make – and they're a lot cheaper than shop-bought Easter eggs, too. This recipe makes 24-36; the chocolates will keep in the fridge for 7-10 days.

1 lb/450 g good-quality chocolate, broken into pieces
6 fl oz/175 ml double cream
2-3 tablespoons rum
6 oz/175 g plain, milk or white chocolate

1 Place the chocolate pieces in a bowl. Pour the cream into a pan and bring it to just boiling point. Pour over the chocolate and beat until combined and chocolate has melted. Stir in the rum and

chill in the fridge for 3 hours until firm.

2 Melt the remaining chocolate in a bowl over a pan of simmering water. Scoop off a small piece of the truffle mix with a teaspoon and shape into a ball (work quickly to keep mixture cool). Dip the truffles into the melted chocolate and place on a rack to cool. Continue with the remaining truffle mix and chocolate.

3 When the chocolates have cooled and set, place them in individual paper cases and present them in pretty boxes as gifts.

THIS WEEK THROUGH THE YEARS

- **27 March, 1952** The UK cheese ration was cut to one ounce a week.
- **28 March, 1925** Cambridge won the Boat Race after the Oxford boat sank.
- **29 March, 1967** In France, President De Gaulle launched the country's first nuclear submarine.
- **31 March, 1990** A huge march and rally against the poll tax was held in London.

TIP TIME
To make an old umbrella waterproof again, spray it with a furniture polish that contains silicone.
Mrs Westley, Herne Bay, Kent

THE RED CARNATION

By Jeanne Jones

hree minutes to go! That should be just long enough. Calm down and take a nice, deep breath. Nearly there!

Trains are always late anyway, and it's only a short walk from the taxi-rank to Platform One. There's a Ladies on that platform, too. I might even have time to pop in and check how I look. If only I hadn't taken so long deciding what to wear, I wouldn't be in such a rush now.

Still, it was important to create the right image. The grey dress with the pearls made me appear too matronly, and I should have given the red suit with the long jacket and short skirt to the Charity Shop long ago. It made me look like mutton dressed as lamb.

In the end I think I made the right choice – the blouse and slacks, smart but casual, with flat shoes and a fine, wool cardigan draped around my shoulders.

But it isn't just the clothes that I'd been unsure about. I'd spent the early part of the morning in an agony of indecision about whether to go to the station at all – whether the whole idea was such a good one. After all, we don't know each other. We're strangers. What if he's disappointed in me – or me in him?

What if we don't like each other at all? Oh, now I'm being ridiculous – so what if we don't care for each other! It's only lunch. There's no law that says we have to have a relationship for the rest of our lives, is there? We need never see each other again after today if we don't want to.

There's no law that says we have to have a relationship for the rest of our lives, is there?

Maybe I should have told him everything before the wedding but I lacked the courage, and then it was too late. I had to learn to live with my secret

On the other hand, we might hit it off straight away. We might want to go on seeing each other – to fill an empty space in each other's lives. I wonder what sort of a life he's had. What sort of man he is? I don't even know what he looks like.

And he must be as curious about me as I am about him. I didn't tell him much about myself when he phoned out of the blue like that. Just that I'd been married; that it had been a good marriage – although, sadly, not blessed with children – and that I had been a widow for a few years.

There is so much more that I could tell him, that I might want to tell him if we're comfortable with each other. About why I had moved away from my home town in the Fifties; away from everything and everyone I had known and loved. I was only 18.

few years later I met my husband in London. David was older than me, attractive and well-to-do and he offered me the security of marriage. Rightly or wrongly, I accepted; pretending when he held me that I had never felt such passion for another man – pretending when he said he loved me that no one else had ever said those words to me before. If he knew of my deceit, he never said so; never questioned me about my past. Maybe I should have told him everything before the wedding but I lacked the courage, and then it was too late. I had to learn to live with my secret.

The man I'm meeting today, the one I'll recognise by the red carnation he'll be wearing, would he understand if I told him my story, that I did what I thought was for the best? Would he understand that, by opening my heart to him, I might finally be able to put the pain of the past behind me and look forward to a new beginning? Only time will tell.

Twelve-thirty! The train is coming. Will he be on it? He may have changed his mind

We're strangers. What if he's disappointed in me – or me in him?

about coming, as I so nearly did. My pulse is racing. The train is slowing down, stopping now. Doors are opening and people are spilling out on to the platform. Their faces are coming into focus as they move towards me.

Oh, there he is. I'm waving to him. No need for the red carnation, I'd have known him anywhere. My son is the image of his father.

IT'S IN THE STARS

Patrick Arundell looks to the heavens to predict what's in store for you this month

PISCES
(20 February – 20 March)
The need to be with others gets stronger and you'll have a real fascination for what makes them tick. Pencil the 12th into your diary as a decisive turning point in a potentially stunning month.

ARIES (21 March – 20 April)
As winter draws to a close, you probably won't feel very outgoing. But you'll bounce back. If you enjoy a dabble, fortune can shine.

TAURUS (21 April – 21 May)
Expect your energy levels to surge. This is a wonderful time to join in with group activities.

GEMINI (22 May – 21 June)
Your mood will be up and down. Try to focus your energies and save time for yourself.

CANCER (22 June – 23 July)
In friendships or charity activities, you could be a driving force. Don't be surprised if you and an old friend are becoming very close.

LEO (24 July – 23 August)
You're in line for financial good fortune this month. Try to contain a bossy tendency.

VIRGO (24 August – 23 September)
Don't take anyone for granted. Travel, or a new outdoor pursuit, also features strongly.

LIBRA (24 September – 23 October)
Even if there are difficult matters to attend to your sense of humour will win through.

SCORPIO (24 October – 22 November)
If you're too demanding of those nearest and dearest to you, you'll score an own goal.

SAGITTARIUS (23 November – 21 December)
Past memories, perhaps from your childhood, could be evocative early on, but as the month goes on a more outward-looking spell begins.

CAPRICORN (22 December – 20 January)
Closer contact with siblings is a possibility and you might take up a new hobby with them.

AQUARIUS (21 January – 19 February)
You're full of enthusiasm but don't expect folk to instantly agree with your plans. This is a good time to make a major purchase.

HOUSEWIFE'S CHOICE

Robert Opie takes a nostalgic peek at shopping-basket bygones

GOLDEN SHRED
For generations, households had made their own marmalades jams and bottled their own fruits. The public viewed 'shop' jam with some prejudice. Nevertheless, James Robertson began to make and sell marmalade in 1864 when his wife suggested turning some unsaleable oranges into marmalade. The business expanded and the clear marmalade, called Golden Shred, appeared on breakfast tables across the land. The idea of making the golly a trademark was adopted in 1914, the paper golly stuck to each jar started in 1928 and from 1930 an enamel brooch became available.

GUINNESS
It was in 1759 that Arthur Guinness began brewing porter and ale in Dublin, but it was some 60 years before the special Guinness brew of 'extra superior porter' was devised by his son. The Guinness trade mark label featuring the harp appeared in 1862. Sent all over Britain, Guinness was bottled by many different breweries, and in 1929 Guinness launched its first national advertising campaign with the slogan 'Guinness is good for you'. In 1936 the new brewery at Park Royal, London was opened. By that time many of the famous ads drawn by John Gilroy had appeared, such as the man carrying a girder (1934) and the toucan (1935).

PUZZLE IT OUT!

Cryptic crosswords and tea-time teasers to keep your brain busy

Entertainment This puzzle is all about the golden, olden days of entertainment.

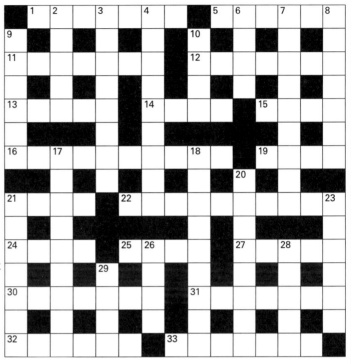

ACROSS

1 Hitchcock film starring James Stewart and Kim Novak (7)

5 ___ Andrews, ventriloquist Peter Brough's dummy (6)

11 Walter ___, quiet-spoken leading man in films of the '30s and '40s, including *Mrs Miniver* (7)

12 John ___, playwright of *Look Back in Anger* in 1956 (7)

13 *Frankenstein ___ The Wolf Man*, 1943 Bela Lugosi horror film (5)

14 Nickname given to silent actress Theda Bara from her predatory screen persona (4)

15 ___ Negri, Polish-born actress in Hollywood films from WW1 onwards (4)

16 1947 Louis Armstrong film about the city where jazz was born (3,7)

19 Jenny ___, 19th century soprano known as the 'Swedish Nightingale' (4)

21 ___ Dillon, marshal played by James Arness in TV's *Gunsmoke* (4)

22 American actor in gangster films of the '30s and '40s (6,4)

24 *A ___ Grows in Brooklyn*, 1945 family drama film (4)

25 ___ *of Triumph*, 1948 Ingrid Bergman melodrama (4)

27 ___ Fudd, Warner Bros cartoon character, enemy of Bugs Bunny (5)

30 See **17 Down**

31 Hertfordshire film studios established in the 1920s (7)

32 ___ *Joe Young*, 1949 monster film (7)

33 Nickname of *Band Waggon* comic actor Richard Murdoch (7)

DOWN

2 ___ Albert, co-star of Audrey Hepburn and Gregory Peck in *Roman Holiday* in 1953 (5)

3 ___ *Island*, 1950 film starring Robert Newton as Long John Silver (8)

4 1953 British comedy film about a vintage car (9)

6 *The* ___, 1953 biblical epic, the first film in Cinemascope (4)

7 Instrument on which Larry Adler played his own score for 4 down (9)

8 ___ City, home of the Wizard of Oz (7)

9 *Tarzan the* ___, 1932 film starring Johnny Weissmuller in the title role (3,3)

10 ___ *at the Top*, 1959 film starring Laurence Harvey (4)

17 and **30 across** Classic novel filmed in 1939 with Laurence Olivier and Merle Oberon (9,7)

18 ___ *Frontier*, 1959 historical adventure film set in India and starring Kenneth More (5-4)

20 Oscar ___, Canadian jazz pianist and international star from 1949 (8)

21 Robert ___, American actor, star of *The Night of the Hunter* in 1955 (7)

23 Lana ___, American leading lady of the 1940s (6)

26 and **28** 1936 Canadian-set musical starring Nelson Eddy (4-5)

28 See **26 Down**

29 ___ *Old Black Magic,* 1955 hit for Sammy Davis Jnr (4)

For solutions turn to Page 161

47

April 2002

MONDAY	TUESDAY	WEDNESDAY	THURSDAY
1 Easter Monday Public Holiday and April Fool's Day	2	3	4
8	9	10	11
15	16	17	18
22	23 St George's Day	24	25
29	30 May YOURS on sale		

DAY	SATURDAY	SUNDAY
	6	7
	13	14
	20	21 Queen Elizabeth II's birthday
	27	28

Flower of the month

MAGNOLIA
(Magnolia x soulangeana)

Even the most inveterate gambler would not dare to wager on the biggest risk of the year: Will your magnolia escape the spring frosts?

Magnolia x soulangeana is the most popular of spring-flowering trees and has knocked the flowering cherry from the top spot, and no wonder. The tree has a beautiful habit and the flowers are larger than any other tree. Magnolias vary a great deal but this French hybrid has captured the hearts of gardeners with its tulip-like flowers in shades of pink and white, depending on the variety, each releasing a beautiful scent with undertones of soap and cucumber! Produced in great numbers, the flowers cover the branches and a well-grown plant can be a majestic and wonderful sight.

Yet, it can all go horribly wrong, and oddly, warm spring weather is usually to blame. Though the tree is hardy, the flowers are ruined by frost and one cold night can ruin the display of magnolias. A warm spring means early flowers and a greater danger that they will be caught by a hard frost in April. Colder weather early in the spring usually ensures that magnolias are less advanced and survive cold April weather more successfully. They are not fussy about soil, but prefer a sheltered position in the sun.

Born this month...

- Debbie Reynolds *(1 April, 1932)*
- Alec Guinness *(2 April, 1914)*
- **Doris Day** *(3 April, 1924)*
- **Gregory Peck** *(5 April, 1916)*
- Leonardo Da Vinci *(15 April, 1452)*
- Charlie Chaplin *(16 April, 1889)*
- Hayley Mills *(18 April, 1946)*
- Queen Elizabeth II *(21 April, 1926)*
- William Shakespeare *(23 April, 1564)*
- Barbra Streisand *(24 April, 1942)*

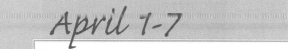

April 1-7

THOUGHT FOR THE WEEK

Bill Adams from Neath in West Glamorgan offers this piece of advice to people embarking on a new project:
'If you are itching to do something well, you'll come up to scratch.'

THIS WEEK IN YOUR GARDEN

April showers and warmer soil provide perfect growing conditions for spring flowers…

- Deadhead daffodils as soon as they fade so they don't produce seeds.
- Before hoeing, check the ground for self-sown plant seedlings and pot them up for friends.
- Lightly scatter night-scented stock seeds now to enjoy the lovely fragrance during long summer evenings.
- Keep on weeding! Annual weeds can be hand-pulled but perennials need digging out.
- Winter flowering pansies can be sown outside but you'll have better results by sowing them in gentle heat.

FROM ME TO YOU

Eye, eye!
As a junior nurse on the nightshift in the '60s, I was left in charge when the senior nurse went for her break. The responsibility lay heavily on my shoulders and she had just left when I heard a patient call.

I looked quickly down the ward and found one of the men trying to get out of bed. He was very confused and I was worried he would hurt himself, so, as I ran to the phone for help, I shouted: "Mr Jones, please keep an eye on him while I phone for help." Just as I picked up the phone I remembered Mr Jones had only one eye! I still blush when I think of that night.

Mary Byrne, Weymouth, Dorset

TIP TIME
After washing net curtains, fold them over the bar of a coat hanger to prevent them from creasing.
Mrs K Ryan, Teversham, Cambs

TIP TIME
Struggling to open new jars of sauces and pickles? Carefully pierce the lids with a pointed knife to break the vacuum. They'll open easily.
Mrs W Swanborough, Basingstoke, Hampshire

HEALTH CHECK

A good excuse to put your feet up!
Do you find that after a long shopping spell the soles of your feet ache? You could be suffering from a new medical syndrome that doctors have identified, called Shoppers Foot. They recommend placing your feet on ice – a bag of frozen peas will do – and then putting them up in the evening.

FASCINATING PHOTOS

Barbara Finch from Chapel St Leonards in Lincolnshire shares a precious memento of her mother working in a clothing firm during the depression…

"This photo of my mother, Lily Jeffrey, was taken around 1926. At the time my sister was four – and I wasn't even thought of!

"My mother is the lady at the front on the right-hand side in the dark dress. As always, she has a lovely, beaming smile on her face.

"As you can see, it was a large clothing firm and of course the women were all on 'piece' work. Life was hard – my father was out of work for nine years during the depression, so it was down to my mum to keep the family together."

RECIPE CORNER

Impossible Pie

"For simplicity, you can't beat this!" says Mrs E Walmsley from Thornton-Cleveleys, Lancs. "When cooked, this pie will have pastry on the bottom, custard in the middle and coconut on top!"

4 eggs
2 oz/50 g soft margarine or butter
6 oz/175 g white sugar
2 oz/50 g plain flour
¼ teaspoon salt
½ teaspoon baking powder
¾ pt/425 ml milk
4 oz/110 g desiccated coconut
1 teaspoon vanilla essence

1 Preheat oven to 180°C/350°F/gas mark 4. Grease a 10 in pie dish.
2 Place all ingredients in a large mixing bowl or food blender and whisk until smooth. Pour into the prepared dish and bake in the oven for 50-60 minutes until the topping is browned.

TIP TIME
When washing up or doing dirty household chores, pop your rings on to the arms of your glasses. They'll be easy to find!
Mrs T Wood, Clitheroe, Lancashire

GO ON, SMILE!

Baby talk

Having just read these 'wanted' adverts in our local paper, I realise we must have some pretty strange babies in our area:

'Plastic baby high chair.' 'Antique pine baby unit with long drawers.' 'Bouncy baby chair with coloured dots.'
Jean Ramsey, Ipswich, Suffolk

THIS WEEK THROUGH THE YEARS

- **4 April, 1968** US civil rights hero Dr Martin Luther King, who had worked for years to achieve equality for all Americans, was assassinated in Memphis.
- **4 April, 1968** The science fiction film 2001: A Space Odyssey, directed by Stanley Kubrick, was released.
- **6 April, 1909** US naval commander Robert Peary became the first person to reach the North Pole.
- **6 April, 1974** Swedish pop group Abba won the Eurovision Song Contest with their song Waterloo.

April 8-14

THOUGHT FOR THE WEEK

My favourite words of wisdom are: "If life had a second edition, I would correct the proofs."
Mrs D Tanner, Tonbridge, Kent

THIS WEEK IN YOUR GARDEN

Nights can still be cold, so protect tender plants from frost with cloches or fleece...

- Prune early-flowering shrubs and trim grey-leaved shrubs to keep them full and bushy.
- Lawns need mowing more frequently. Unless you did so in late March, feed established lawns. This is a good time to sow grass seed.
- Now is the time to plant out all summer-flowering bulbs.
- It's all go in the vegetable garden – peas, broad beans, salad leaves and radishes can all be sown now.
- Stake tall growing perennials.

GO ON, SMILE!

Taken for a ride
In the past, we'd occasionally taken our elderly aunt out in the car for a trip to St Ives in Cambridgeshire. We knew that she used to enjoy it, so recently we decided we would take her out again.

I said to my aunt: "It's been ages since we came here."

"Yes," she replied. "We haven't been here since the last time."

Well, I suppose there is some logic in that!"
Mrs J M Smith, Cambridge

HEALTH CHECK

Creature comforts
Pet owners are healthier than people without an animal friend. Walking a dog keeps you fit and active and simply stroking a cat or watching your goldfish swim in its tank has been proven to lower blood pressure. And caring for a pet is good for your mental well-being too. A much-loved pet who relies on you for food and shelter provides companionship and a sense you are needed. Indeed, having a pet waiting to greet you at the end of the day can make the difference between returning to an empty house and coming home.

FROM ME TO YOU

Dot and Arthur celebrate 60 diamond years

A real gem!
Arthur Thompson from Croydon, Surrey, writes:
My wife, Dot, and I celebrated our diamond wedding last year. One of our nieces, Elsie Eva, composed this poem after my wife told her how we met. And how true it is! At a dance Dot lost her precious pair of dancing shoes and accused me of taking them. I managed to convince her I was innocent and we began chatting. A whirl-wind romance followed and we have now enjoyed 60 happy years together.

Dot & Arthur's Diamond Romance

She was just on her way to the dance hall,
With her dance shoes so carefully wrapped,
And all that it took was a flash of her eyes
To convince him his heart was trapped.

She was lured away by the music
Which was played on a Spanish guitar,
Oh how could she know that musician
Would steal her away from her Ma?

And all because of a pair of shoes
That were lost on the way to the dance,
Their lives were changed forever
As they started their great romance.

She had wanted to join the Forces,
But he much preferred her to stay,
Permission was sought for the marriage
And arrangements were made for 'the day'.

And how many days was the courtship?
An amazing one hundred and two!
Now their marriage has proved to be a diamond,
Demonstrating that their love was true.

FASCINATING PHOTOS

Betty Bosher, from Loughton, Essex, has fond memories of her father's company – and a special day when The Duke and Duchess of York visited…

"This is a photo of my late father, William Hurd from Highbury, North London (fourth on the right), and his colleagues, taken during the 1930s. It shows a visit by the then Duke and Duchess of York to a company I knew of as Hill's. It employed First World War ex-servicemen with disabilities. My father lost his leg above the knee while fighting in France.

"The men at Hill's were engaged in making jewellery from glass beads and gold wire. They had stands in Marks & Spencer stores, manned by disabled men. I remember popping in to see them – the stands were all glass, glittery and lit up."

RECIPE CORNER

Seared Salmon with a Red Pepper Topping

A perfect special-occasion dish. Serve hot or cold with a crisp green salad. This recipe makes enough for 6.

3-4 red peppers
2 cloves garlic, peeled
3 tablespoons olive oil
1 cup fresh breadcrumbs
salt and pepper
6 salmon steaks

1   Preheat grill to 'high'. Cut peppers in half, place on a baking tray (cut side down) and grill until skin blackens. Leave to cool, remove skin and roughly chop flesh.
2   To make the pepper topping, place red pepper and garlic in a food processor. Purée, adding 2 tablespoons olive oil and enough crumbs to makes a smooth paste. Season.
3   For the salmon, heat remaining oil in a pan and sear salmon for 2-3 minutes on each side. Transfer to a grill tray and spoon over red-pepper crust. Place under grill until crust is golden brown.

> **TIP TIME**
> Put a button on the end of a roll of sticky tape so that the end is easier to find.
> *Mrs M Clarke, Motherwell, Lanarkshire*

> **TIP TIME**
> Soaking beans and peas before planting gives them an early start into growth.
> *E Johnson, Dunholme, Co. Durham*

THIS WEEK THROUGH THE YEARS

- **10 April, 1912** The luxury ocean liner Titanic set out on her maiden voyage only to sink when she hit an iceberg in the early hours of the morning of 15 April.
- **10 April, 1950** The head of the National Hairdressers' Federation in the UK said that many men have longer hair than their wives.
- **11 April, 1959** Bobby Charlton scored the only goal in England's 1-0 defeat of Scotland at Wembley.
- **13 April, 1997** Twenty-one-year-old Tiger Woods made history when he became the youngest and the first ever black golfer to win the Masters tournament in the US.

THOUGHT FOR THE WEEK

Contentment consists not in great wealth but in few wants.
Anon

THIS WEEK IN YOUR GARDEN

Visit your local garden centre for winter-flowering bargains – but check them carefully…

- Rhododendrons can be propagated by 'layering'. Peg down low-growing branches with a hook, resting part of the stem on the soil surface.
- Evergreen hedges are best planted in the spring.
- Remove any blanketweed from your pond with a cane or rake.
- Now you've pruned the roses, it's time to feed and mulch them, and spray against blackspot.

FROM ME TO YOU

Upwardly mobile

I know the mobile phone is a modern timesaving invention, but I didn't realise how lazy it could make some people.

I was at a friend's house recently when her husband phoned their son to say his dinner was ready. I asked: "Is he round his friend's house?" "No," he replied. "He's upstairs doing his homework!"

Rosemary Medland,
Letchworth, Herts

FASCINATING PHOTOS

Mr F Kilminster from Flore, Northampton, remembers flying half way across the world to find work…

"One of the effects of nationalisation of the rail network was that promotion prospects were bleak for many those who worked on the railways. For this reason many young men, like myself, (*pictured right, inset*) were prepared to try a new country in order to make something of their lives.

"Some went by normal shipping lines but pictured here is one of the few air charters that flew locomotive crew to take up the challenge of a new life overseas.

"This photograph was taken in 1953 on our departure from Blackbush Airport. The flight was very up and down and we had to stop many times to refuel. We stopped at Malta, then at Khartoum and eventually at Ndola. From there, we were transferred to the railway network, and travelled on to Bulawayo in what was then known as Rhodesia but is now called Zimbabwe."

HEALTH CHECK

The natural way to a good night's sleep:

- Avoid any drinks that contain caffeine – tea, coffee, chocolate, cola – for several hours before you go to bed.
- Have a mug of warm milk, or a cup of camomile tea, before you go to bed.
- Don't go to bed hungry, as this can keep you awake, but avoid a full stomach at bedtime, as this can cause indigestion.
- Have starchy foods such as pasta, potatoes and bread for your supper – they stimulate your body to produce

hormones that make you feel sleepy.
- Sleep in a well-ventilated room that is not too warm
- Take regular exercise – this physically tires you and also helps to reduce stress, which can prevent you sleeping properly.
- A drop of lavender aromatherapy oil in your evening bath or on your pillow can help you sleep. Dried hops under your pillow are also said to be beneficial.

TIP TIME

To defrost your freezer, scrape off the frost and place a fan about two feet from the open door. This will help speed up the defrosting process.
Mr G Hale,
Ilford, Essex

GO ON, SMILE!

Milk mix-up

One morning I asked the milkman to start bringing me semi-skilled milk. Every time I see him he reminds me of what I said.

Mrs L Clarkson,
Birstall, Batley

RECIPE CORNER

Lemon Soufflés
Use the recipe for home-made lemon curd on Pages 80-81 for these individual soufflés. They can be prepared, ready to cook, 2-3 hours before serving. Makes 6-8

2 egg whites (stored at room temperature)
1 oz /25 g granulated sugar
2 oz/ 50 g lemon curd

1 Whisk egg whites with sugar to stiff peaks. Gently heat lemon curd to loosen, but don't overheat as it will cause it to 'split'. Carefully fold lemon curd into

THIS WEEK THROUGH THE YEARS

- **17 April, 1971** The Apollo 13 spacecraft splashed down safely in the Pacific after experiencing major technical problems during its mission.
- **18 April, 1966** The film The Sound of Music, which followed the story of the von Trapp family in Austria, won the Oscar for Best Film.
- **19 April, 1906** A massive earthquake shook the city of San Francisco. The earthquake, and the fire that followed, caused many millions of pounds worth of damage.
- **19 April, 1988** Two elephants arrived in Italy at the end of a trip organised by cricketer Ian Botham to retrace the footsteps of Hannibal's journey across the Alps from France.

the egg whites.

2 Place 6-8 ramekins on baking tray and fill with lemon mixture. Chill in fridge until ready to cook.

3 Heat oven to 200°C/400°F/gas 6. Bake soufflés for 10 minutes until risen and golden brown. Serve immediately.

THOUGHT FOR THE WEEK

Early to bed and early to rise,
Makes a man healthy, wealthy and wise.

Benjamin Franklin (1706-90)
American statesman

THIS WEEK IN YOUR GARDEN

The swallows have arrived, the birds are nest building. Let's welcome their cheerful twittering as they feast on slugs and snails...

- Plant out cauliflowers, Brussels sprouts and cabbages sown last month. Water well and protect from cabbage-root fly.
- April is a good month to take conifer cuttings.
- Remember to harvest forced rhubarb.
- Tie in clematis regularly to avoid a tangled mass of shoots.
- Increase greenhouse ventilation as the weather starts to improve.
- Sow parsley outdoors now in a partly-shaded position.
- Prepare trenches for those runner beans.

FROM ME TO YOU

Question time

Usually the neat, clipboard interviewers in the town centre tend to pass me by, probably because I'm an older man.

However, one day I was flattered to be approached by a young lady who asked if I'd mind answering a few questions.

I drew in my stomach and answered all the questions as well as I could. However, my ego was dampened when I was finally asked: "And now, John, how about taking out a funeral plan?"

John Bingham, Northampton

HEALTH CHECK

Kitchen cures

It isn't always necessary to resort to drugs if you're feeling under the weather. Common herbs and spices have been used for centuries to relieve everyday health niggles. Add them to your cooking or dilute in hot water (an infusion):

- **Chilli peppers:** Said to be good for the respiratory system.
- **Sage:** A tonic for the nervous system.
- **Camomile:** Infusion for relaxation and sleep.
- **Turmeric:** Add a pinch to your cooking to treat your catarrh.
- **Cloves:** Acts as a local anaesthetic to ease toothache.
- **Marjoram:** An infusion is good for relieving cold symptoms.
- **Ginger root:** An infusion is said to keep colds and nausea at bay.
- **Parsley:** Infusion can be helpful against fluid retention.
- **Mint:** Try a mint infusion after a rich meal to ward against indigestion.

Note: Always see your GP if symptoms persist.

THIS WEEK THROUGH THE YEARS

- **23 April, 1984** The discovery of the virus that causes AIDS (Acquired Immune Deficiency Syndrome) was announced.
- **26 April, 1986** There was a major nuclear explosion at the Chernobyl power plant in the Ukraine, which released massive amounts of radiation into the atmosphere.
- **27 April, 1994** Apartheid was finally ended in South Africa when ANC (African National Congress) leader Nelson Mandela was elected as president.
- **27 April, 1931** The Budget put two pence on a gallon of petrol, bringing the cost to one shilling and four pence halfpenny (nearly 7p).

TIP TIME

I've found the perfect slug deterrent. Fill a foil case – like those from shop-bought cakes – with some left-over beer. It's very effective and the slugs die with a smile on their faces!
Caroline Chadderton, Dowsby, Lincs

TIP TIME

If you find it hard to stand while preparing vegetables, place a stool next to an open drawer and place your chopping board on it to use as a work surface.
Gwen Mann, Grimsby, North East Lincs

FASCINATING PHOTOS

Evelyn Balmain from Market Drayton, Shropshire, recalls a day on the open road…

"This photograph of me and my daughter Gael, in the background, was taken in the '50s by my husband, James, who was brave enough to sit on the pillion while I showed off my driving skills.

"Some friends with a solo bike were taking us to Cambridgeshire to visit their relatives and we followed them from our home in Coventry. On reaching a dual carriageway, I opened the throttle of our Triumph 500 twin, and suddenly we were zooming past our friends. They were stopped at the roadside and he was busy tinkering with the engine. We couldn't turn around for a few miles, but finally returned and pulled up alongside.

" 'What's the problem?' asked my husband. 'Huh!' grunted our friend. 'No problem. I just didn't think that Evelyn would be driving so fast, so I put different plugs in. Now I'm having to change them to keep up!'

It just goes to show… never underestimate a woman!"

GO ON, SMILE!

Plane sailing
My 80-year-old friend flies to Canada every year to visit friends and relatives. On her last flight home, she was invited on to the flight deck to meet the pilot. "And do you know," she said to me, "the co-pilot was a woman and when they turned around to talk to me they certainly weren't watching where they were going."
Lyn Williams, Fareham, Hants

RECIPE CORNER

Orange and Ginger Biscuits
Makes four dozen

8 oz/230 g unsalted butter, softened
6 oz/150 g caster sugar
1 egg
2 tablespoons finely-grated orange zest
1 teaspoon vanilla essence
1 teaspoon ground ginger
Pinch of salt
1 lb 2 oz/500 g plain flour

1 Cream the butter and sugar together until pale and fluffy. Beat in the vanilla, egg and orange zest. Add the ginger and salt to the flour and then gradually work into the mixture until you have a soft dough. Divide in two and roll each part into a cylinder 2 in/5 cm in diameter. Wrap in cling film, then foil and chill for at least 2 hours.

2 Preheat the oven to 180C/350F/Gas Mark 4. Unwrap the dough and slice it about $1/4$ in/0.5 cm think. Place on baking sheets $1/2$ in/1 cm apart and cook for 8-10 minutes until brown. Cool on a wire rack.

NO HEAD FOR HEIGHTS

When Wyn Terrett's family moved to Turkey, she desperately wanted to visit them. There was only one problem, she was terrified of flying

"I'm going to live in Turkey for four years, Tim's got promotion," my daughter announced excitedly.

"Wonderful, what an opportunity it will be for you all," I replied, happy to see her so thrilled. At that moment I really meant it but when they'd gone home and my husband and I were left to our thoughts, we knew how much we were going to miss them. Our grandchildren – Alexandra and James – are three and five years old and they're growing up so quickly. In spite of our assurances that we would be out to visit them soon, I knew they were hollow promises.

I suffer from claustrophobia which had worsened recently following two visits to the MRI scanner, which can only be likened to going headfirst into a washing machine.

I suddenly remembered I'd seen something about a British Airways fear of flying course. It was two months before I plucked up the courage to send for the information, another month before I rang up. My palms were sweating and I hoped that they'd be fully booked but they had a place on a one-day course – a day's instruction and an hour's flight, on which I could take a person to support me.

Replacing the phone, I laughed out loud, slightly hysterically. The course date was April 1. What had I done?

From then on it was always at the back of my mind and as the day drew nearer I didn't sleep well, wondering if I'd be able to go through with it.

On April 1, I joined the queue of more than 100 people at the airport hotel waiting to join the course. Wobbly-legged, I found a seat. I was surprised to see so many young men and women, which was explained later – they needed to fly for work or lose their jobs.

The morning began by meeting the captain, co-pilot, cabin crew and psychologist. We were given talks on all aspects of flying – how an aeroplane flies, the mechanics, turbulence, the take off and landing. Each manoeuvre and change of engine noise was explained so that when we flew we'd be prepared for every sound.

This was accompanied by visual aids and light-hearted banter which made the morning pass quickly. At no time were we pressured to fly and we could leave at any time if we wanted to. Over lunch, the speakers mingled with us and we were encouraged to talk about our fears, which was very helpful.

The captain then made an announcement: "Ladies and gentlemen, this is not an April Fools' joke but unfortunately our flight today will be delayed." We all groaned as we had been due to fly out at 4pm and the waiting became more difficult as time wore on. He then introduced us to the psychologist who talked to us about panic attacks, phobias and our fear of flying and the best way of coping with it.

One remedy which caused hilarity was to take a deep breath while simultaneously clenching our buttocks, followed by slowly exhaling and unclenching them.

He finished by telling us to close our eyes and imagine the flight itself. In my imagination I left my seat, walked out of the hotel, boarded a coach to the airport and went through all the procedures until I was seated in the plane. We did this twice, so when I walked outside to meet my husband, Stan, who was coming with me, it already seemed familiar.

As we sat in the departure lounge there was an air of camaraderie as we tried to bolster each other up. The hardest step for me was the final one on to the plane. I knew there'd be no turning back.

On board, the ratio of crew to passengers was very high. There was always someone with a reassuring word or a quip to distract us. The captain told us what was happening to the plane and the psychologist kept up a steady stream of advice. Before long we were all clenching our buttocks and breathing deeply!

Suddenly the engines started up and we were moving. Faster and faster we went and I needed every ounce of nerve to stay in my seat. Oxygen masks, inflatable life jackets and escape slides were a jumbled blur in my mind but the exits were indelibly stamped on my brain.

The engine noise changed, we were taking off, this was it! Feet glued to the floor, elbows gripped

Far left: Wyn in the cockpit

Left: Claire with James and Alexandra – three very good reasons to take the fear of flying course

to my side, fingers clamped round the arm rests, forehead damp with perspiration and, in spite of the commentary inviting us to look out of the window (he must be joking!), eyes tightly closed.

Just as I'd had enough of being pushed back in my seat by the acceleration, it stopped

Suddenly the engines started up and we were moving. Faster and faster we went and I needed every ounce of nerve to stay in my seat

and we were in the air. The tension in the plane eased noticeably and we were invited to walk around. I couldn't – my legs were jelly.

Sandwiches and drinks were served but as my stomach was continuing to loop-the-loop, my husband ate mine. Surprisingly, it seemed no time at all before the captain asked us to fasten our seat belts for landing. I'd no need to do this as I'd kept mine securely fastened.

The descent wasn't as bad as I'd feared and I even managed a quick peep out of the window just before landing. The wheels touched the ground with a bump and there was spontaneous applause. We were safe and we'd done it!

I'd found it very hard and was advised to take another short flight as soon as possible. Others enjoyed it, a few hated every minute. Once at home, I slept on and off for two days, exhausted from the stress. I remembered the co-pilot's advice and booked a flight to Manchester with my son.

When I booked the ticket I mentioned that I'd taken the fear of flying course and the crew took the greatest care of me. I was invited into the cockpit – the view was stunning – but I couldn't wait to get back to my seat. This trip was much better and I was given a congratulations card signed by the crew members.

I punched the air, shouting: "Hooray!" as I left the plane, much to the amusement of the other passengers. I didn't care – I'd conquered my fear and, although I knew it would be hard to take a four-hour flight, I knew I could do it.

Three months later I nervously boarded the plane to Istanbul but this time I was

calmer. Little did I know what lay ahead. After an hour we ran into storms, the turbulence was really something.

Being shaken from side to side in the toilet which was the size of a shoe box, I realised I could either face my fear or run amok, screaming down the aisle, which was everyone's nightmare on the course. At this point I remembered a tip from the psychologist; if you keep pushing your fear away when it surfaces, eventually your brain will give up and you'll win. And that's exactly what I did.

At Istanbul Airport my daughter Claire was there to meet me. We hugged and she said in my ear: "Well done. Mum, you made it." We spent a wonderful two weeks with the family, during which time I had no fear about the return journey – nothing could be worse than the flight out and it wasn't. Blue skies, mountain tops pushing through the clouds, the River Thames, the Dome and Heathrow.

Overcoming my fear was a long journey but well worth it. My son is living in France for the next two years, so guess where I'm off to?

IT'S IN THE STARS

Patrick Arundell looks to the heavens to predict what's in store for you this month

**ARIES
(21 March – 20 April)**
Your greatest ability comes from being bold and taking the initiative, so there is little that can prevent you from going for your goals. This could see you creating a more secure lifestyle.

TAURUS (21 April – 21 May)
You'll be in reflective mood as you contemplate your life's direction. On the positive side, this could be a fortunate time for you, romantically.

GEMINI (22 May – 21 June)
This is a soul-searching time for Geminis. Friendships will be important and can help you unlock situations relating to your past.

CANCER (22 June – 23 July)
Someone powerful or wise will have a big impact on your life. If they try to help, let them.

LEO (24 July – 23 August)
You can be both charming and assertive, yet there is a restlessness that needs resolving.

VIRGO (24 August – 23 September)
Someone very different to you, perhaps from overseas, can help you look at life differently.

LIBRA (24 September – 23 October)
This is an intense month for relationships but try not to feel overwhelmed. Your good humour, drive and determination will win through.

SCORPIO (24 October – 22 November)
April will find you feeling passionate and creative. You'll be full of enthusiasm, so don't be disheartened if things don't go to plan.

SAGITTARIUS (23 November – 21 December)
Until the 20th, the emphasis will be on fun but don't forget to try to achieve practical goals, too.

CAPRICORN (22 December – 20 January)
You could be feeling withdrawn. The 21st sees a change and you'll be itching to get out more.

AQUARIUS (21 January – 19 February)
The pace could be hectic this month. Don't be surprised if your home acts as a meeting place.

PISCES (20 February – 20 March)
Someone you've known for some time, could take a shine to you. While this could be flattering, your focus will be on finances.

HOUSEWIFE'S CHOICE

Robert Opie takes a nostalgic peek at shopping-basket bygones

SUNLIGHT SOAP

Before working for his father's warehouse of grocers and household goods, William Lever was a commercial traveller. During that time he saw at first hand the bleak and unsanitary conditions in which people lived. Since 1874, the Lever Wholesale business had been selling soap, but in 1884 William Lever registered the name Sunlight for his best soap made from vegetable oils instead of tallow. The following year he started to produce his own soap from a factory in Warrington. It was sold in a carton; previously soap had been wrapped in parchment papers. Lever's factory moved to a site on the banks of the Mersey in 1889. A village was built for the workers and the whole area was named Port Sunlight. Advertising made Sunlight Soap familiar around the world with such slogans as 'Why does a woman look older sooner than a man?'

HP SAUCE

The origins of HP Sauce go back to Frederick Garton of Nottingham who was making sauces in the 1870s. The story goes that he had heard a rumour that a bottle of his sauce had been seen at the Houses of Parliament. Some years later, the secret HP recipe was exchanged for a debt due to the Midland Vinegar Company based in Birmingham. The brand was relaunched in 1903 with the Houses of Parliament proudly displayed on the label. Since then it has become a national institution, using slogans such as, 'Mary had a little lamb with lots of HP Sauce'. Sales were boosted when Mary Wilson, wife of Prime Minister Harold Wilson, complained that the PM covered everything she cooked with HP Sauce.

PUZZLE IT OUT!
Cryptic crosswords and tea-time teasers to keep your brain busy

Code-cracker

This puzzle has no clues in the conventional sense. Instead, every different number printed in the main grid represents a different letter (with the same number always representing the same letter, of course). For example, if 17 turns out to be an 'F', you can write in F wherever a square contains 17.

We have completed a small part of the puzzle to give you a start, but the rest is up to you.

Use the smaller grid to keep track of deciphered letters.

15	9	3	10	4	21	4	8	20	■	21	■	5
■	7	■	7	■	7	■	3	■	22	3	25	13
21	25	17	26	21	1	12	5	5	■	5	■	12
■	23	■	21	■	3	■	15	■	5	13	20	12
15	■	1	■	5	15	4	4	13	■	7	■	25
4	14	12	5	12	■	8	■	10	4	15	2	20
1	■	24	■	16	4	8	2	7	■	9	■	7
11	17	4	13	12	■	25	■	19	9	3	10	10
17	■	13	■	10	4	20	7	25	■	4	■	8
12	21	3	15	■	6	■	18	■	13	■	7	■
10	■	7	■	25	3	11	17	4	10	3	15	12
4	1	13	4	■	8	■	10	■	3	■	9	■
10	■	12	■	8	12	16	12	25(L)	4(O)	21(P)	12	10

1	2	3	4 O	5	6	7	8	9	10	11	12	13
14	15	16	17	18	19	20	21 P	22	23	24	25 L	26

Letter set

All the letters needed for the answers in each row and column are given. Cross-referencing coupled with anagram skills will ensure the complete solution. (Start by locating the rarer letters.)

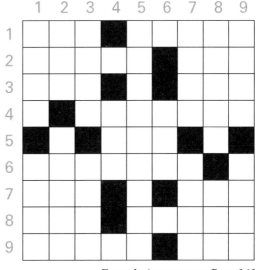

Across

1 ACEELNPP
2 AAEEILRS
3 OEIRSRX
4 AEEWRRTT
5 ARSWY
6 AMEICDRR
7 AEEGLNO
8 AADLLMOC
9 MREEMNUY

Down

1 AOMEWCRP
2 AAEGNORW
3 DEEIORRP
4 EMRRS
5 ACEILNRTY
6 ELLRY
7 AADEEERS
8 AAEILMSU
9 AMECLNTX

For solutions turn to Page 161

May 2002

MONDAY	TUESDAY	WEDNESDAY	THURSDAY	
		1	2	
6 Public Holiday	7	8	9	
13 YOURS Summer Special on sale	14	15	16	
20	21 Chelsea Flower Show opens	22	23	
27	28	29	30	Ju

IDAY	SATURDAY	SUNDAY
	4	*5*
	11	*12*
	18	*19* Whitsunday
	25	*26*

Flower of the month

RHODODENDRON
(Rhododendron yakushimanum)

For many gardeners May means the Chelsea Flower Show and, in turn, rhododendrons. Vibrant gardens, packed with colour, are a tradition and rhododendrons, smothered with blooms are favourites.

Unfortunately, rhododendrons are fussy, needing an acid soil, though they can be grown in containers in special ericaceous compost. For all their beauty, some rhododendrons can become large plants and their leaves, though evergreen, are unexciting.

What gardeners need is a small rhododendron with colourful flowers that has interesting leaves and will grow well in containers.

Luckily, Japan has the answer. From the island of Yakushima, at the southern tip of Japan, comes *Rhododendron yakushimanum*, a low-growing shrub often less than 3ft (1m) high. Although the great rhododendron boom occurred in the 19th and early 20th century, the British public did not see this species until 1947 when it was exhibited at the Chelsea Flower Show. It had pale pink flowers in tight clusters, opening from deeper buds, and the foliage, especially when young, is covered in white felt. Most of all it had a compact habit. From that day onwards it has captured the hearts of gardeners and it has spawned a raft of hybrids, most with characteristic features of the species.

URS on sale

Born this month...
- Bing Crosby *(3 May, 1903)*
- **Audrey Hepburn** *(4 May, 1929)*
- Peter Ilyich Tchaikovsky *(7 May, 1840)*
- Glenda Jackson *(9 May, 1936)*
- Fred Astaire *(10 May, 1899)*
- Florence Nightingale *(12 May, 1820)*
- Pope John Paul II *(18 May, 1920)*
- John F Kennedy *(19 May, 1917)*
- Sir Laurence Olivier *(22 May, 1907)*
- Isadora Duncan *(27 May, 1878)*

THOUGHT FOR THE WEEK

If you always do what you've always done, you'll always get what you've always had.

Mary Ann Fulcher, Norfolk

THIS WEEK IN YOUR GARDEN

For many gardeners, May is the best month of the year. But although the weather is milder, beware sudden sharp frosts…

- Any remaining spring-flowering bedding plants such as wallflowers should be cleared away and put on the compost heap.
- Lift and divide polyanthus and primulas which have finished flowering.
- Rainfall generally decreases this month so water shrubs, trees and plants as they need it, especially those in containers.
- To guarantee vegetables throughout the summer, sow them regularly at ten day intervals. Hoeing now becomes a regular chore as weeds try to take control!
- Protect crops from carrot fly.

TIP TIME

Don't throw cold tea down the sink. Geraniums love it – and it's cheaper and more effective than any plant food.
Mrs M Cunliffe, Pudsey, West Yorkshire

HEALTH CHECK

Are you getting enough?
Fruit and veg, that is! Doctors recommend eating at least five portions of fruit or vegetables a day, but a recent study has shown that on average we chomp through just three portions. Part of the problem might be because there's some confusion about what counts as a portion – or even what counts as a fruit or vegetable.

For instance, in nutritional terms, potatoes are a starch not a vegetable, so you can't include chips in your daily tally!

So what counts as a portion? Well probably not as much as you think. For most vegetables, two tablespoons constitutes a portion. For salad leaves and other watery vegetables, such as cucumber, you should eat a small bowlful. One medium-size fruit, such as an apple, counts as a portion; you'll need two for smaller fruits. It makes no difference, in terms of the nutritional value, whether your fruit and veg is fresh, frozen, canned or dried; eaten raw or cooked.

It's easy to boost your daily tally. Drink a glass of fruit juice with your breakfast and eat a piece of fruit for a mid-morning snack. Tuck into a side salad with your lunchtime sandwich and add a handful of carrots and mushrooms, for instance, to your shepherd's pie.

FROM ME TO YOU

Blushing bather
As a teenager I was admitted in a rush to a local fever hospital. A young trainee nurse was ordered to give me a 'blanket bath', but instead she took one look at me and ran off.

Afterwards I found out that she had been a classmate of mine from the same school and was too embarrassed to give me a bed bath.

Duncan Robson, Gateshead, Tyne and Wear

RECIPE CORNER

Anzac Biscuits
"These biscuits have been made in our family for years," says Jenny Sunderland from Burnley in Lancashire.

"They're called Anzac biscuits because they were brought over here by troops serving in the Australia and New Zealand Army in the First World War."

The measurements aren't exact but I use a teacup which holds about 8 fl oz."

1 cup self-raising flour
1 cup sugar
1 cup Quaker oats
1 cup desiccated coconut
1 tablespoon golden syrup
4oz/110g margarine or butter
1 teaspoon baking powder
1 tablespoon boiling water

Florence Drake from Liverpool recalls the excitement of planning a big night out with her best friend…

"Browsing through my photos I found this one taken of my friend Vera McDonald (now Scott) and me, when I was Florence Briercliffe (I'm on the left). I was 17 and the year was 1955. Vera had managed to get tickets for us to go on a river cruise in Liverpool. We were so excited, we spent our week's wages on new dresses – in anticipation of all the young men asking us to dance. Imagine our disappointment when we boarded the river boat and discovered, to our horror, that it was a cruise for the Boy Scouts! Unfortunately, there was no going back – unless we jumped overboard and swam for it! All the same, we had lots of fun – even if it wasn't the most romantic of nights."

---

1 Preheat the oven to 190°C/375°F/gas mark 5 and grease a baking tray.
2 Place the flour, sugar, oats and coconut in a bowl. Melt the syrup and margarine or butter and mix into the dry ingredients. Dissolve the baking powder in the boiling water and add to the mixture. Stir to combine.
3 Using your hands, shape into small balls, roughly the size of a walnut, and place on the baking tray (space them apart, as they spread during cooking). Bake in the oven for about 10-15 minutes or until golden brown. Cool a little before removing to a rack.

GO ON, SMILE
Portrait present
A man asked his wife: "What would you like for your birthday, dear?" She said: "I'd like a portrait of the Queen." When he inquired: "Where am I going to get one of those?" She quickly replied: "There is one on every £50 note."
Harry Swift, Hull

TIP TIME
Old stockings or tights make strong ties for fixing fruit canes to trellis.
Eric Fisher, Canvey Island, Essex

THIS WEEK THROUGH THE YEARS
- **3 May, 1957** South Africa dropped God Save the Queen as its national anthem.
- **4 May, 1979** Margaret Thatcher, leader of the Conservative party, became the first female British prime minister.
- **5 May, 1975** The first British Rail high-speed train went into service between Paddington and Weston-super-Mare.
- **30 May, 1944** The Labour Party called for the nationalisation of coal, gas and electricity.

May 6-12

THOUGHT FOR THE WEEK

I often quote one of my Mum's sayings about getting the best out of life...

Give me flowers while I'm living
Do not wait until I'm dead
If the love be worth the giving
Let it o'er my life be shed

E Frontcrak, Lindley,
Huddersfield

THIS WEEK IN YOUR GARDEN

This week in your garden borders are bursting at the seams with colour and trees are in full leaf...

- Train sweet peas that are growing vigorously.
- Newly-sown lawns can be cut when the grass is roughly 2in (5cm) high, with the blades on their highest setting.
- Plant up hanging baskets and other containers, keeping them in the greenhouse or conservatory to grow on.
- Sow ornamental cabbage for winter colour and lovely spring bedding.
- If you have a pond, feed fish regularly as they become more active.

TIP TIME
To help prevent blisters on a long walk, rub your heels with soap before you put on your shoes.
Z Sheppard,
Stoke-on-Trent

FROM ME TO YOU

The Boiled Egg
A short story by Sheila Bungenaar from Stoke-on-Trent, Staffordshire.

I clutched my precious blue ribbon and ran down the hill to my Auntie's house. Mummy was there. She would fasten my ribbon for me. Before I could slow down, I tripped and fell headlong, crushing my face on the sandstone step.

I screamed, terrified by all the blood that poured from my nose. I was rushed to the surgery where a broken nose was diagnosed. My face was heavily bruised and I was in a state of shock.

I beamed with pleasure when my Auntie made me a soft-boiled egg and soldiers for being so brave. I had an egg – all to myself. It was 1945 and that was my Auntie's ration for the week!

FASCINATING PHOTOS

Renée Cole from Looe in Cornwall remembers dressing up for King George and Queen Mary's Silver Jubilee…

"This photo was taken in 1935 as part of our local celebrations in Weybridge in Surrey to mark the Silver Jubilee of King George V and Queen Mary. Instead of a carnival queen that year, it was decided to have Britannia, Miss Scotland, Miss Wales and Miss Ireland. All the local girls were invited to a special dance, where four of us were chosen to ride on the Silver Jubilee float. I was picked to be Miss Ireland (that's me on the right) and I was 15 years old. I'm not Irish but I was chosen because of my brunette hair and blue eyes."

HEALTH CHECK

New hope for Alzheimer's
There are encouraging signs that a revolutionary vaccine for Alzheimer's may not be far away. The vaccine works by stimulating the immune system to fight the development of plaques that appear in the brains of people who have Alzheimer's. Early research results suggest that it might be able to prevent the disease or delay its progression. As part of the study, 80 patients suffering from Alzheimer's are being treated with the vaccine in four hospitals around the UK. Doctors are refusing to reveal the hospitals, for fear that they will be besieged by sufferers wanting to take part in the trial.

THIS WEEK THROUGH THE YEARS

- **6 May, 1954** Roger Bannister, a British medical student, broke the four-minute mile, running the distance in 3 minutes 59.4 seconds.
- **7 May, 1945** The German Army surrendered and, on May 8, VE Day was celebrated with street parties and fireworks to mark the end of the war in Europe.
- **12 May, 1937** The streets were lined with well-wishers as George VI and Queen Elizabeth (now the Queen Mother) were crowned in Westminster Abbey.
- **12 May, 1999** Ler Sarkisor from Georgia, 60, became the oldest person ever to reach the summit of Mount Everest.

TIP TIME
To clean artificial flowers, put a good handful of salt into a paper carrier bag. Holding the flowers upside down by their stems, place the flower head in the bag. Tighten the bag around the stems and shake several times. They will come up as good as new.
Peggy Owen, Gwynedd

GO ON, SMILE!

Good grub?
I recently saw a blackboard outside a pub, which read, 'The Chef's Special'. Underneath, some bright spark had written, 'He might be, but his food isn't!'
B Scott, Slough

TIP TIME
Buy a carton of mustard and cress a week before needed. Put it on a windowsill and water. It will soon double in size.
Mrs R Latter, Aylesford, Kent

RECIPE CORNER

Lemon Curd Cake
This lemon-flavoured cake is always a hit with my family and friends, writes Barbara Ling of Needham Market, Suffolk. It's delicious served plain, or you can decorate with lemon icing.

Ingredients
5 oz/150 g self-raising flour
4 oz/110 g caster sugar
4 oz/110 g margarine
2 eggs, beaten
2 tablespoons lemon curd

Method
1 Grease and line an 8in cake tin. Preheat the oven to 190°C/375°F/gas mark 5.
2 Place all ingredients in a bowl and beat until mixture is light and fluffy. Turn mixture into cake tin, smooth surface and bake in oven for 45 minutes or until well risen. Leave to cool then turn out on to wire tray.

THOUGHT FOR THE WEEK

Those who never change their minds love themselves more than the truth.

Franz Schubert (1797-1828)
Austrian composer

THIS WEEK IN YOUR GARDEN

Why not visit gardens open to the public – there'll be cuttings for sale and ideas to glean...

- Tuck straw under strawberries to protect the fruit from rotting.
- Lift and divide mint. Grow it in pots to prevent it taking over the garden.
- Continue to prick out and pot on seedlings, cuttings and young plants as and when needed.
- Remove frost protection from fruit trees and begin pruning trained plums and cherries.
- Clear out spring bedding from containers to make way for summer bedding plants.

THIS WEEK THROUGH THE YEARS

- **16 May, 1955** Olga Korbut, the waif-like USSR gymnast who won huge popularity and three gold medals at the 1972 Munich Olympics, was born.
- **13 May, 1981** Pope John Paul II was shot while blessing a huge crowd in St Peter's Square, Rome, from an open-top vehicle. He made a full recovery.
- **13 May, 1995** Alison Hargreaves became the first woman to climb Mount Everest alone and without oxygen.
- **17 May, 1995** Jacques Chirac became the fifth president of France.

GO ON, SMILE!

Spotty dogs
I asked a friend if she had enjoyed the film 102 Dalmatians and she replied: "It was good in spots."

Mrs B Butler, Culchech, Warrington

TIP TIME
When our friends from America visited us last year, they asked if, instead of giving me flowers on their departure, I would let them 'plant-up' my garden with a few bedding plants. All during the summer, I had a lasting reminder of their visit and received many compliments from passers-by.
Mrs C Beard, Crownhill, Plymouth

HEALTH CHECK

A lotta bottle!
Bottled mineral waters promise all sorts of health benefits – at a price. But are they any better for you than the water you can get for free from your kitchen tap? Research reported last year showed that, in general, fancy mineral waters don't contain any more health-promoting minerals than the ordinary stuff. In the taste stakes, tap water scores well, too. In one blind test, tasters picked out good old London tap water as being their favourite – beating all the fancy bottled varieties.

FROM ME TO YOU

Anyone for tea?
B Thompson from Penn in Buckinghamshire, remembers a humorous incident, which happened in the workplace more than 50 years ago:
Going back to the early 1950s when office juniors acted as tea-girls for the office staff, a new youngster offered us tea which was pitch-black.

When I asked how many spoonfuls of tea she'd used, she said her mother always put in one for each cup and one for the pot – we had 26 staff!

TIP TIME
Don't throw away old lipsticks. Clean the remnants into a small container using a cocktail stick and melt gently in the microwave. It can be used for months with a lipbrush.
Mrs Noble, Penrith, Cumbria

FASCINATING PHOTOS

Olive Martin from Swindon in Wiltshire waited anxiously in the wings during her daughter's moment of glory…

"This is a photo of my daughter Carol taken in 1951 on the stage at the Odeon Cinema, Hammersmith in West London. She is nervously presenting a bouquet to the late Joyce Grenfell. She was a wonderful actress and also one of the judges in the Bonny Babies competition that my little girl had entered, as part of the Festival of Britain.

"In the background, you can see me peering over my little girl's shoulder looking rather worried in case she dropped the bouquet, as it looked rather heavy for a little toddler to handle.

"This photo, which appeared in the Kensington Gazette, is special to me as my daughter came first in her heat and was chosen from many other little girls to make presentation to Joyce."

RECIPE CORNER

Devilled Chicken
This is the perfect treatment for one or two chicken breasts or chunks of chicken left after a Sunday roast. Piled in a soft roll with crisp lettuce and mayonnaise, it makes a delicious Monday lunch. Serves 1-2.

2 cold, cooked chicken breasts
1 tablespoon Dijon mustard
1 clove of garlic, crushed (optional)
2 tablespoon fruit chutney
1 tablespoon Worcestershire sauce

1 tablespoon ketchup
1 tablespoon horseradish sauce
Few drops Tabasco sauce

1 Heat the grill to medium. Mix all ingredients to a paste. Slash the chicken flesh with a knife and spread paste over the meat and in the slashes.

TIP TIME
Keep an old bucket in a corner of your kitchen with a plastic bag folded over the top. It's a perfect place to put all your scraps and peelings and it's easy to empty.
Mrs W Twydle, Paston, Peterborough

2 Grill the chicken about 4 in/10 cm from the flame for about 10 minutes, turning once, until it is piping hot and sizzling. Carve it into slices while still hot.

May 20-26

THOUGHT FOR THE WEEK

Experience is the name everyone gives to their mistakes.

Oscar Wilde (1854-1900)

THIS WEEK IN YOUR GARDEN

The days are becoming warmer, so pests and diseases can start to take hold…

- Temperatures are rising in the greenhouse. Take care to shade young plants and keep the ventilators open during the day.
- Keep a watch for aphids on roses; protect young plants from slugs, snails and caterpillars. Hang yellow sticky traps round the greenhouse.
- Finish planting out dahlias and begonias.
- Mulch all soft fruit to retain moisture in the soil.
- Growing tomatoes need feeding regularly with high-potash fertiliser.

FROM ME TO YOU

Government health warning

The Government and health authorities aren't the only ones to warn of increased drinking in Britain.

One £10 note I received in my pension had scrawled across it: 'Don't spend it on drink'.

Mr F Butler, Glazebury, Warrington

GO ON, SMILE!

Cooking up a story

Visiting my granddaughter in hospital after the birth of her son, Harry, I asked her how she'd coped with the birth. "Well at first they used suction," she replied, "but in the end they had to use spatulas."

Well I knew she liked cooking, but I think forceps would have been better.

Mrs J Howarth, Hyde, Cheshire

> **TIP TIME**
> When you've finished cutting bread or buttering toast, keep the crumbs in a plastic bag. You will soon have enough for breadcrumbs to use in a recipe.
> *Alan Kilburn, Burnley, Lancashire*

HEALTH CHECK

Perfect posture

Standing and sitting properly can help you feel and look better. When you're standing still, try to imagine that there's a cord attached to the top of your head which is being pulled upwards, straightening your spine. Lift your shoulders back and relax them, feeling your arms pulling down from their sockets. Keep your abdominal muscles pulled in, tuck your buttocks under, relax your knees and keep your weight on the balls of your feet.

When sitting, your chair should support the base of your spine and the height should let your feet rest comfortably on the floor. If your chair is at a table your elbows should be level with the top, allowing your forearms to be at a right angle to your upper arms.

THIS WEEK THROUGH THE YEARS

- **24 May, 1933** The Trades Union Congress called for a boycott of Germany to protest against Hitler.
- **25 May, 1977** The film Star Wars, directed by George Lucas, was released.
- **26 May, 1980** Who shot JR? The long-awaited episode of the US soap, Dallas, revealed that the culprit was his ex-lover, Kristin.
- **26 May, 1994** Michael 'Wacko Jacko' Jackson married Lisa Marie Presley, daughter of Elvis Presley, in a secret ceremony.

> **TIP TIME**
> I remember what I need to check before a long car journey by saying the word, 'flower'. It stands for fuel, lights, oil, water, electrics and rubber (tyres and wipers).
> *J Machin, Congleton, Cheshire*

Creamy Paprika Chicken
Ideal with new potatoes or rice,
and tender spring vegetables.
Serves 4

1 oz/25 g butter
2 tablespoons sunflower oil
4 chicken breast fillets,
cut in strips
4 streaky bacon rashers
1 large onion, sliced
8 oz/225 g button mushrooms,
halved
1 oz/25 g plain flour
1 teaspoon paprika
¼ pint/150 ml chicken stock
5 oz/150 g soured cream
Salt and pepper

1 Melt the butter and oil in a
   large frying pan. Add the
   chicken and cook for 8
   minutes, stirring. Remove
   from pan with a slotted
   spoon and keep warm.
2 Lower the heat and add the
   bacon, onion and mushrooms.
   Cook gently, for 3-5 minutes,
   until the onion is soft but not
   coloured. Add the flour and
   paprika and cook for a
   minute, stirring constantly.
   Pour in the stock and bring
   to a boil, stirring until
   thickened. Return chicken to
   the pan. Cover and simmer
   for 5 minutes or until the
   chicken is tender.
3 Stir in the soured cream and
   season to taste. Gently heat
   the mixture until hot but
   not boiling.

FASCINATING PHOTOS

**John Stewart from London tells the story of his father who
was a gentlemen's outfitter in the West End…**
"Here's a picture of my father, Charles Albert Edwin Stewart,
in the 1920s carrying 28 straw boater hats.

   "At the time he was working as a gentlemen's outfitter with
my Uncle Rody in a London shop, where they sold suits,
hats and blazers. My father enjoyed working in the clothes
industry and he always managed to look immaculate and
well-dressed himself.

   "During the General Strike, my father had to do other
things to earn money, including labouring, but as soon as the
strike was over he went back to outfitting. He finished his
working life as the first hand at F H Rowse Ltd, which was
the biggest gentlemen's drapers in west London."

THOUGHT FOR THE WEEK

Age is a matter of feeling, not years.

*George William Curtis
(1824-92)
American man of letters*

THIS WEEK IN YOUR GARDEN

With June come the longest days of the year when we can take most pleasure – and most produce – from the garden…

- Plant out marrows and courgettes and keep them well watered.
- Damp down the greenhouse to increase humidity levels.
- Harden off bedding plants for planting out.
- Pinch out broad bean tops to discourage blackfly.
- Sow half-hardy and hardy annuals now to ensure autumn colour.
- Protect apple and pear trees from codling moth by using pheromone traps.
- Harden off hanging baskets by leaving them out for increasingly longer periods.

TIP TIME
Prevent paint dripping down your wrist when you're painting a ceiling by pushing the brush handle through a paper plate.

FROM ME TO YOU

Creamy treat

Mock cream was very popular in the war years and I'd like to share the recipe, which I recently found written on the flyleaf of a cookbook belonging to my late mother.

Mock Cream

Melt 1 tablespoon of gelatine in a tablespoon of boiling water. Add to half a tin of evaporated milk. Add a heaped teaspoon of sugar, some vanilla flavouring and beat. Make up when needed.

Pauline Stainton, Goole, East Yorkshire

HEALTH CHECK

Hiding from hay fever?

When summer comes, up to one-fifth of Britons suffer the itchy eyes, nose and throat that characterise hay fever, an allergy to pollen.

Antihistamine drugs can help, although these can cause drowsiness, and corticosteroid preparations can also relieve the symptoms.

Desensitisation, which involves injecting small doses of pollen extract over a three-year period, is a very effective long-term treatment. You can help yourself by watching the pollen forecast carefully and, if it is high, stay indoors in the late afternoon, wear sunglasses, and if you're out in a car, keep your windows shut.

Studies have also shown that eating live yoghurt can help reduce hay fever attacks, as can eating onions, which are high in quercetin, thought to help quell allergic reactions.

TIP TIME
Instead of spreading cream cheese on to your crackers, pipe it on using an icing bag. It looks more attractive and the tasty treats are perfect for special occasions.
*Mrs J Pearce,
Bognor Regis,
West Sussex*

THIS WEEK THROUGH THE YEARS

- **28 May, 1955** Frank Sinatra entered the US music charts with his song In the Wee Small Hours.
- **28 May, 1961** The CEGB (Central Electricity Generating Board) blamed human error for a massive blackout in the south-east of England.
- **29 May, 1985** Forty-one people died and many more were injured at the Heysel Stadium in Belgium after British football hooligans went on the rampage.
- **2 June, 1953** Queen Elizabeth II was crowned in Westminster Abbey aged 27. The coronation service was watched on television by viewers all over the world.

FASCINATING PHOTOS

Rose White from Whitstable, Kent, was very proud of her young daughter Jackie when she became a bride...

"These two little girls are taking part in a fancy-dress parade in Whitstable, Kent, at the 1945 Victory party.

"Most of the children in Whitstable dressed up to mark the occasion. The bride is my young daughter Jackie, aged four, and her groom is my brother's little girl, Pauline Coffin, then aged five.

"Times were hard then and we had to make do and mend. I made Jackie's little outfit from old flour sacks and an eiderdown cover. I think the veil was passed down from a communion. Pauline's mum made the groom's outfit out of leftover Forces material.

"They really do look a lovely pair and people will probably recognise them as an American GI and his bride."

GO ON, SMILE!

A bitter pill to swallow
I caught a bronchial infection while on holiday in Italy and went to see the local doctor who couldn't speak English. He gave me some antibiotics. They looked like horse pills but I managed to swallow them anyway.

When we got home, I told this tale to a friend's daughter who had lived abroad for some years. She couldn't stop laughing – apparently, overseas antibiotics are taken as suppositories.

Mary Holmes,
Llandudno, Conwy

A HOLIDAY TO REMEMBER

By Sally Wragg

"I haven't a clue where I put the blessed things." Charlie stood in the kitchen with his hands on his hips, the same perplexed expression on his face Elspeth had, of late, become too used to seeing.

"Darling, if you're looking for your glasses, they're still on top of your head." She said it gently and then sighed. He'd propped them up there after he'd read the label on the cereal packet.

He was becoming so forgetful. Anything not attached – shoes, papers, books, glasses – life was a constant round of hide-and-seek. Yesterday she had found the washing-up liquid in the fridge. He'd denied putting it there, of course, pointing out she had done the washing-up that morning.

"And who washed the coffee-cups?" she reminded him, and then seeing his hurt expression, had continued dryly, "Well, it must have been the fairies," and left it at that, not wanting to turn it into another argument. There had been plenty enough of those of late.

Poor Charlie. It was only age catching up with him, much as he tried to hide it. He sat down grumpily, propped the paper up against the marmalade jar and took the top off his boiled egg. Elspeth watched him in amused resignation. The thinning, grey hair brushed over his forehead to conceal the receding hairline, the extra notch on his trouser belt, the aches and pains brought on by the slightest activity, the forgetfulness.

Yes, old age was painful, but she supposed it had been bound to claim one of them. As a young man Charlie had been so capable and organised – bursting with energy. Now all he wanted to do was settle down in front of the television with the paper. He had been such a handsome man once, tall and well-proportioned with thick, wavy hair. That was back in the days when he had hair.

And he had chosen Elspeth out of all the girls in college. Oh yes, he had certainly been a catch, had Charlie. They had married after their finals and gone off on a grand tour of Italy that had stretched down into Sicily. It had seemed to last forever. Tuscany, Venice, Rome, staying in each place as long as they wanted. They had finished up in a charming little hotel in the quaint old town of Cefalu. It had been perfectly idyllic.

It had to come to an end some time, of course. And then all the usual paraphenalia of life had claimed their attention, along with the major things, such as finding jobs, building a home together, the children. Sicily had become like a fairy-tale, a distant illusion of happiness.

Not that she was complaining, she thought, pouring tea out into their breakfast mugs. There had been plenty of good times for the two of them and she wouldn't have changed a bit of it. All part of life's rich tapestry, her mother had said.

And besides, they still had plenty to look forward to. They had both dreamed of returning to Cefalu and so when Elspeth had seen the late booking in the travel agent's window for the very same hotel, well it had seemed more than fate. The children were off their hands with homes and families of their own. They were both retired with a tidy little nest-egg. Why not?

She had gone straight into the shop and booked it, afraid it might be snapped up if she didn't. She worried momentarily about Charlie but she needn't have, he was as delighted as she was when she rushed home to tell him.

"I can see I shall have to watch my beautiful wife when we get over there," he said teasingly, sweeping his arms up around her. "You know what those Italian men are like."

Elspeth spread butter on her toast and thought of last-minute arrangements. They were flying from Gatwick at the weekend, such a change from their annual outing to Bournemouth, a chance to recapture their youth. She was as excited and giddy as a school girl. And it was probably just what Charlie needed…

"Charlie! You can't have mislaid the tickets!" Elspeth's anguished cry could be heard outside in the garden. It was Saturday morning and Gemma would be arriving shortly to take them to the airport.

Charlie had been such a handsome man, tall and well-proportioned with thick, wavy hair

No tickets and no passports. There would be no holiday. It was ridiculous

"We put them safe with the passports, remember?" Charlie ran a hand through his thinning hair and tried not to look worried.

"Of course I can remember," she snapped, unable to quell her rising anxiety. "The passports are missing with them!" Couldn't she trust him with anything? She had done everything else that needed to be done – organising the traveller's cheques and the money, the endless washing and ironing, the shopping, cancelling the papers. She'd even written the luggage-labels and fastened them carefully on to the cases. It was just too bad of him.

"I'm sure I put them away in the cupboard," he fretted.

"Well they're not there now." She had looked already – three times in fact. "Think Charlie…" She tried to keep her voice reasonable but failed. "Where else might you have put them?"

"I don't know," he cried. "It was just behind the Crown Derby."

"Then where are they? I can't trust you with anything nowadays."

There, it was said. Charlie's bottom lip stuck out, like it did when he was offended. It would have been funny if it hadn't been so desperate. No tickets and no passports. There would be no holiday. It was ridiculous.

"It's no good us falling out, love," he said tiredly.

"You would say that!" Elspeth's voice was still sharp, but how could she help it? They had a plane to catch in four hours and they still had to get to Gatwick.

By the time Gemma arrived, everything was out of the cases and spread around on the dining-room table. So much for all Elspeth's careful packing. And the missing documents still hadn't turned up.

"Not ready yet?" their daughter began

cheerfully. The smile slid from her face when she saw their anxious expressions.

"Your father's lost the passports," Elspeth said.

"I'm sure I put them in the cupboard," Charlie began to protest.

"Don't start that again," she snapped.

Gemma interrupted: "Oh, is that all?" Without another word, she went straight over to the sideboard drawer and pulled it open. It was where they kept the best cutlery, used only on special occasions – birthdays, Christmas, that sort of thing.

"Here we are," she cried happily, pulling out two passports with the flight tickets protruding.

"Don't you remember, Mum? You got them out of the cupboard to show me your passport photographs. You said they made you look like a couple of convicts and they'd never let you out of the country. You shoved them back in here," she said pointing to the sideboard. "I thought at the time it was a funny place to put them."

"Oh…" Elspeth stammered. She couldn't bear to look at Charlie's face. After all she'd said. She could remember now showing them to Gemma and then taking her upstairs to let her have a look at the new sun-dress she'd bought for the holiday. What she'd done with the passports and tickets after Gemma had seen them was a blank. If Gemma said she'd put them in the drawer, she must have done. The evidence was before her.

In the mirror above the fire-place, a pale face stared back at her, the brown hair liberally sprinkled with grey.

"Don't look so worried, Mum," Gemma laughed, folding things back into the cases. "It's your age. I was only saying to Mike the other day, how forgetful you were getting. And you have had a lot on recently."

There was a snort of something that might have been imploded laughter emanating from Charlie's direction. Elspeth went bright pink and then hastily buried her face in her hands, her shoulders beginning to shake.

"Don't take on, love." Somehow, Charlie managed to keep his face straight.

Elspeth just couldn't help it. It seemed it wasn't only Charlie fighting off the years. They obviously hadn't a memory between them. Dear Charlie, he was always paying her compliments, making her feel good about herself, she'd really come to believe eternal youth was hers.

"Oh, Charlie…" She could fight it off no longer. Laughter burst from her, like steam released from a pressure-cooker. Charlie crossed the room and flung his arms around her.

"You know what you need my girl, don't you?" he said. "You need a good holiday!"

IT'S IN THE STARS

Patrick Arundell looks to the heavens to predict what's in store for you this month

TAURUS (21 April – 21 May)
You sometimes hold on to old habits longer than you should. This month, don't take anything for granted concerning your cash flow. Prudence is your best bet for the foreseeable future.

GEMINI (22 May – 21 June)
Luck is with you right through May, but you've got to make it work for you. Don't make assumptions.

CANCER (22 June – 23 July)
You might be feeling that everyone knows what you're thinking this month. Stick to friends who are sensitive and caring.

LEO (24 July – 23 August)
Meeting people through voluntary or social groups is invaluable, but expect at least one friend to get the wrong end of the stick.

VIRGO (24 August – 23 September)
Your home or family life is changing. Balance your own needs with more worldly concerns.

LIBRA (24 September – 23 October)
Travelling could be exciting, but make sure you double check your travel arrangements.

SCORPIO (24 October – 22 November)
Confusion could affect your home life but don't fret. Accept it and try to reorganise things.

SAGITTARIUS (23 November – 21 December)
Be co-operative and flexibile in your relationships. If not, there might be conflict.

CAPRICORN (22 December – 20 January)
You're feeling efficient this month. It's a good time to get jobs done and have fun, too.

AQUARIUS (21 January – 19 February)
There are opportunities to feel closer to loved ones – partners and children especially.

PISCES (20 February – 20 March)
If you're moving home, unexpected delays will be frustrating. Don't bottle up how you feel – share your thoughts with others.

ARIES (21 March – 20 April)
Be careful what you say and don't sign anything without scrutinising the small print.

HOUSEWIFE'S CHOICE

Robert Opie takes a nostalgic peek at shopping-basket bygones

MARS BARS
Frank Mars began making sweets in his kitchen in 1911 in the USA. By 1920 he had a factory and Milky Way was launched in 1923, followed by the Mars bar in 1930. His son, Forrest Mars, came to Britain in 1932 to produce Mars bars, sold for 2d each. They were promoted for their 'sheer delicious goodness made with chocolate to sustain, glucose to energise, milk to nourish'. The slogan, 'A Mars a day helps you work, rest and play' was soon well-known.

MAZAWATTEE TEA
Tea drinking became popular during the 18th century, although tea from China had been imported since 1660 when Samuel Pepys had first tried it. It was the tea merchants Densham & Sons who established the Mazawattee brand name, registered in 1887. The name came from the Hindu word 'mazathe', meaning luscious and the Singhalese word 'wattee', meaning garden. A grandmother and her bespectacled granddaughter, appeared on the tea tins and advertisements. Mazawattee was still on sale during the 1950s.

PUZZLE IT OUT!
Cryptic crosswords and tea-time teasers to keep your brain busy

Royal quiz

A majestic monarchy quiz

1 Who, pictured below right as a baby, is fifth in line to the British throne?

2 What is the name of Prince Charles' home near Tetbury in Gloucestershire?

3 Who is the Queen's eldest grandchild?

4 Who was British Prime Minister at the time of Edward VIII's abdication?

5 What is the official London residence of Queen Elizabeth, the Queen Mother?

6 Who did Princess Anne marry in 1992?

7 What are the three middle names of Prince Charles?

8 Which cousin of the Queen was born on October 9, 1935?

9 On which island was Prince Philip born?

10 At which castle did Prince Charles' investiture as Prince of Wales take place, in 1969?

11 Which female friend of Prince Charles was seriously injured at Klosters in Switzerland in March 1988?

12 At which castle was Princess Margaret born?

13 Who is the father of Lady Davina Windsor?

14 In which year was Queen Elizabeth, the Queen Mother born?

15 Which member of the Royal Family was born on November 3, 1961?

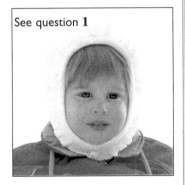
See question **1**

Cryptograms

In these sentences, one set of letters has been substituted for another. For example, A BIG CAT might be written M SWX UMP, M being used for A, S for B, W for I, etc. Each cryptogram is in a different code.

1 C PWCIS VWG XLVP WFTG KGGI TGZE VPZCMPYE KZRLQWP LA, VWG'V

VR UGVAGZFPGYE FIBCRLV PR UR PWG HZRIQ PWCIQ MRZZGMPYE.

A	B	C	D	E	F	G	H	I	J	K	L	M	N	O	P	Q	R	S	T	U	V	W	X	Y	Z

2 VTOJO BL SGZA SGO VTBGU BG VTO NSJZX NSJLO VTEG DOBGU

VEZYOX EDSPV, EGX VTEV BL GSV DOBGU VEZYOX EDSPV.

A	B	C	D	E	F	G	H	I	J	K	L	M	N	O	P	Q	R	S	T	U	V	W	X	Y	Z

For solutions turn to Page 161

June 2002

MONDAY	TUESDAY	WEDNESDAY	THURSDAY	
3 Golden Jubilee Day Public Holiday	4 Public Holiday	5	6	
10	11	12	13	
17	18	19	20	
24 Wimbledon Tennis Championship	25	26	27	

Born this month...

- Marilyn Monroe *(1 June, 1926)*
- Bob Monkhouse *(1 June, 1928)*
- Pat Boone *(1 June, 1934)*
- **Tony Curtis** *(3 June, 1925)*
- Bjorn Borg *(6 June, 1956)*
- Tom Jones *(7 June, 1940)*
- Paul Gauguin *(7 June, 1848)*

- Cole Porter *(9 June, 1892)*
- **Judy Garland** *(10 June, 1922)*
- Steffi Graf *(14 June, 1969)*
- Paul McCartney *(18 June, 1942)*
- Errol Flynn *(20 June, 1909)*
- Prince William *(21 June, 1982)*
- Meryl Streep *(22 June, 1949)*

DAY	SATURDAY	SUNDAY
	1	*2*
	8	*9*
		Epsom Derby
	15	*16*
		Father's Day
	22	*23*
	29	*30*
	July YOURS on sale	

Flower of the month

BLUE POPPY
(Meconopsis betonicifolia)

In this age of change we take so much for granted. Supersonic travel, the Internet and special effects in movies no longer amaze us. Yet imagine the reaction of someone when the first elephant reached our shores. The astonishment of the onlooker must have been something like the wonderment of gardeners when the first blooms of *Meconopsis betonicifolia* and other Himalayan blue poppies flowered on our shores.

These fabled blooms are perhaps the most beautiful of flowers – four ruffled silky petals around a boss of golden stamens, in pure azure blue. Their beauty is enhanced by their capricious nature, taxing the skill of the most experienced gardener.

But it is possible to grow these beautiful flowers in most gardens if their needs are understood. They love cool, moist conditions and thrive best in the north and west of the UK. In the south and east, plant them in moist shade to the north of walls and in semi-shaded woodland but not under large trees. They need plenty of moisture all summer.

Packeted seed often germinates poorly, so buy a plant, let it flower and sow the seed immediately, in midsummer. This species will last for several years, but only if there are several shoots growing from the base. If you let young plants flower they will die – the advice is to remove the flowers the first year.

79

June 3-9

THOUGHT FOR THE WEEK

You're only here for a short visit.
Don't hurry. Don't worry. And be sure
to smell the flowers along the way.

Walter C Hagen (1892-1969)
American professional golfer

THIS WEEK IN YOUR GARDEN

Summer is on the way and with it a garden full of flowers and colourful foliage...

- Water summer bedding plants well before planting to ensure that their rootballs aren't dry.
- Sow bienniels, including polyanthus. Perennials such as lupins, oriental poppies, hollyhocks and delphiniums are among the easiest to raise from seed.
- Examine pot plants daily from now on; watering is best done in the morning.
- Keep a watch on your greenhouse thermometer and close the ventilators quite early if the temperature starts to take a rapid drop at night.

TIP TIME
To ripen hard pears, place them next to an apple in the fruit bowl. They will ripen to perfection very quickly.
Mrs S Field, Highgate, London

THIS WEEK THROUGH THE YEARS

- **3 June, 1971** No Sex Please, We're British, the longest running comedy in theatrical history, opened at the Strand Theatre, London.
- **5 June, 1963** John Profumo, Secretary of State for War, resigned from Parliament after admitting lying to the Commons about his relationship with Christine Keeler.
- **6 June, 1984** The Sikh Golden Temple of Amritsar was attacked by Indian troops following its occupation by militant Sikhs demanding their own state.
- **9 June, 1989** Hundreds of pro-democracy demonstrators were killed in China's Tiananmen Square by the People's Liberation Army.

RECIPE CORNER

Luscious Lemon Curd
Irresistibly tangy – guaranteed to set your tastebuds tingling. Keeps for up to three weeks in a cool place.

4 oz/110g butter
4 oz/100 g sugar
Grated rind and juice 4 lemons
3 eggs, beaten

1 Place butter, sugar, lemon rind and juice in a double boiler (or a heatproof bowl over a pan of simmering water). Stir until sugar has dissolved.
2 Pour lemon mixture into the beaten eggs, strain through a non-metallic sieve or a piece of muslin and return to the double boiler. Stir until mixture coats back of spoon, but do not allow to boil. Pour into hot sterilized jars.

GO ON, SMILE!

By George!
We were having a family quiz as a change from watching television. One of the questions asked was: "What year did Lloyd-George become Prime Minister?

While we were pondering the question, David, aged eight, piped up: "I didn't know that Boy George had ever been Prime Minister!"

Mrs R Axon,
Vicars Cross, Chester

TIP TIME
Before going on holiday, put a few drops of lavender oil on a saucer in each room of your house. It will prevent your home from smelling fusty on your return.
Mrs R Adcock, Boston, Lincs

Cliff Jolin, from Hemel Hempstead in Hertfordshire, treasures this family photo…

"This is a photo of me, aged 12, taken in 1940 with my big brother Cyril and my sister Vivian. Cyril was home on leave and Vivian was dressed up to enter a stage contest. Tragically, Cyril was later killed in the Battle of Britain, but my sister Vivian, who was very beautiful, later became one of the Bluebell Girls, dancing in London and Paris. She later married an American and now lives in Florida. I grew up to serve in the Royal Navy and was awarded the Pacific Star. When I left the Royal Navy, I went to work in East Africa to help install oil pipelines."

FROM ME TO YOU

Coronation treat

I can't believe that it's 50 years since I was fortunate enough to go with my school to 'line the Coronation route'. I was the eldest child of a large family and there was never enough money or time for us to go anywhere as a family, nor to have treats. Imagine how excited I was when the headmistress of our primary school announced that 12 children would be selected to watch the Coronation procession.

We all sat in the school assembly hall and waited while the names were being drawn from a hat. One by one they came out and I sat scrunched up in hopeful anticipation, eyes tightly closed – but none of them was me!

As the final piece of paper was drawn out, the suspense was tangible – and, oh, how I willed that it would have my name on it. When I did hear my name called I couldn't move because I was petrified with disbelief and sure that if I opened my eyes I would discover a mistake had been made. When my name was called once more, and I had to stand up and join the rest of the 'chosen few', I knew my dream had been realised.

After all these years I still recall that feeling of utter joy – and the event itself, even though it was a grey, wet day, with the Coronation coach passing us by in seconds, will be etched forever in my memory.

Gillian Emans, Canterbury, Kent

TIP TIME

Use paper plates and cups for the last meal before you go on holiday – it'll save last minute washing up.
Mrs M Foy, Leicester

HEALTH CHECK

My goodness!

In June 2001, 113-year-old Amy Hulmes of Bury was officially declared to be the oldest woman in the world. So how did she get to such a ripe old age? Well, you may be glad to hear it's not the result of abstinence and puritanical living.

Her grandson explained: "Many have wondered about her secret of longevity, and I have to say it may have something to do with her lifelong love of Guinness." Let's drink to that!

81

June 10-16

THOUGHT FOR THE WEEK

Inspiration for Father's Day: Anyone can be a father, but it takes someone special to be a dad.

Anon

THIS WEEK IN YOUR GARDEN

Most of the pricking out and potting on should be done by now, so take a little time to relax in your garden and enjoy one of the prettiest seasons...

- Keep deadheading fading flowers – including rhododendrons, camellias and phlox – to encourage more blooms.
- Cut sweet peas regularly to maintain continuous flowering. If the weather is hot, mulch the soil after watering.
- Pests and diseases are now on the attack. Watch out for greenfly on roses and red spiders on fruit trees.
- Harvest vegetables as they mature. Early peas should be ready now.

GO ON, SMILE!

Guest of honour
Recently seen on a church noticeboard: 'Jumble sale, 2pm Saturday.'

An adjoining notice advised: 'Jesus is coming.'

Mrs M Woodrow,
Chatham, Kent

FASCINATING PHOTOS

Maisie Edmondson Firth recalls how she shared her big day with a very special lady thousands of miles away...

"It was 1944 and I was serving in the ATS in 578 Heavy Ack Ack Battery when I became engaged to be married. Clothing coupons didn't stretch to wedding gowns, so women in the USA were asked to send their own gowns to British girls serving in the forces. The response from the American wives was wonderful, and when I sent in my request for a dress, with my size details, I was given one. As soon as I opened the parcel, I could tell it was a very beautiful dress. And when I looked at the label I was astounded to see it was Eleanor Roosevelt's gown!

The dress fitted perfectly, and it made my wedding day in September that year extra special. I later wrote to Mrs Roosevelt to tell her what had become of her gown and to thank her for her generosity. Some weeks later I received a personal note from her, which I treasure to this day."

RECIPE CORNER

Roasted stuffed peppers
How can anything this simple taste so good! Serve these peppers as a starter for a fancy dinner, or on their own as a light summer lunch. You'll need plenty of crusty bread to mop up all the juices. Serves 4

4 red peppers
4 ripe plum tomatoes, chopped into quarters
Handful pitted olives (optional)
1 clove garlic, very finely chopped (optional)
Few fresh basil leaves (optional)
Salt and pepper
8 dessert-spoons olive oil
Few slices fresh mozzarella cheese (or your favourite melting cheese)

1 Preheat oven to 220°C/425°F/gas 7. Cut each pepper in half lengthways, through the green stem (which you should leave on). Gently remove any seeds and white pith. Place, cut side up, on a shallow baking tray.
2 Fill the pepper halves with the tomatoes, a few olives, a few slivers of garlic and fresh basil leaves. Season well and pour a dessertspoonful of oil into each pepper half. Roast in the oven, on a high shelf, for about 30-40 minutes until peppers are beginning to brown. Remove from the oven, top with a few slices of cheese and return to the oven until cheese begins to bubble and brown.

TIP TIME
Prevent ants from invading your home by plugging their entry holes with Blu-tack. It can be removed easily at any time and doesn't harm anything
Sheila Waite, Redruth, Cornwall

HEALTH CHECK

Stop bugging me!

If you're off to exotic climes this summer, don't forget to check whether mosquitoes are a problem in the area you're visiting. Even if you're taking anti-malaria pills, you'll need to avoid being bitten in the first place, as pills are not 100 per cent effective. Like Dracula, mozzies hate garlic so adding a clove or two to your meals each day will help you stay bite-free. And pack a little pot of Marmite to spread on your toast – it's packed with B vitamins, a natural mosquito repellent. Cover up ankles and arms at dusk, and if you're eating outside burn candles scented with citronella, lavender, peppermint or eucalyptus oils.

FROM ME TO YOU

Charity begins at home

I manage the local Oxfam shop and I would like to remind people that we rely on volunteers.

There are lots of ways to help apart from running the shop itself – sorting buttons, checking jigsaws, bookkeeping and many more. And if you have specialist knowledge of china, glassware or jewellery you would be worth your weight in gold.

And it's not all one-way either. We are a friendly bunch of people who care about each other. Friendships are made and we can even boast of a wedding between two of our volunteers.

M Blackmore, London

THIS WEEK THROUGH THE YEARS

- **11 June, 1975** The first oil was pumped ashore from Britain's North Sea oilfields.
- **14 June, 1982** After more than two months of fighting, the Argentine forces surrendered to British troops in the Falkland Islands.
- **15 June, 1919** Captain John Alcock from Britain and Lieutenant Arthur Brown from the US became the first people to fly non-stop across the Atlantic Ocean. It took them 16 hours and 12 minutes in a Vickers-Vimy biplane.
- **15 June, 1957** The diary of Anne Frank, a young Jewish girl from Holland, was published. She wrote the diary while in hiding from the Nazis and, after being betrayed by informers, died in a concentration camp.

THOUGHT FOR THE WEEK

We should not let our fears hold us back from pursuing our hopes.

John F Kennedy (1917-1963)
35th American President

THIS WEEK IN YOUR GARDEN

You should be able to plant out all tender plants now, as there's little chance of frost...

- Aromatic herbs such as sage and thyme thrive in a sunny spot.
- Trim evergreen hedges lightly at any time during the month.
- Begin planting winter greens such as Brussels sprouts and broccoli.
- Brooms become straggly if not they're not pruned every year, so clip the bushes lightly.
- Take cuttings from pinks. Look for healthy, non-flowering shoots and pot in sandy soil.
- Plant anemones to flower in the autumn.

FROM ME TO YOU

No smoke without fire

Not long after we got married, I said to my husband: "Hurry home from work tonight, love, as I'm going to make you a meal to remember this evening."

Later that day, to my horror, I had a small kitchen fire and had to call out the fire brigade.

When my husband came home from work he was greeted by clouds of acrid smoke, a fire engine parked outside and firemen everywhere.

My husband walked into the house and calmly said: "So you set that meal to remember on fire did you, love? Better luck next time."

Margaret Shattock, Knowle, Bristol

FASCINATING PHOTOS

Emily Turton from Widnes in Cheshire, remembers the magic of her Auntie's wedding day…

"Here's a picture of my Auntie Eva's wedding in June 1919. I was only nine and it was the first wedding ceremony I had ever been to. It was wonderful and I am thrilled when I think of it, even today – more than 80 years later.

Auntie Eva was my mother's youngest sister and my mother, who was a dressmaker by trade, made all the lovely dresses. I was so excited watching her at work.

I'm not in the photograph but I wore a beautiful white dress and I felt like Alice in Wonderland. My father, who is pictured sitting at the front left, wore a straw hat and my mother is sitting next to him. The bride is sitting on the front row second from the right, wearing a lovely hat and locket. She's sitting next to her bridegroom, my uncle Jack. The ceremony took place at Christ Church in Bootle, which was where Jack and Eva met after Jack had been 'demobbed' after serving in the war.

I have been to plenty of weddings since then, but my Auntie Eva's was magical and I will never forget it."

GO ON, SMILE!

Whistle while you work

When I was walking into town, workmen on the other side of the road stopped digging and started wolf-whistling at me. "Can't be bad for a 65-year-old," I thought.

I went into the first shop and a lady quickly pulled me to one side, saying: "I think you ought to know – your skirt is tucked inside your waistband." Was my face red!

Mrs M James,
Great Wyrley, Walsall

HEALTH CHECK

Aspirin – the wonder drug

New research suggests that aspirin might help prevent heart attacks and strokes. In the past, aspirin has been prescribed to patients who've already had a heart-attack, or are in danger of having a heart attack. It works by thinning the blood to prevent clots developing. But now studies have shown that taking a daily low-dose aspirin might help to protect the hearts of healthy people and offer some protection against strokes. However, a word of caution: You should never regularly dose yourself with aspirin without checking with your GP first. Aspirin can be harmful if you have an ulcer or stomach complaints, or if you are prone to bleeding. Asthmatics should also take extra care.

RECIPE CORNER

Minty Couscous Salad

If you haven't tried couscous before, give it a try – it's perfect for quick summer salads. You'll find packets next to the pasta and rice in the supermarket. Serves 4-6.

8 oz/230 g instant couscous
6 spring onions, trimmed and sliced
3 ripe tomatoes, diced
½ red pepper, deseeded and diced
12 green olives pitted and halved
1 tablespoon shredded mint
1 tablespoon chopped coriander
1-2 garlic cloves, peeled and crushed (optional)
3 tbsp olive oil
2 tsp lemon or lime juice
salt and pepper

Prepare the couscous according to packet directions. Break up any lumps with a fork and add more water if too dry. Stir in the rest of the ingredients and season to taste. Leave for half an hour for flavours to infuse, then serve.

THIS WEEK THROUGH THE YEARS

- **17 June 1950** The first kidney transplant was carried out by Dr Richard Lawler in Chicago.
- **17 June 1994** O J Simpson, the American football star, gave himself up to police after failing to appear in court to be charged with the murder of his wife and her friend.
- **19 June 1999** Prince Edward and Sophie Rhys-Jones were married at St George's chapel, Windsor.
- **21 June 1982** Princess Diana gave birth to her first child, Prince William, at St Mary's Hospital, London.

THOUGHT FOR THE WEEK

Retired is being tired twice,
I've thought.
First, tired of working,
Then tired of not.

*Richard Armour
– American writer*

THIS WEEK IN YOUR GARDEN

Vegetables and soft fruit taste so much better if you've grown them yourself...

- You can improve the yield of your gooseberry bushes by cutting the side shoots to about 3 in (7.5 cm) but spread the work over about six weeks.
- Remove cloches from strawberries and they'll soon be ripe enough for picking.
- Remove suckers from roses, lilac and other plants before they get too large.
- Tender floating plants can be put in your garden pond now and will quickly establish themselves in the warmer weather.

FROM ME TO YOU

Cheery chorus

My electricity meter was installed ten years ago and we were told that it was due for a renewal. Arrangements were made for the electricians to call and they started their work, which was going to take about an hour.

I suddenly became aware that there was some very pleasant singing coming from nearby. It was the two electricians, and for about three quarters of an hour I was treated to a recital of very well-sung songs. I wondered if they belonged to a choir, they sang so well together. They were also pleasant, happy and when they finished they asked for a bag to tidy up their rubbish. Applause for my two entertainers.

Joyce Taylor, Bristol

GO ON, SMILE!

No place to hide

My mother's Uncle Tom was a draper who travelled around the countryside selling his wares. Seeing him coming, a woman who owed him money ran upstairs telling her young daughter to say that she had gone to the nearby town of Bedale.

The child dutifully told Uncle Tom the message. When he asked what time she'd be back, the child ran to the bottom of the stairs and shouted: "Mother! What time will you be back from Bedale?" The woman was so embarrassed she had to come down.

Doreen Moore, Ripon, North Yorkshire

HEALTH CHECK

Let's face it...

You have nearly 60 muscles in your face – and you can help keep them toned with regular exercise.

- Firm your mouth by rolling your lips inwards over your top and bottom teeth, keeping your mouth slightly open. Now try to smile as broadly as you can, keeping your lower jaw pushed outwards.
- Tone your neck by curling your tongue towards the back of your mouth. Then lift your chin, stretching upwards, and slowly stretch your neck first to the right, then to the left.
- Tighten the skin on your face by making an 'O' shape with your mouth, pulling your upper lip down over your teeth. Close your eyes and try to pull your face into a smile using your upper cheek muscles.

THIS WEEK THROUGH THE YEARS

- **26 June, 1997** Ralf Laue of Germany successfully stacked 529 dominoes on top of a single supporting domino to achieve a new world record.
- **27 June, 1967** The world's first cash dispenser was installed at the Enfield branch of Barclays Bank.
- **30 June, 1960** Alfred Hitchcock's horror film Psycho opened to rave reviews
- **30 June, 1997** The British handed Hong Kong back to the Chinese after 156 years of colonial rule.

RECIPE CORNER

Strawberry Compote
A fitting recipe for Wimbledon week! It's wonderfully versatile – add raspberries when they come into season, or frozen berries at any time of the year. Serve with ice-cream, dollop on meringues – or use it to add a fruit burst to your morning muesli. Serves 4-6

2 tablespoons cornflour
3/4 cup water
Juice of 1 lemon
1/4 cup sugar
4 cups strawberries (or any combination of mixed berries)

Blend the cornflour with water, place in a saucepan with lemon juice and sugar. Bring to boil stirring constantly, until thickened and cornflour has 'cooked out'. Add berries and cook gently until they've softened. Leave to cool before serving.

FASCINATING PHOTOS

Peggy Dalby from Lymington, Hants, shares this photograph of her mother, which is more than 100 years old...
"Here's a photograph of my mother, Mary Dalby, in 1893 when she was 21 years old. She is standing next to her bicycle, which was one of the first ladies bicycles produced in Leicester. My mother was a trained dressmaker and milliner and would have designed and made the outfit and hat she is wearing.

"She used to tell me that if anyone dropped a hat in the workroom, the customer would be well pleased with it – just a good luck gesture I suppose, a bit like 'break a leg' in the theatre."

TIP TIME
If the castors on your bed keep sliding on the carpet, place a small curtain ring under each castor.
W Villis, Preston

TIP TIME
Put leftover bones, oil and fat into a plastic screw-top bottle before putting them in the dustbin. This will stop hungry animals scratching, and over-turning, your bin.
Mrs F Bond, Hanwell, London

It's in the stars

Patrick Arundell looks to the heavens to predict what's in store for you this month

GEMINI (22 May – 21 June)
You're a quick-witted sign and little fazes you when it comes to creative ideas. June can see you benefit from these, but even your best-laid plans will require revision until the 8th of the month.

CANCER (22 June – 23 July)
Don't be surprised if confidential conversations or discreet developments are crucial this month.

LEO (24 July – 23 August)
Misunderstandings can creep in, especially in dealings with friends. But this is no bad thing, as you'll discover those who really care.

VIRGO (24 August – 23 September)
An older person, perhaps from a different cultural background, will influence you.

LIBRA (24 September – 23 October)
The eclipse on the 10th augurs well if you're making life more exciting. Take the plunge!

SCORPIO (24 October – 22 November)
A property or long-term financial issue that has been dormant springs to life. Now you can consider a fresher way of living.

SAGITTARIUS (23 November – 21 December)
It seems that someone special will come into your social circle in the near future.

CAPRICORN (22 December – 20 January)
This is a time of contemplation for Capricorns as your values continue to change. Some gentle exercise is key your health.

AQUARIUS (21 January – 19 February)
You can be a mystery this month – at times enjoying your own company and at other times thriving as a team player.

PISCES (20 February – 20 March)
Your social life is highlighted in June, especially within the family or at home. Later you'll spread your wings more.

ARIES (21 March – 20 April)
Ties with neighbours or siblings can be testing, so be clear in what you say and decisive in your actions.

TAURUS (21 April – 21 May)
Recent concerns over finances should fade. With that worry out of the way, the accent is on reaching out and sharing ideas.

Housewife's choice

Robert Opie takes a nostalgic peek at shopping-basket bygones

Smith's Potato Crisps

Launched in 1920, Smith's Potato Crisps quickly became a favourite snack in Britain. Frank Smith found just the right crispness, selling his packets at 2d each with a twist of blue paper that contained the salt. Larger quantities of crisps were sold in tins, an ideal way of keeping them fresh for a picnic or party. They were encouraged to be eaten on motoring or cycling trips, while fishing or walking – or at any time of day, such as 'with your morning bacon'.

Oxo

Baron Justus Von Leibig developed a concentrated form of meat extract in 1847. Fortunately, there was a vast surplus of meat in South America during the 1860s and Leibig's Extract was soon being made, arriving in Britain from 1865.

Around 1900 the name was changed to Lemco and then, soon after, to Oxo. In 1910, Oxo in cubes was launched, with each cube wrapped in a tiny, individual card box and sold in tins of six or more.

By the late 1950s, technology made it possible for each cube to be wrapped in foil, and the six or 12 cubes sold in a box. At this time the slogan was, 'Oxo gives a meal man-appeal!', and Katie became a regular in the TV commercials.

ALL WORK AND NO PAY

When Jill Nevile started work at a dogs' home, little did she know just how much there was to learn – and how wriggly her charges would be!

Jill caring for a Yorkie puppy

I've always been mad about dogs so when I retired from teaching in 1998, what better idea than to volunteer my services to a local dog sanctuary? And when I said I would do anything – including the less pleasant chores – they took me at my word.

To begin with, I learned how to prepare the kennels for the night. They are layered with newspaper and each has a clean plastic bed filled with shredded paper.

A colleague then showed me the correct way to bath a dog. Afterwards we groomed him, inspected his ears and cleaned his teeth. Then it was my turn. The other dog had been docile but mine kept jumping out of the bath. The flea shampoo had to be left on for five minutes, so to calm him, I stroked and talked to him.

All the dogs are taken for a walk before being kennelled for the night and they love it. I walk about a dozen dogs. Some are well-behaved, others tug on their lead, trying to trip me up. Bowls of food await them in the kennels, so they're eager to get back.

I learned how to put on a Lupi, a special harness which loops around the dog's front legs and is useful for walking animals that pull a lot. I also fitted the plastic lampshade collars that some dogs wear to stop them chewing their stitches after an operation.

Another less savoury duty is to clean the day runs. I 'scoop the poop', then swill the floors with disinfectant and scrub them with a stiff broom.

Then came my first escape. I'd been grooming a dog and as I was leaving the run, he shot through my legs. He got himself into a state running up and down the path and barking. I managed to catch him and haul him inside but it was an embarrassing moment. I soon discovered the importance of leaving the kennels backwards to keep a wary eye out!

The sanctuary staff are very caring and make the dogs as comfortable as possible. All of them need good homes but they're so desperate for love that they can be overpowering, putting off adopters. Sometimes dogs are returned because their new owners find them too demanding.

It was June when I started volunteering and friends doubted whether I would work through the winter. But doing an active job and wearing layers of clothing, I hardly noticed the cold and my feet stayed warm in green Wellies.

With the shorter winter afternoons, the dogs have to be walked and kennelled earlier and the runs cleaned by artificial light. During very cold weather we use a mop and bucket to swab the runs. This prevents surface water freezing overnight and turning the runs into ice rinks.

Now that I'm experienced, I sometimes help with tasks such as kennelling new arrivals or showing dogs to prospective owners. I keep a dog still while stitches are removed, or when medication is applied.

There's also the joy of seeing mothers caring for their pups, knowing they will bring new owners years of love and laughter. I carefully bath the

I carefully bath the puppies in a small sink.
Vulnerable and affectionate, they love a cuddle

puppies in a small sink. Vulnerable and affectionate, they love a cuddle.

I thought my new career was finished the day a puppy fell from my arms. Three pups had to be put into their kennel. I got hold of one puppy but as I picked up another, he wriggled and dropped to the ground. To my great dismay, he landed on his back and bounced. Luckily, his puppy fat protected him from injury but since then, I handle puppies one at a time!

As I drive home – often with an aching back – I know that I get as much pleasure from my work as the dogs do!

July 2002

MONDAY	TUESDAY	WEDNESDAY	THURSDAY	
1	2	3	4	
8	9	10	11	
15	16	17	18	
22	23	24	25 Opening ceremony Commonwealth Games, Manchester	2
29	30	31 August YOURS on sale		

IDAY	SATURDAY	SUNDAY
	6	*7*
		Final day Wimbledon Tennis Championships
	13	*14*
	20	*21*
	27	*28*

Flower of the month

HEUCHERA
'Amethyst Mist'

We have flower arrangers to thank for the rise of foliage plants in our gardens. It is largely through their need to maintain a year-round supply of foliage that bergenias, hostas and heucheras have exchanged a supporting role for their spot in the limelight, but heucheras owe their fame to a more distant source.

Until about 20 years ago, most heucheras were grown for their flowers – airy spikes of small pink and red blooms. Then 'Palace Purple' became available and though its flowers were tiny and creamy white, its deep purple, lacquered foliage proved invaluable in summer and winter, forming neat domes of perfect foliage.

This was the only purple heuchera we had to try, but over the years several breeders on America's west coast have produced a bewildering array of varieties. There has been a steady stream of these new plants reaching our shores and they are some of the best herbaceous plants we can grow. They keep their leaves all winter. Plant one with a skimmia for a perfect winter combination. But it is in summer that they are at their best. The soft, pinks and greys of 'Amethyst Mist', the deep, fabulously flounced leaves of 'Chocolate Ruffles' and the prim, bright blades of 'Regina' all complement summer flowers, be they bedding plants or roses.

Born this month...

- **Diana, Princess of Wales** *(1 July, 1961)*
- Tom Cruise *(3 July, 1962)*
- Gina Lollobrigida *(4 July, 1927)*
- Tom Hanks *(9 July, 1956)*
- Barbara Stanwyck *(16 July, 1907)*
- **Nelson Mandela** *(18 July, 1918)*
- Helen Mirren *(26 July, 1946)*
- Emily Bronte *(30 July, 1818)*
- Jacqueline Kennedy Onassis *(28 July, 1929)*

July 1-7

THOUGHT FOR THE WEEK

The rule for travelling abroad is to take our common sense with us and leave our prejudices behind.

William Hazlitt (1778–1830)
English essayist

THIS WEEK IN YOUR GARDEN

This is the month when your garden is at its glorious peak. Find a shady spot, sit back and admire your handiwork...

- Check all new plantings in very hot weather, especially trees and shrubs which were planted in the autumn.
- Continue to watch for pests such as caterpillars, red spider, blackfly and greenfly.
- Pick herbs regularly to ensure a supply of fresh, flavoursome shoots for cooking.
- Plant autumn-flowering bulbs such as crocus, to flower in September and October.

FROM ME TO YOU

Look on the bright side

I've always had a naturally happy disposition and when I was young I was often told: "You must be up to something." I was suspected of all sorts of misdeeds, which I never even contemplated, to explain my smiling face. And now I'm older, people assume my happy outlook on life is due to strong drink.

Neither is true. It is simply that I have never seen any point in looking on the black side. Too many people make miseries of their lives worrying about things that may never happen.

Valerie Harman, North Shields, Tyne and Wear

TIP TIME
Buy heaters and other winter gadgets in summer when they are on offer.
Mrs S May, Co Antrim

RECIPE CORNER

Marlborough Pie

This simple but delicious apple pie with a twist is a family favourite from Joyce Rea from Hampstead Norreys, Berkshire.

Ready-rolled puff pastry
Zest and juice of 1 lemon
2 large cooking apples
8 oz/225 g sugar
3 eggs
4 oz/110 g butter

1 Preheat oven to 200°C/400°F/gas 6. Line a deep 8 in pie dish with puff pastry.
2 Grate the zest of a lemon into a large bowl and add the squeezed juice. Peel the apples and grate into the bowls (discard the cores). Toss to prevent darkening. Pour sugar over fruit and mix well.
3 Beat eggs until light. Cream butter until very soft and add eggs, blending well. Fold mixture into the fruit and spoon into the lined pie dish.
4 Bake for 15 minutes then reduce the heat to 180°C/350°F/gas 4. Bake for a further 45 minutes, or until a knife inserted in the centre comes out clean.
Cool before serving the pie with cream.

FASCINATING PHOTOS

Arthur Grove, from Bracknell in Berkshire, recalls how his mum was upstaged during her moment of glory...

"1935 was King George V and Queen Mary's jubilee. We lived in Bethnal Green in the East End of London, where the borough encouraged people to tend and show their gardens. In July that year, an official from the council called my father, William, to say that someone would like to visit the garden the following afternoon, and would there be anyone in? Dad said my mum, Maude, would be at home. Next day, there was a knock on the door and Mum opened it to find Queen Mary standing on the doorstep! In a state of shock, Mum showed the Queen around her garden. By this time, quite a crowd had gathered and news soon travelled to my father at work that he should get home sharpish. He arrived just in time to see the Queen's car disappearing down the road.

"But at least my mum had a wonderful story to tell, and we all looked forward to the press photograph that would appear in the local paper. What a huge disappointment it was when the photo (pictured here) appeared. Mum, who was standing next to the Queen, was completely blotted out by the man who was accompanying her. All you can see is the bottom of my mum's pinafore!"

GO ON, SMILE!

"I'll have what they're having!"
On holiday I overheard two ladies discussing the meals in the hotel. I couldn't help but smile when one said that they had enjoyed 'porn cocktails' as a starter!

Mrs S Beckett, Bucknall,
Stoke-on-Trent

HEALTH CHECK

Happy travels
If just the thought of boarding a boat makes you feel green around the gills, try wearing Seabands on your wrists. Based on the acupuncture principle of stimulating pressure points in the body, they are effective at staving off nausea. Ginger is another natural remedy. Nibble on the odd ginger biscuit and you'll probably be able to outlast an old salty sea dog!

If you're taking to the air on holiday and suffer from earache on take-off and

landing, you can buy special ear plugs, called Earplanes. They have a filter that slows down the rate of change in air pressure – so there's none of that endless holding your nose and blowing till your ears 'pop'!

Seabands and Earplanes are available from Boots.

TIP TIME

The day before a picnic, fill bottles with water or squash and place them in the freezer. Pack them into your hamper and they will keep your food fresh as well as providing you with a delicious chilled drink.

Mrs M Matthews,
Southampton

THIS WEEK THROUGH THE YEARS

- **1 July, 1929** Popeye, the Sailor Man, made his debut in a cartoon strip.
- **2 July, 1912** Ballerina Anna Pavlova topped the bill at the first Royal Command Performance to be held in Britain.
- **3 July, 1964** US president Lyndon B Johnson signed the Civil Rights Act, which made racial discrimination, in public and in the workplace, illegal.
- **5 July, 1946** A new type of two-piece swimming costume was revealed in Paris and was named after Bikini Atoll, a group of islands in the Pacific Ocean.

July 8-14

THOUGHT FOR THE WEEK

Why is it that a tourist will travel thousands of miles to get away from people – just so he can send cards saying, 'wish you were here'?

E C McKenzie
American writer and compiler

THIS WEEK IN YOUR GARDEN

Relax during the long summer evenings and enjoy the perfume of night-scented stocks, roses and sweet peas...

- Continue to water and feed containers to extend their display into autumn.
- Give the wisteria a summer pruning. Cut back the whippy growths, leaving four leaf joints on each stem.
- During your evening stroll jot down which planting schemes have worked and which haven't, to make changes in the spring.
- Disbud chrysanthemums and dahlias to encourage larger blooms.
- Water new lawns thoroughly during dry spells.

HEALTH CHECK

Shake a leg!
If you're jetting off on holiday this summer, you might have been alarmed by scare stories about Economy Class Syndrome, the popular name for Deep Vein Thrombosis. It's thought that sitting still for long periods of time – such as on a long flight – increases the risk of blood clots pooling in the veins and then travelling to the heart, lungs and brain. But by taking a few simple precautions, you can make sure you arrive at your destination safe and sound. Doctors recommend wearing elasticated support tights. You should drink plenty of fluids and take regular light exercise – just the odd trip to the loo is enough. Or, if you find you're hemmed in at a window seat, try twirling your ankles and flexing the muscles in your legs every now and then.

FROM ME TO YOU

Door dilemma
A YOURS magazine reader shares her point of view about doors and letterboxes...

It does annoy me when people get new doors and don't get a house number. If they were made to deliver post for a week, I think they might decide to be a bit more reasonable about their door numbers.

As for the extra-sprung, double-flap, finger-eating letterboxes helpfully placed six inches from the ground... that's another story!
Maureen Butcher, Burntwood, Staffs

FASCINATING PHOTOS

William Sharp of Leeds recalls the joys of answering a call of nature in the great outdoors while serving in Cyprus.
"This snap features the standard 'troop' size four-man thunderbox. They came in other sizes like the ten-man 'squadron' (also portable), up to the more permanent 25-seater 'regimental' model (real nose-holding constructions they were). Enjoying the facilities in the photo are (from left) myself, Bill 'Bessima' Sharp, Eddie 'Geordie' Fisher and Chris 'Jock' Craig. We were in 4 Troop, 30 Field Squadron, RE – stationed in Cyprus and part of 35 Field Engineer Regiment. It was 1953 and we had virtual free run of the island. Our task was to construct a water supply pipeline, 30 miles long, from Kissousa to Episkopi."

GO ON, SMILE!

Say it with flowers
A young friend told me that when her husband unexpectedly brought her flowers, she said to him: "Oh, you must have read my mind! I really wanted flowers."

To which he replied: "Well, you obviously didn't read mine because I was hoping for some tea."

Doreen Fay, Tiper, Portsmouth

RECIPE CORNER
White Fish with Brown Butter
You can use any piece of white fish for this spectacularly simple but delicious recipe. Try it with a creamy mash and some steamed vegetables. This recipe will serve 4 people.

3 oz/75 g butter
2 tablespoons lemon juice
3 tablespoons pine nuts, roughly chopped
4 firm white fish fillets

1 Melt butter in a large frying pan until butter is a light golden colour. Add lemon juice and pine nuts and cook 1 minute.
2 Add fish to pan and fry a couple of minutes on each side until it is cooked to your liking.

THIS WEEK THROUGH THE YEARS

- **11 July, 1936** Athlete Jesse Owens won a place on the US team for the Berlin Olympics, where he won four gold medals, angering Hitler who refused to congratulate him because he was black.
- **11 July, 1975** An army of life-sized terracotta warriors was unearthed by archaeologists in China.
- **12 July, 1998** France, the host nation, won the football World Cup for the first time, beating Brazil 3-0.
- **13 July, 1985** The Live Aid benefit concert took place at two locations – in the UK and the US – simultaneously. Fronted by Bob Geldof, it was the biggest rock benefit ever held.

TIP TIME
When packing for your holiday, don't carry big bottles of toiletries such as shampoo. Pour them into small, plastic, medicine bottles – they're much lighter and the lids fit snugly so there are no leaks.
Pam Pollock, Hemel Hempstead, Herts

July 15-21

THOUGHT FOR THE WEEK.

One of the many things nobody ever tells you about middle age is that it's such a nice change from being young.

Dorothy Canfield Fisher (1879-1958) American novelist

THIS WEEK IN YOUR GARDEN

There's still plenty of routine work to be done but slow down and take your time – it's hot…

- Put out a shallow dish of water for birds and other wildlife, changing it regularly.
- Support heavily-laden fruit tree branches.
- Cut flowers such as statice for drying. Hang small bunches upside-down in an airy, shady place.
- Start to pick apples and pears. If the fruit comes away easily with its stalk, it's ready for picking.
- Cut courgettes and pick beans regularly to encourage growth.

FASCINATING PHOTOS

Every time Ceinwen Holden, from Alresford in Hampshire, looks at this snapshot, she relives her days working in a holiday camp…

"Here I am working in a holiday camp called Broadreeds in Selsey, Sussex.

"The camp photographer took this picture in 1951, while I was behind the counter in the snack bar. I'm wearing my pretty little uniform, which was pink and white gingham under a white pinny.

"We sold those delicious Kunzle Cakes and, as it was Festival of Britain year, we also had special packets of biscuits with The Festival stamp and date on them.

"That same year I met my husband, Sidney, at Broadreeds, and we were soon engaged and then married in 1954. Sadly, houses have now replaced the holiday camp but I had some really good times there – was just like the television series, Hi-De-Hi!"

FROM ME TO YOU

Top of the pops

Yippee! I'm in my second childhood at the age of 72! I received a parcel that contained some bubble-wrap material and, from that moment on, I was completely hooked on popping the bubbles.

This takes me way back to my childhood when I used to pop the tar bubbles in the road during the sizzling hot summers. Happy days!

Doreen King, Tunbridge Wells, Kent

HEALTH CHECK

Fun in the sun?

Summer is a time to get out and about, but how can you avoid the sun-traps of sunburn and heat exhaustion?

- Always wear a hat with a broad enough brim to shade your neck.
- Use a sun cream with a sun protection factor (SPF) of at least 15 on exposed skin.
- Avoid alcohol and wear loose, lightweight clothes.
- Drink plenty of water to avoid dehydration.
- Avoid being out for too long between 11am and 3pm if possible.

TIP TIME

To avoid soaking your towels after a shower or bath, wipe surplus water off your body with a wrung-out flannel or sponge before towelling yourself dry.
Mrs M Jones, Rhiwbina, Cardiff

THIS WEEK THROUGH THE YEARS

- **17 July, 1975** The US Apollo and the Soviet Soyuz spacecrafts docked 140 miles above the Atlantic ocean and an astronaut and a cosmonaut shook hands through hatches in their crafts.
- **17 July, 1987** It's A Royal Knockout, a special charity edition of the slapstick gameshow featuring celebrities, sports personalities and members of the royal family, was broadcast.
- **18 July, 1955** Walt Disney's first amusement park, Disneyland, opened at Anaheim, near Los Angeles.
- **21 July, 1969** Neil Armstrong became the first man to walk on the moon, uttering the phrase: "That's one small step for a man, one giant leap for mankind."

RECIPE CORNER

Moroccan Lamb Kebabs
Tender lamb is marinated in aromatic herbs and spices and quickly barbecued or grilled.
Serves 2

12 oz/350 g cubed lamb
1 small onion, finely chopped
1 clove garlic, crushed (optional)
½ teaspoon ground cumin
½ teaspoon paprika
Pinch of cayenne pepper
2 tablespoons each chopped fresh parsley and coriander
4 tablespoons olive oil
Juice of ½ a lemon
1 courgette, sliced
½ red pepper chopped into 1 in/2 cm pieces

1 Mix the lamb with the onion, garlic, herbs and spices, olive oil and lemon juice. Leave to marinate for half an hour (the flavour strengthens the longer the meat is marinated).
2 Preheat a barbecue or grill. Shake liquid from the meat and onion and thread on to metal skewers, alternating with courgette and pepper pieces. Cook until the lamb is firm and lightly crisped and the vegetables softened.

GO ON, SMILE!

A slip up
One Monday lunchtime in 1939, my mother was asking for my washing, so I took down the straps of my petticoat underneath my clothes intending to step out of it.

Later that day I was walking through my office when a young man handed me a small brown paper parcel, shyly telling me to open it in the ladies room.

How embarrassing to discover my 'old' slip enclosed. Apparently I had 'stepped' out of it in the office rather than at home at lunchtime.

But we saw the funny side and I ended up marrying the gallant gent who had been picked to hand me the parcel.

Mrs M Broad, Camp Hill, Northampton

TIP TIME
Rinsed out plastic detergent bottles make perfect holders for your knitting needles.
Mrs F Burrd, Telford, Shropshire

THOUGHT FOR THE WEEK

While one finds company in himself and his pursuits, he cannot feel old, no matter what his age may be.

Amos Bronson Alcott, American teacher (1799-1888)

FASCINATING PHOTOS

As a 19-year-old, Clare Shetliffe-Smith was picked from all the girls at a printing factory for a memorable sweet treat...

"I worked in a printing shop where we printed all the labels for Rowntrees Chocolates. One day I was asked if I would pose for a poster advertising a new chocolate that Rowntrees was just about to launch. Unknown to me, someone from Rowntrees had walked around the factory and had chosen me from all the girls. The year was 1926. I had to sit for two photographic shoots in the local wood. I was bitten all over by midges – how I managed to sit still I don't know! But it was worth it. I appeared on the box lids for Rowntrees York chocolates – and I was given a ½ lb box of chocolates all to myself!"

THIS WEEK IN YOUR GARDEN

Avoid gardening in the hot daytime sun. It's much better to work in the early morning or in the cool of the evening...

- Plan for the holidays and arrange for a neighbour to water and feed the plants and mow the lawn.
- Fish can suffer from a lack of oxygen in hot weather, so spray your pond with a jet of water to keep it re-oxygenated.
- To dry lavender, pick the flowers just before they're fully open, on a dry day.

TIP TIME
To iron lace, cover it with tissue paper to stop the lace from shining.

GO ON, SMILE!

Hospital humour

While visiting my husband in hospital, I heard the nurse ask the man in the next bed if he'd moved his bowels today. "No," he replied, "They still live at the same address."

Marjorie Cantwell, Rathfarnham, Dublin

TIP TIME
Use dental floss to re-string bead or pearl necklaces. It's much easier than using cotton as the floss is stiffer.
J Williams, Prescot, Merseyside

FROM ME TO YOU

The long and short of it

Has anybody else noticed that the longest two minutes of the day seem to be when you're in a hurry? For example, when the washing has finished and you have to wait two minutes to open the door of the washing machine.

The shortest two minutes is when you put a pan of milk on the stove and it boils over the second you turn your back.

Valerie Heney, Addlestone, Surrey

HEALTH CHECK

Well fed in the Med!

Studies have shown that people from the Mediterranean region, such as Italy, Southern France and Spain live longer than their Northern European neighbours. It's thought the secret of their long lives is their diet, which protects against heart disease and cancer. So here's how to eat the Mediterranean way:

- The bulk of each meal should be a starch or cereal, such as pasta, rice, bread, potatoes or couscous.
- Serve a salad or a variety of vegetables with each meal. Try to vary the range – add roasted peppers, mushrooms or aubergines.
- Eat less red meat and more chicken and fish – especially oily fish such as tuna.
- Use olive oil instead of your regular vegetable oil.
- Eat plenty of fresh fruit.
- Add garlic to your cooking – it's good for the heart.
- Enjoy a tipple of red wine with your evening meal.

THIS WEEK THROUGH THE YEARS

- **23 July, 1875** Isaac Singer, the inventor of the domestic sewing machine, died.
- **23 July, 1986** Prince Andrew married Sarah Ferguson in Westminster Abbey.
- **25 July, 1978** Louise Brown, the world's first 'test-tube baby' was born at Oldham Hospital.
- **26 July, 1952** Eva Peron, known affectionately as 'Evita', wife of Argentinian president Juan Peron, died aged 33.

TIP TIME
Water comes to the boil faster if it is unsalted. When cooking vegetables, bring the water to the boil and only add the salt when you add the vegetables.

RECIPE CORNER

Bacon, Egg and Potato Salad
A new twist on an old favourite. This recipe serves 4.

4 rindless bacon rashers
3 oz/75 g Cheddar cheese, diced
2 cocktail gherkins, chopped
4-5 spring onions, chopped
3 hard-boiled eggs, sliced
1 lb 4 oz/350 g boiled potatoes, diced
1 tablespoon chopped parsley

2 tablespoon olive oil
1 tablespoon white wine or malt vinegar
Salt and pepper

1 Grill the bacon until it's crisp, then dice it and leave to cool.
2 Place the bacon in a serving bowl along with the cheese, gherkins, onions, eggs and potatoes. Sprinkle the parsley over them.
3 Blend the oil and vinegar together and drizzle it liberally over the salad.
4 Toss everything together gently to avoid breaking up the egg slices.
Eat with crusty bread.

RETURN TO CORDEVILLE

By Jill Hazell

"Look, Robert, we've got a postcard from David and Anne." Marie-Claire came into the kitchen clutching a pile of mail in one hand while short-sightedly studying the postcard in the other.

"What's the news?" Robert asked.

"I can't read it," Marie-Claire replied, looking for her glasses. Robert took his off and handed them to her. After so many years of marriage, he knew there was no point offering to read it to her.

"I knew it was from them because of the French stamp," she explained now she could see it properly. "And it's got a picture of Cordeville on it."

Robert smiled and stretched out his hand to see, but Marie-Claire held it tight. "Let me read it to you, cherie.

"Dear Grandma and Grandpa, Hope you survived the wedding and are having a good rest back home. Stopped off yesterday in Cordeville so Anne could see the old house…"

Marie-Claire looked up. "Isn't that romantic, Robert? Going out of their way to look at the old house on their honeymoon."

"Yes, darling," Robert replied. "David is romantic. He takes after us, after all."

Marie-Claire read the rest, but Robert wasn't concentrating. His mind did that sometimes. It was funny, he often forgot what had happened two minutes ago but could remember things from years ago as though they'd happened yesterday…

It was a warm July evening. He stopped his motorbike and slid his goggles up on to his forehead. After searching the Ile de France for nearly a week, he had almost despaired of ever finding the hamlet again. Yet here it was, exactly as he remembered it. He switched off the engine and looked around him. It was just the same as it had been five years ago when he first saw it – and just as quiet.

Thatched cottages lay by the banks of the river but the only sounds came from the rippling of the water and a few bees working the flower beds in the gardens behind. The scent of hay filled the air and, in the distance, a flock of crows flew between the poplar trees on the hills to the east, just as they had on that July dawn five years ago.

Robert got off his bike and walked towards the river. Now he was so close he was suddenly afraid. Suppose something dreadful had happened to them?

In July 1941, when he was just 19, he had made several night flights across France in his black-painted Lysander. It was tricky work, looking for the tiny landing fields to come down in, although not half as dangerous as it was for the men he took out there. They were brave, shadowy men who risked everything to work in occupied France as spies and saboteurs.

On that July night five years ago, his mission had been to collect an agent for debriefing. It was a clear moonlit night and he found the field easily and started his descent. But before his wheels touched the ground a man ran out in front of him, wildly waving a torch. Robert saw his body jerk and fall to the ground and felt the tiny plane shudder as a volley of bullets found their mark. It was a miracle he managed to get back in the air again and stay there till he could bale out. The Lysander crashed a few minutes later in a ball of flame.

Robert had never used a parachute before. In the moonlight he felt as if he was hardly moving, until with a snap of breaking wood, he scraped through the branches of a poplar tree, coming to an abrupt halt 20 feet above the ground.

Robert could hear barking in the distance. Pulling himself higher, he sat astride a branch, praying they wouldn't look up and see the silk canopy in the leaves above him. Minutes later he watched the men come into the field and pass along the edge of the copse. Swinging their torches in arcs across the grass, they followed the dogs into a further field.

Once they'd gone Robert decided to make a run for it. Releasing the harness, he began to climb down but in the darkness misjudged his height. Landing awkwardly, his ankle gave way under his weight.

He lay breathless with pain. It was useless to attempt to stand. He knew he'd blown his chance of escape. He lay there waiting for daylight – and

The woman bandaged his ankle and the girl brought him a baguette and some water. Then they shut the door and left him

capture. At dawn, he heard the sound of wheels approaching. He crawled behind the trees and from there saw a girl standing on the edge of a small cart, attempting to get a foothold on one of the trees. An older woman held her ankles to steady her. Above them hung enough silk to make a dozen petticoats. Robert stood up slowly and put his hands in the air.

It was almost light when they reached the hamlet. Looking back up the hill, he could clearly see the white parachute still hanging out of the tree. He hoped the Germans would think he was miles away by now.

They put him in the cow shed. He wished he could communicate but his schoolboy French was hopeless and they spoke no English. The woman bandaged his ankle and the girl brought him a baguette and some water, then shut the door and left him.

They were taking a terrible risk, but he had no choice. Until his ankle was healed, he needed somewhere to hide. For three weeks the girl came daily with food and water. She must have been 13 or 14, old enough to know the danger, but she never showed any fear. She never spoke to him or even looked him in the eye.

One evening when it was dark the woman came and helped him walk the length of the garden. Nodding her head, she produced a pair of trousers, a jacket and a map.

Late one evening soon after, the girl presented him with a pack of food for his journey. The woman shook his hand, but the girl merely wished him 'Bonne chance' and Robert walked out of their lives.

He'd been fast asleep in a small wood two days later when they found him, a half-eaten baguette and the map in his pocket. The German who questioned him asked where they and the clothes had come from. He swore he'd stolen everything, but knew they didn't believe him. Perhaps a neighbour had given him away. How else could he have been discovered so

quickly. He could only pray the mother and her daughter were safe.

For four years he'd worried about them while he was in a prisoner of war camp. Then another year kicking his heels waiting to be demobbed. But he promised himself that, one day, he would find out what had happened to them.

Now he was so close he was suddenly afraid. Suppose something dreadful had happened to them?

And now, five years later, he was back. He left the bike and walked towards the cottage. A girl's face appeared in the window. Slowly, recognition dawned. With a smile, she opened the door and came out to meet him.

"Are you the English pilot?" she asked in French.

"That's me," Robert replied in the language he had been learning for this day. He held her hands and looked her up and down. All these years he'd thought of her as a little girl. But she'd grown up.

"I've come back to thank you for your kindness and find out what happened to you," he said.

"We were fine," she replied. "We knew you'd been caught. Some German soldiers came to the village to tell us but they never discovered where you'd been staying." She looked up at him with a smile. "We've often wondered what happened to you."

Robert smiled back. "Oh, it wasn't too bad," he said. "And at least I had time to learn French, so now I can thank you properly."

"I'm so glad you're here," she said in English. "See, I've been studying your language, too." She took his hand. "I'm just home from college. Won't you come in and meet the rest of my family? And now I can introduce myself properly. My name is Marie-Claire."

It's in the stars

Patrick Arundell looks to the heavens to predict what's in store for you this month

CANCER (22 June – 23 July)
Few people marshal resources better than Cancerians and you're a born leader. This becomes more evident from the 7th, when you take the initiative. Your self-esteem benefits from the 23rd.

LEO (24 July – 23 August)
You'll lack energy but soon start to revive. By the 23rd you will be ready to take on the world.

VIRGO (24 August – 23 September)
Group activities and long-range plans are important, but by the month's end you are in more reflective mood.

LIBRA (24 September – 23 October)
Any ambitions you have come sharply into focus and you'll be ready to get cracking.

SCORPIO (24 October – 22 November)
You can travel in mind or in body, but limitations will be hard to bear and obligations bring you back to reality.

SAGITTARIUS (23 November – 21 December)
Look below the surface – much will be revealed, especially where finances are concerned.

CAPRICORN (22 December – 20 January)
Links with relatives overseas occur early on, but until the 22nd concentrate on those at home.

AQUARIUS (21 January – 19 February)
A practical time can put work, health and pets at the centre of things, at least until the last week of the month.

PISCES (20 February – 20 March)
You are in your element socially this month. Even though there are obligations to attend to, allow yourself to have some fun.

ARIES (21 March – 20 April)
Everybody needs a secure base to work from. With a little effort, yours can improve too.

TAURUS (21 April – 21 May)
Getting in touch with others is at the centre of your activities this month.

GEMINI (22 May – 21 June)
You've closed a chapter on an area of your life recently but it has freed you to concentrate on other matters.

Housewife's choice

Robert Opie takes a nostalgic peek at shopping-basket bygones

Bisto

It is said that the idea of creating Bisto was inspired by the wife of the manager of the Cerebos Salt company. Over dinner, she complained that there was nothing on the market to help her make gravy. The task of finding a solution was given to the Cerebos company chemist who, after many experiments, created a dry powder

that could be mixed with water and the roasting juices, producing thick brown gravy. The name for this new product was derived from the letters of the slogan 'Browns, Seasons, Thickens in One – Bisto'. It was launched in 1910 with a full-page advertisement on the front of the Daily Mail. In 1919 the artist Will Owen was employed to create the Bisto Kids.

Typhoo Tea

The family grocers of William Sumner had been established in Birmingham since 1820. In 1902 his grandson John took over. He was able to provide a cure for his sister's indigestion with a small leaf tea. It proved to be so good a cure that he

decided to sell the new tea in packets, calling it Typhoo Tipps Tea. First sold in 1903, it was so popular that in 1905 Sumner's Typhoo Tea Ltd was incorporated. During the 1920s many promotional ideas were used, such as inserting picture cards in each packet. For instance, in 1924 a series of Ancient & Annual Customs were produced, and ten million cards printed.

Cryptic crosswords and tea-time teasers to keep your brain busy

Skeleton

The black squares have to be filled in as well as the words. Four black squares and four numbers have been inserted. The black squares form a diagonally symmetrical pattern.

ACROSS

1 Experimental, hesitant
7 Fabulous bird
10 Affirm
11 Depart
12 Paved area behind a house
14 Contend
15 Wild beast's lair
16 Large brass instrument
17 Intone
19 Number of wonders of the world
21 Discourage
23 Masticate
25 Sofa
27 Our continent
30 Deserve
32 Market booth
34 Waltz or minuet, eg
37 South African province
39 Unwanted garden plant
40 Era
41 Popular drink
42 Rajah's wife
45 Imprecation
46 Football score
47 Farm bird
48 Fruit or disapproving sound

DOWN

1 Gentle knock
2 Avoid, shirk
3 Tennis-court divider
4 Hackneyed
5 Enter as an enemy
6 Vote
7 Scanning device
8 Part of a kitchen stove
9 Many-legged creepy-crawly
13 ⅟₁₆th of a pound
18 Successor
19 Scots name for an Englishman
20 Large wine-cask
22 Large jug
24 Part of the foot
26 Cheerio (2-2)
28 Beneath
29 Possess
31 Ever
32 Rear of a ship
33 Change
35 Traditional proverb
36 Lucid
38 Shivering fit
43 And not
44 East Anglian cathedral

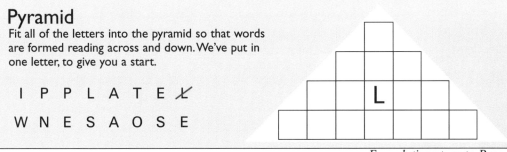

Pyramid

Fit all of the letters into the pyramid so that words are formed reading across and down. We've put in one letter, to give you a start.

I P P L A T E X

W N E S A O S E

L

For solutions turn to Page 161

August 2002

MONDAY	TUESDAY	WEDNESDAY	THURSDAY	
			1	
5	6	7	8	
12	13	14	15	
19	20	21	22	
26 Public Holiday	27	28	29	

Born this month...

- Martin Sheen *(3 August, 1940)*
- Queen Elizabeth, The Queen Mother *(4 August, 1900)*
- Madonna *(16 August, 1958)*
- Mae West *(17 August, 1892)*
- **Robert Redford** *(18 August, 1937)*

- Bill Clinton *(19 August, 1946)*
- Gene Kelly *(23 August, 1912)*
- Sean Connery *(25 August, 1930)*
- Mother Teresa *(27 August, 1910)*
- Richard Gere *(31 August, 1949)*

IDAY	SATURDAY	SUNDAY
	3	*4*
	10	*11* Edinburgh International Festival opens
	17	*18*
	24	*25*
	31 September YOURS on sale	

Flower of the month

LOVE-IN-A-MIST
(Nigella)

Summer is when a garden works hardest. The gardener might be rather less hectic with planting done, growth of the lawn slowing down as the soil dries, and fruit and vegetables swelling nicely, but plants are busy.

The most frenetic of all are annuals. After all, an oak tree has decades, even centuries to grow, flower and then set seed to make sure it leaves another generation of its kind. But an annual such as *nigella* has just a short time, perhaps from May to September, in which to complete its life.

It is no surprise that annuals are among the most popular plants with gardeners who want fast results.

Nigella is better known as love-in-a-mist and that perfectly describes the delicate flowers, intricately marked in shades of blue, set amid a lacy network of leaves. As well as the traditional blue there are pinks, white and purples, but nothing can surpass the natural beauty of *N. hispanica*, a weed of cultivated ground in southern Europe.

The key to success with all annuals is to make sure that everything is right for them – after all they only get one chance. So prepare the soil, pick a site in sun, and thin out the plants so they have a chance to grow, branch and develop. Their one aim in life is to set seed. If this is achieved they die, so to prolong the display, pick off the faded flowers so they have to try and try again.

105

THOUGHT FOR THE WEEK

Our object in travelling should be not to gratify curiosity and seek mere temporary amusement, but to learn, and to venerate, to improve the understanding of the heart.

Nigel Gresley (1876-1941)
English locomotive engineer

THIS WEEK IN YOUR GARDEN

Although there are always jobs to do in the garden, August is the month when you can take a well-earned break…

- Keep the ponds and birdbaths topped up. Thin out crowded water lilies.
- Mow the lawn less frequently if the weather is hot and dry.
- Cut and dry herbs for winter. Tie sprigs in small bunches and hang them upside-down to dry.
- Check daily for seeds ripening on shrubs, annuals and perennials. Cut them off when the pods are brown and put into paper bags to be sorted.

FROM ME TO YOU

Better the devil you know…

I was standing in my garden talking to a couple passing by our bungalow. My husband was singing as he mowed the lawn. As he has a good voice I was enjoying listening to his singing as I chatted. Out of the blue, the woman I was talking to said disapprovingly: "Isn't your husband a noisy devil?"

"Well that depends on how you look at things," I replied. "Most of the bungalows in this avenue are occupied by widows. So I would rather have a noisy devil than a quiet angel!"

Elsie Clarke, Polegate, East Sussex

HEALTH CHECK

Holiday hints

Don't let tummy troubles turn your fortnight in the sun into the holiday from hell. In the vast majority of places the food you eat will be perfectly safe but, if you're at all worried, your best bet is to follow the advice given to soldiers serving overseas: If you can't boil it, cook it or peel it, don't touch it!

- Stick to bottled water – and don't fall into the trap of having ice in your drinks!
- Make sure that meat is thoroughly cooked.
- Avoid salads as they might have been washed in tap water.
- Only eat fruit that is peeled, such as oranges, unless you can be sure it has been washed in bottled water.

If you do suffer an attack of diarrhoea, make sure you drink lots of fluids to keep you hydrated. If the bout is severe, see a doctor who might recommend a sachet of minerals mixed with water to rehydrate your body.

FASCINATING PHOTOS

Audrey Lake from Molesey, Surrey, likes showing this photo of her late husband at school to their grandchildren…

"How different school is today! In fact, my grandchildren, who are at university, couldn't recognise their grandfather. The photo shows a schoolroom in Preston, taken in 1922. My husband, Hugh, sitting in the last row, on the right of the middle block, is four and a half years old in the picture.

"When he grew up he moved to Ipswich, where we met and married, and later raised three wonderful daughters called Valerie, Celia and Linda. He joined the Army as a captain in the Royal Engineers, and was then attached to the Indian Army as Lieutenant Colonel."

TIP TIME

In dry, fine weather, deter slugs and snails from munching your favourite plants by pouring a ring of salt – about an inch wide – around them. No slug or snail will cross the salt line!
Mrs D Calcott-Fynn London

GO ON, SMILE!

A room with a view

Touring the south coast last summer, my husband and I were trying to find a hotel, but they were all too expensive.

One of the receptionists told us there was only one room vacant, but it would be more expensive than the standard rooms because it had a sea view. "If we don't open the curtains," my husband asked, "could we have it at a cheaper rate?"

Pat Barnes, Greenwich, London

RECIPE CORNER

Vegetarian Burgers

These moist burgers are just the thing for keeping vegetarian grandchildren happy at a family barbecue – in fact, they're so good, you'll have to fend off the meat-eaters! Serve them in burger buns with crisp iceberg lettuce and tomatoes, and a good dollop of mayonnaise. Makes 8.

1 cup chickpeas, soaked overnight
2 oz/50 g unsalted peanuts, dry-roasted in a frying pan
2 onions, chopped
2 cloves garlic, crushed
2 tablespoons oil
Pinch cayenne pepper
2 tablespoons fresh herbs
2 oz/50 g fresh breadcrumbs
2 oz/50 g flour
1 egg, beaten
Salt and pepper

1. Drain and rinse the chickpeas. Place in a saucepan and cover with fresh water. Bring to the boil and simmer 40-50 minutes until tender. Drain and cool. Blend in a food processor, with the peanuts, to resemble breadcrumbs.
2. Sweat onion and garlic in 2 tablespoons of oil. Place in a bowl and add the chickpea mixture and the remaining ingredients. Mix thoroughly and form into 8 patties. Barbecue or fry in a little oil for 3-4 minutes on each side.

THIS WEEK THROUGH THE YEARS

- **29 July, 1907** The Boy Scout organisation was officially set up by Sir Robert Baden-Powell.
- **29 July, 1981** Prince Charles married Lady Diana Spencer in London's St Paul's Cathedral. The day was declared a national holiday.
- **30 July, 1966** England's football team beat Germany 4-0 to win the World Cup. The team was captained by West Ham's Bobby Moore.
- **31 July, 1977** Nadia Comaneci, a 14-year-old gymnast from Romania, made history when she scored a perfect 10 points for her perfomance at the Montreal Olympic Games.

TIP TIME

To save a struggle when inserting a duvet into its cover, first put two corners of the duvet into position within the cover. Secure them in place from outside with giant bulldog clips. This makes the job so much easier.
John Yates, Leatherhead, Surrey

THOUGHT FOR THE WEEK

Remember to be gentle with yourself and others. We are all children of chance and none can say why some fields will blossom while others lay brown beneath the August sun. Care for those around you. Look past your differences. Their dreams are no less than yours. Their choices in life no more easily made. And give… give in any way you can. To give is to love. To withhold is to wither. Care less for your harvest than for how it is shared and your life will have meaning and your heart will have peace.

Pearl Bodimeade, North Harrow, Middlesex

TIP TIME
An easy way to cook sausages on the barbecue is to stick them on metal skewers. It makes them easier to turn. But beware, the skewers get very hot.
J Williams, Prescot, Merseyside

THIS WEEK IN YOUR GARDEN

If you're going on holiday, make sure your garden can cope with the summer heat…

- Keep well ahead with the watering, weeding and deadheading.
- The night before you go, give everything a good soaking and cut the lawn.
- Show the neighbours where you keep the hosepipe and watering cans. They'll probably be only too pleased to harvest the vegetables!
- Also, pot up your favourite herbs to provide a regular supply for the winter.
- Continue slug watch – they love lush, green foliage. Regular hoeing will turn up baby slugs for the birds.

TIP TIME
To prevent the base of a fruit pie turning soggy, sprinkle a little dry semolina on the pastry base before adding the filling. The semolina will absorb excess juice from the fruit.

FROM ME TO YOU

Bargain books

I'm all in favour of car boot sales. If you go early enough, many bargains can be found for a small amount of money. There are numerous stalls selling lovely baby clothes and equipment, plus bric-a-brac and you might even pick up an antique! It must break the owners' hearts to sell their property so cheaply.

But my pride and joy is definitely the bookstall where, for a few pence, I can pick up many of the latest paperbacks and loads of reference books. My library is growing. Long live car boot sales!

Margaret King, Huddersfield, West Yorkshire

HEALTH CHECK

What a strange diagnosis

Folk have some funny ideas about the causes of indigestion. According to a recent survey, one in five people aged 65 and over think heartburn is caused by eating food that it is too hot. More than one in ten think it is caused by feeling sad.

All untrue! The underlying problem is caused by a loose valve that allows digestive juices to flow back up from the stomach into the food pipe, causing the familiar burning sensation in the chest. It can be

made worse by eating rich food and drinking excessively.

There are many different types of remedy available from your local chemist. Be sure to check with the pharmacist to find out which one is right for you.

Did you know?
- Our digestive system is a nine-metre long tube.
- An adult's stomach can hold approx 1.5 litres of food or liquid at a time.
- Food usually takes around 24 hours to be fully digested, although spicy or fatty foods can take up up to 72 hours.
- Glands in the stomach produce hydrochloric acid, which is so strong it can eat through a cotton hanky.

Fascinating photos

Mary Langley from Carshalton in Surrey recalls a very close call for her younger brother Adrian…

"This photo was taken 65 years ago. It is of my brother, Adrian, who according to my parents was 'into everything' as a toddler. My father was painting the back entrance of our home when he needed to spend a penny. Checking that Adrian was safely in the living room with Mum, he popped to the lavatory.

"Two minutes later he walked out to see Adrian balanced precariously at the top of the ladder, happily 'painting like Daddy', he said. My father said his heart missed a beat as he quietly walked towards him, so as not to startle him, and caught hold of his legs. It was just one of his escapades apparently. My father even had to secure the manhole covers – nothing was safe while Adrian was around. Even a gate was built in between the kitchen and dining room for when Mum was cooking to keep a 'certain person' at bay!"

Recipe corner

Broad Bean and Feta Cheese Salad
The best possible way to use fresh broad beans. But don't worry if you can't get hold of them, frozen ones work just as well. Serves 2.

9 oz/250 g broad beans, shelled and peeled
4 oz/100 g feta cheese, cut into cubes
1 tablespoon olive oil
1 tablespoon lemon juice
Salt and pepper

Optional:
1/4 cup fresh basil leaves
1/4 cup flat-leaf parsley
1/2 red onion, peeled and chopped
1 clove garlic, peeled and chopped
Small handful capers (drained)

1 Briefly blanch beans in boiling water. Cool. Mix with the feta. Drizzle with olive oil and lemon juice. Season with salt and pepper.
2 Toss optional ingredients together and spoon over salad.

This week through the years

- **5 August, 1962** Film star Marilyn Monroe was found dead in her home.
- **6 August, 1945** The first atomic bomb was dropped on Hiroshima in Japan by the Americans, killing 100,000 people instantly and causing massive destruction.
- **8 August, 1974** Following the Watergate scandal, Richard Nixon became the first US president to resign.
- **8 August, 1991** British journalist John McCarthy arrived home after being held hostage in Lebanon for more than five years.

Go on, smile!

All you need is love!
Our first wedding anniversary fell in August 1956 and I was struggling to think of a suitable gift for my wife. Although we were both working we had very little money to spare. Then I had a bright idea. I went to the bank and withdrew one of those great big white £5 notes, took a photograph of it and paid it back in the same day. You can imagine how she laughed when I presented her with a paper anniversary gift!

David Critchlow, Poole, Dorset

THOUGHT FOR THE WEEK

The happiest time of life is between 70 and 80, and I advise everyone to hurry up and get there as soon as possible.

Joseph Choate (1832-1917)
American diplomat

THIS WEEK IN YOUR GARDEN

Temperatures now are often similar to July, with hot sultry days broken up by occasional thundery showers…

- Greenhouse ventilation will be needed constantly. Be ready with shading at the first sign of scorched leaves. Damp down regularly in hot weather.
- Prune rambling roses after flowering. Side shoots which have flowered can be cut back to one or two buds from the main stem.
- Take cuttings from any tender perennials such as fuschias.
- Treat ants' nests in lawns and paving cracks.

THIS WEEK THROUGH THE YEARS

- **14-17 August, 1969** The world's largest rock festival took place in the village of Woodstock in the USA. Among the musicians appearing were Jimi Hendrix, Janis Joplin, The Who and Santana.
- **15 August, 1947** The British colony of India was replaced by the independent countries of India and Pakistan.
- **18 August, 1959** The Morris Mini car was launched by the British Motor Corporation.
- **16 August, 1977** Elvis Presley, 'the King of Rock 'n' Roll', died after years of deteriorating health.

GO ON, SMILE!

Half-price headlines
I overheard a man in the supermarket commenting to his friend that their daily paper was half-price.

"That's good," replied the friend, "you can get two!"

S Thomas, London

TIP TIME
If things keep rolling out of your bathroom cabinet, put a blob of Blu-Tack on the shelf. Stick things to it and they'll never fall out of the cabinet again.
Mrs Lardner, Lytham St Annes, Lancashire

HEALTH CHECK

Water works!
Our bodies need about 3½ pints (2 litres) of fluid every day – more in hot weather or after exercising. You should not count tea, coffee or alcohol as part of your daily intake, as these are 'diuretics', which means they make you go to the toilet more frequently, adding to fluid loss.

As we get older, it's easy to become dehydrated, as our natural response to thirst diminshes. Signs to look out for include, dry lips and skin, a high temperature and confusion. But the simplest way to tell if you are drinking enough is to check your urine when you go to the toilet. It should be pale yellow. If it is a deep orangey colour, you should drink more fluid.

FROM ME TO YOU

Name game
I wonder if anyone else has noticed how the spellings of names seem to be changing.

Since when has Rebecca been spelt 'Rebekah' and when did the spelling of Yvonne change to 'Eevon'? And I've even seen Julia spelt 'Guila' and Fiona, 'Feeona'.

My name's Peter by the way, not 'Peetre' – just a thought.

Peter Metcalf, Edgware, Middlesex

TIP TIME
To keep cut flowers as fresh as possible, change the water and cut off a small piece of the stems every day.

RECIPE CORNER

Spicy Cucumber Salad
The combination of cucumber, yoghurt and mint is a cooling combination for a hot August day. Serves 4.

2 cucumbers
1 tablespoon sea salt
3 tablespoons thick plain yoghurt
½ teaspoon chilli paste
½ teaspoon paprika
1 garlic clove, peeled and crushed (optional)
1 tablespoon chopped fresh mint

1 Cut the cucumbers in half lengthways and slice thinly. Place in a sieve over a bowl and sprinkle with salt, turning the slices with a spoon to make sure all the cucumber is well salted. Leave to draw out juices for 4-5 hours. Rinse the cucumber thoroughly and dry with a clean tea towel.

2 Mix the cucumber with the yoghurt, chilli paste, paprika, garlic and chopped mint and leave to stand for 30-40 minutes for flavours to blend before serving.

THOUGHT FOR THE WEEK

If you are not poor enough to take charity, then you are rich enough to give it.

Anon

THIS WEEK IN YOUR GARDEN

This is the ideal time to make planting plans and order your spring-flowering bulbs...

- To prolong flowering, feed seasonal potted plants with liquid fertiliser.
- Lift onions and leave them to dry on the surface.
- Most hydrangeas will have finished flowering and will benefit from pruning.
- Water and feed tomatoes regularly and pick off yellowing leaves.
- Visit friends and beg a few shrub cuttings, which should be about 3in (8cm) and going woody.

FASCINATING PHOTOS

Della Browne from Thornes in Wakefield, recalls a day out with patients at the hospital where she worked in the '40s...

"Here is a photograph, taken in 1949. It shows staff and patients of the Cheyne's Children's Hospital, which was in Cheyne Walk, Chelsea, until it was evacuated to Sevenoaks during the war.

"We were taking some of the children out for the afternoon to Lullingstone Silk Farm. The owner of the farm was a friend of our Matron, Miss Price-Williams. We had a lovely afternoon out and enjoyed a picnic on the lawn.

"The coaches in the picture were new. We had some children on stretchers, which we balanced on top of the seat backs, with children sitting underneath. You can just see the stretchers in the photograph and I'm on the bus helping to balance them.

"I was only 16 years old at the time – just a few years older than some of the patients, but I loved my job and spent 43 years in nursing before my retirement recently."

HEALTH CHECK

Remember, remember?
It's very common to become more and more forgetful as time passes, but there are ways you can improve your memory:

- Cut down caffeine. Research has shown it to have a negative effect on memory. It also keeps you awake, and tiredness can affect memory.
- Make lists of things you need to remember, and leave yourself reminders around the house.
- Look for patterns in things you have to remember, for example, that you have three things to buy in the chemist and two in the grocers.
- Reduce alcohol consumption as it can dull the senses and make you less able to remember efficiently.
- Create special places for items that you lose regularly, like your glasses, your wallet or your watch.
- Play memory games to help your mental agility – for example, try to remember, then say out loud, the names of the last ten people you spoke to, saw on television, or heard on the radio or read about in the newspaper.

THIS WEEK THROUGH THE YEARS

- **22 August, 1952** Surrey won the county cricket championship outright for the first time since 1914.
- **22 August, 1997** Two Russian cosmonauts, sent to the damaged space station Mir, began to carry out repairs to its power system.
- **24 August, 1875** British swimmer Matthew Webb became the first person to swim the English Channel.
- **25 August, 1940** The Luftwaffe carried out its first bombing raid on London.

RECIPE CORNER
Choc Chip and Peanut Oaties
Irresistibly moist and crumbly cookies. Makes about 15

4 oz/100 g butter or margarine
1 egg
2 tbsps golden syrup
4 oz/100 g rolled oats
2 oz/50 g demerara sugar
2 oz/50 g peanuts, chopped
2 oz/50 g dark chocolate chips

1 Preheat oven to 180C/350F/gas mark 4. Cream together the butter, egg and syrup. Work in the oats, sugar, peanuts and chocolate chips.
2 Drop spoonfuls on to a greased baking sheet and bake for 12-15 minutes until golden. Transfer to a wire rack to cool.

FROM ME TO YOU
On your bike
Remember the days when bicycles were ridden on the road? These days you're in danger of getting knocked over by a child cyclist while walking on the pavement. Here are my tips on what you should do:

First, check to see if you're still alive – you may be lucky and just have a few broken bones. Next, get someone to call for an ambulance – for the child, then one for yourself.

Get a witness to verify what happened – you might find this a little difficult as most of the passers-by will only be concerned with kissing cuts on the child's grazed knees.

Be sure to check the bicycle for damage – as you will certainly get a bill to pay for its repair.

My advice to anyone concerned about their safety on the pavement is to buy a pair of bicycle kneepads, an illuminated jacket and bicycle helmet. Then walk in the road – where the cyclists used to roam.

Mr D Clewley, Borehamwood, Hertfordshire

GO ON, SMILE!
Rhyming reminder
My friend had to go to the dentist the other day for a check-up. "What time is your appointment?" I asked him. "Er, half past two," came the reply. "Well, that's easy to remember," I told him. "Your tooth hurty at two-thirty!"

David Kimberley, Darwen, Lancashire

THOUGHT FOR THE WEEK

Age does not depend upon years, but upon temperament and health. Some men are born old, and some never grow so.

Tyron Edwards (1809-94)
American theologian

THIS WEEK IN YOUR GARDEN

Plant growth slows down now, so it is time to complete your summer pruning…

- Plant daffodil and narcissus bulbs at any time before the end of next month. Daffodils should be planted at three times their own depth.
- Finish summer pruning of wisteria.
- Complete trimming hedges this month. Late trimming can result in autumn growth which may suffer frost damage.
- Summer prune apples and pears and trained fruit trees.
- Greenhouse heaters should be checked and overhauled.
- Pot hyacinths for Christmas flowering indoors – also narcissi, crocuses and early tulips.

FROM ME TO YOU

Sign of the times

I suppose many autograph books disappeared in the war years, which is a great pity. I always enjoy looking back at mine, which is packed with messages and autographs from old school friends and people I met in the WAAF at Bletchley.

Some people put in clever things and others just their names – but I wouldn't be without mine and it brings back memories almost like a photograph.

Mrs P Edmed, Bognor Regis, Sussex

GO ON, SMILE!

Sweet treat

I overheard a woman say to her child: "Divide that chocolate bar in half and share it with your two brothers." No wonder the poor child looked mystified.

C Manning, West Derby, Liverpool

TIP TIME
When preparing leeks in a cheese sauce, add a few carrot sticks. They add extra flavour and colour to the dish.
Mrs A Smalley, King's Lynn, Norfolk

HEALTH CHECK

Exercise for arthritis

When you have arthritis, the affected joints become swollen, stiff and painful. Although it is important to rest, exercise can also play a major part in helping to relieve the symptoms. As well as easing the physical pain – exercising pumps accumulated fluid out of the tissues surrounding the joints – it also stimulates the production of endorphins, which are your body's own feel-good hormones. The types of exercise to try are those that will increase the mobility of your joints, such as yoga, brisk walking and swimming. Always check with your GP before undertaking a new exercise.

THIS WEEK THROUGH THE YEARS

- **27 August, 1950** The BBC broadcast its first TV programme from the continent, an outside broadcast from Calais.
- **27 August, 1979** Lord Mountbatten, cousin of Queen Elizabeth II, was killed by an IRA bomb while on a fishing trip.
- **31 August, 1997** Diana, Princess of Wales, and her companion, Dodi Fayed, were killed in a car crash in Paris.
- **1 September, 1875** Edgar Rice-Burroughs, who created the character Tarzan, was born.

TIP TIME
Use clothes pegs to reseal packets of food such as pasta and breakfast cereal.

FASCINATING PHOTOS

Vic Birtchnell from Orpington, Kent, found this old photograph while looking through his late sister's photo album…

"This photograph was taken more than 70 years ago in August 1931. It is a clear day and you can see an airship in the sky, flying low in the skies near London Bridge. The airship is a Graf Zeppelin, designed by Count von Ferdinand Zeppelin in the early 1900s.

"I stumbled across the snapshot as I looked through my late sister's albums, but so far I haven't been able to discover anything more about the photo."

RECIPE CORNER

Smoked Trout Salad
You can prepare this simple salad in minutes. It works just as well with salmon or the vacuum packs of smoked mackerel. Serves 4

8 oz/225 g smoked trout, flaked

Salt and pepper
1 tbsp chopped parsley
$1/4$ pint/150 ml mayonnaise
$1/2$ iceberg lettuce, shredded
1 bunch of watercress
2 hard-boiled eggs, quartered
3 tomatoes, quartered

Season the fish with salt and pepper to taste. Mix the parsley with the mayonnaise and stir into the fish. Arrange the lettuce and watercress round a serving dish and pile the fish in the centre. Garnish with the hard-boiled eggs and tomatoes.

TIP TIME
Tie a length of ribbon round your house keys. They will be much easier to find when they have sunk to the bottom of your handbag.
Jenny Fraser
London

IT'S IN THE STARS

Patrick Arundell looks to the heavens to predict what's in store for you this month

LEO (24 July – 23 August)
You are one of the warmest and most generous members of the zodiac and now you can fully show these attributes. Open up to people who are unlike you. You may start something completely new.

VIRGO (24 August – 23 September)
Though your mind is active, physically you could feel strangely out of sorts until the 23rd.

LIBRA (24 September – 23 October)
You love lively conversations and anything that stimulates your mind. You're full of bright ideas.

SCORPIO (24 October – 22 November)
A relative might need extra support, or perhaps you'll become more involved in worthy, public-spirited activities.

SAGITTARIUS (23 November – 21 December)
You have an inquiring mind and it's time to open up new interests and examine different ways of doing things. Inject some variety into your life.

CAPRICORN (22 December –- 20 Jan)
Financial instincts will be demanding most of your attention until the 23rd, after which you need to broaden your horizons.

AQUARIUS (21 January – 19 February)
A degree of flexibility is required in dealing with close relationships. Co-operation takes you much further than digging in your heels.

PISCES (20 February – 20 March)
A more logical approach will help keep partnerships on an even keel, and your down-to-earth approach will be much appreciated.

ARIES (21 March – 20 April)
Your social life can sparkle, especially where you can meet up with others in active situations. You are brimming over with energy.

TAURUS (21 April – 21 May)
The new Moon of the 8th ushers in new beginnings in your home and family life. Perhaps it's time for a fresh start.

GEMINI (22 May – 21 June)
Your personal magnetism is strong this month and people could be highly attracted to you.

CANCER (22 June – 23 July)
You need to feel secure and are looking at ways to reinforce your situation.

HOUSEWIFE'S CHOICE

Robert Opie takes a nostalgic peek at shopping-basket bygones

BRILLO PADS

It was in 1913 that a New York door-to-door salesman discovered that housewives were finding it difficult to clean their pots and pans. He discussed this with his brother-in-law – a jeweller well-used to working with all types of metals – who came up with the idea of using a special soap along with a pad of metal fibres. Their lawyer devised the name Brillo. In 1928 Brillo came to Britain and a factory was opened in 1939. The war put a break on development, and production of Brillo Pads didn't restart until 1946. The red tablets of soap remained rationed until 1950 and the following year a combined soap and pad was introduced.

SHREDDED WHEAT

American lawyer Henry Perky claimed he created Shredded Wheat by accident. Production began in 1893. In 1901 a large factory was built near Niagara Falls, and the packets were redesigned to show off Perky's new 'palace'. The concept of breakfast cereal was unknown, so serving suggestions included spreading the 'biscuit' with marmalade or butter, or topping it with scrambled egg. Then came the idea of serving it with milk as a 'relief from the monotony of the everlasting porridge'. By 1908 Shredded Wheat was being sold in Britain and in 1925 a factory was built at Welwyn Garden City, Herts.

The British pack depicted the factory, described as a 'palace of crystal, its great walls of glass held together by slender, white-tiled columns'. The name Welgar was added in 1941.

Reader article

A CASE OF ITCHY FEET

Lynne and Barry Grocock are great adventurers, so when they decided to go out for a walk, it took them from one side of the country to another!

The summit of Loft Beck – we made it!

My husband and I had lived and travelled on board a 24 foot, old Falmouth Pilot sailing boat in the Mediterranean for the past ten years – an idyllic life on a very small budget. But our elderly parents needed support, our children had become really interesting and we had grandchildren. Time to head back to England.

We knew we'd still have itchy feet, so we bought some walking gear. After various walks we were soon ready to

> We had the satisfaction that only a glorious walk, good food, a new experience and a goal in the distance can bring

be more adventurous. It took an evening in and a bottle of wine for an idea to germinate. Why not walk across England?

We used fell-walker Alfred Wainwright's famous route. The Coast to Coast walk goes through the Lake District, the Yorkshire Dales, across the Pennine Way and on to the fells and moors of North Yorkshire, heading to Whitby, 200 miles in all. Planning began and in September we were off.

Day one took us up the cliff steps at Bees Head, along the clifftops, then inland to Tarn Farm, our first camping barn. The latch door opened onto a room with whitewashed stone walls, an open fire, a worn quarry-tiled floor – and spiders. The bathroom? Outside, cold water, broken mirror, no light.

We made a fire and as the smoke cleared, we had a warm glow and unlimited heat.

By nine o'clock, having eaten lasagne and drunk a pot of tea, we had the satisfaction that only a glorious walk, good food, a new experience and a goal in the distance can bring. We lay watching the flickering flames on the walls wondering what tomorrow would bring. With the tiles rattling, the wind and rain and the farm dog grumbling in the barn next door, we fell asleep.

Day by day, we made our way through the Lake District, travelling alongside Ennerdale Waters to the youth hostel off the beaten track in the woods. Next day we walked through woods, beside sparkling becks and through a magnificent valley surrounded by mountains.

Soon we were walking alongside the falls and rushing waters of Loft Beck – up and up! Almost 2,000 ft upwards in a quarter of a mile.

We had to go on as we were booked into the next hostel. Slowly we made our way up, with frequent stops to admire the view. At the summit, overlooking Buttermere Valley, Ennerdale Water looked like a blue puddle below us. That view is one I will always remember.

We decided to slow down as the pull up Loft Beck had found a few previously unknown muscles! On through places with glorious names – Stonethwaite, Greenup Edge, and Little Tongue. And on to Patterdale. The hostel here was in wonderful surroundings dominated on one side by the Helvellyn mountain range and on the other, the steep flanks of Place Fell, and between them lay Ullswater.

Other interesting stays included a night in a converted Methodist Chapel and a renovated cow shed!

Next, down we went into the lovely town of Richmond with its castle, Grey Friars Tower, Georgian theatre and waterfalls of the River Swale. Then into the Yorkshire Fells and Moors, through the ever-changing landscapes.

Finally, 18 days after leaving Bees Head and a rather misty walk across Sneaton Low Moor, we came to the road down into Robin Hood's Bay. We'd made it!

September 2002

MONDAY	TUESDAY	WEDNESDAY	THURSDAY
2	3	4	5
9 YOURS Autumn Special on sale	10	11	12
16	17	18	19
23	24	25	26
30 October YOURS on sale			

Born this month...

- Raquel Welch *(5 September, 1940)*
- Greg Rusedski *(6 September, 1973)*
- Hugh Grant *(9 September, 1960)*
- Prince Harry *(15 September, 1984)*
- Lauren Bacall *(16 September, 1924)*
- Twiggy *(19 September, 1949)*
- Julio Iglesias *(23 September, 1943)*
- **Brigitte Bardot** *(28 September, 1934)*

IDAY	SATURDAY	SUNDAY
		1
	7	*8*
	14	*15*
	21	*22*
	28	*29*

Flower of the month

BEGONIA

With their jewel-like flowers, tuberous begonias are some of the brightest summer flowers. In their wild form, their flowers are small, yet intriguing, either male or female – the latter complete with a three-winged seedpod behind every bloom. In their cultivated forms, it is the male flowers that are valued most, and the female blooms that attend the males to the sides are pinched out by show-growers so the males can develop. The females do the work of producing seeds.

For the garden these details are unnecessary, as plants produce their flowers with little attention.

The simplest way to enjoy their brightness is to buy plants in spring. The 'Non-stop' series is still the benchmark, with a neat habit, masses of blooms and often with contrasting bronze foliage.

You can also buy tubers that can be started into growth in the warmth and then planted out in late spring (frost is instant death to begonias). You can also sow seeds, but seedlings need careful treatment. Unless sown in January and February, they will not bloom until late in the summer.

Tuberous begonias will continue to bloom until cut down by frost and they thrive in light shade. Just pinch off any developing seed pods, and keep plants watered and fed to keep them growing.

119

THOUGHT FOR THE WEEK

'The world is divided into people who do things and people who get the credit. Try, if you can, to belong to the first class. There's far less competition.'

Dwight Morrow, American lawyer, diplomat and banker (1873-1931)

THIS WEEK IN YOUR GARDEN

September is a wonderful month. The heat of high summer has gone and the fruitfulness of autumn arrives…

● Take hardwood cuttings of roses while the ground is still warm – or sew seeds from rose hips.
● If you're thinking about investing in a greenhouse, don't wait until spring – buy one now.
● Asters will be in flower but check regularly for signs of mildew.
● Begin dividing overgrown perennials and planting new ones so the roots can establish before winter.
● Sow spring cabbages.

TIP TIME
After cooking fish, light a scented candle and leave in the kitchen for a short while to help get rid of the smell.
Mrs J Blower, Bristol, Avon

HEALTH CHECK
Get the most out of your veg
Here's how to preserve nutrional content:
● Store leafy greens and salads in the bottom drawer of the fridge. Keep tougher vegetables, such as potatoes and carrots, in a cool, dark, airy place.
● Don't chop vegetables until you're ready to start cooking them.
● Don't leave vegetables standing in water as some vitamins will leach out.
● Add vegetables to boiling water – the faster the cooking time, the more vitamins are preserved.
● Cook vegetables until just tender. Microwaving, steaming or stir-frying are all excellent methods for preserving vitamins.

FROM ME TO YOU
Out of the blue
When I lived in Australia, we had no neighbours to speak of – the nearest was 14 miles away down a dirt track. Once a month we drove to shop for our groceries – a real red-letter day!

The barren landscape could be very boring and even the passing of a distant car, throwing up clouds of dust, would be the highlight of the day.

One day I was feeling particularly bored, as my husband was away at the quartz mine where he worked as an engineer. I heard the distant noise of an engine and, looking up, saw a light aircraft circling. To my amazement, it started to descend and then landed at the end of our garden.

The pilot leapt out and shouted: "You must be Jeannie!"

"Sorry, no…" I shouted back above the engine noise. "My name is Tessa."

"Must be the wrong house," he said. With this, he jumped back in his plane and flew off!

Tessa Heaps, Wirral, Merseyside

FASCINATING PHOTOS

Doris Woolcock from Wolverhampton poses with her nursing colleagues, at a momentous time in history…

"This snap was taken a day or two after war was declared. We were the night nurses from St James' Hospital in Leeds. We had just come off duty and were waiting for the bus that would take us to the nurses' home just a few miles outside the town centre. As you can see, some of the girls were having fun trying on their gas masks. I am in the front row, third from the right. My maiden name was Roberts."

TIP TIME
If you have an empty bottle garden, fill it with fir cones and pot pourri – it will look nice and smell lovely.
Mrs H Hurcombe, Dursley, Glos

RECIPE CORNER

White Bean and Tuna Salad
This is wonderful with young
spinach, but you can use any
combination of salad leaves. It
takes minutes to prepare and
is full of healthy ingredients.
Serve it for a light lunch with
fresh crusty bread. There's
enough for two.

Large handful spinach leaves
Can of cannellini beans, drained
Can of tuna, drained
1 cucumber, chopped
4 ripe tomatoes, quartered
Handful black olives,
roughly chopped
For the dressing:
2 tablespoons olive oil
2 tablespoons lemon juice
Black pepper

1 Divide the salad ingredients
   among the plates.
2 Mix the dressing ingredients
   together and drizzle over
   the salads.

GO ON, SMILE!

What a bargain
I saw this entry in a holiday
guide recently which gave me
a good laugh:
   'Bed & breakfast plus
evening male.'
   Mr B Scott, Slough, Berks

TIP TIME
Before cooking the
bacon for a bacon sandwich,
I like to cut it into small pieces
with a pair of scissors and then
grill or fry. That way, it's much
easier to cut the finished
sandwich and the filling is
more evenly distributed
inside it.

THIS WEEK THROUGH THE YEARS

- **3 September, 1939** The British Prime Minister Neville
  Chamberlain announced that Britain was at war with Germany.
- **3 September, 1985** The wreck of the Titanic, which sank in 1912,
  was found south of Newfoundland.
- **5 September, 1998** Mother Teresa, who devoted her life to the
  poor of Calcutta in India, died, aged 87.
- **6 September, 1997** The funeral of Diana, Princess of Wales took
  place in Westminster Abbey.

THOUGHT FOR THE WEEK

Here's a little saying which we were told as small children when we didn't want to do something, 'Don't put off 'till tomorrow, what you can do today. 'Cos if you do it today and like it, you can do it again tomorrow'.

Pauline McManus, Rothwell, Leeds

THIS WEEK IN YOUR GARDEN

There are apples and pears in abundance, so harvest and store them carefully…

- Large crops of apples should be wrapped individually in newspaper and laid in a single layer on trays. Check regularly. Damaged fruit should be used immediately.
- Plant strawberries by the end of the month for cropping next year.
- Protect ripening fruits from wasps and birds. Scatter spoiled windfalls on bare ground for wildlife.
- Lift maincrop potatoes.
- Begin lifting root vegetables such as beetroot and turnips and store for winter use.

TIP TIME
Use a toothbrush to clean celery easily – it gets its into all the corrugated crevices.
Mrs A Grimes, Bridlington

FASCINATING PHOTOS

As a child Jean Tiblott of Carlisle, Cumbria, loved to listen to her grandmother's stories…

"During the 1914-18 war, my grandmother Eliza Winterbottom worked on munitions in Oldham. She is pictured on the far left, carrying the shell.

"She was born in the late 1880s and life was hard. I recall her telling me that she was a 'half-timer' – meaning that at the age of ten or 11 she spent the mornings at school and the afternoons working in the cotton mill.

"While she was working at the munitions factory, she also had to look after a boisterous toddler – my father.

"This photo has always been special to me because although taken at work, the girls look like they're in a chorus line!"

GO ON, SMILE!

Doctor, doctor

I'd made an appointment to see my doctor about an ear infection and when I walked into the surgery, I told the receptionist without thinking, 'Doctor Watson to see Mr Bryant'. She laughed out loud and told me it was the other way round.

Tom Watson, Newton Abbot, Devon

TIP TIME
If you are using only part of a frozen vegetable packet, cut a one inch strip straight across the top. That way you will have a ready-made tie-up to replace them in the freezer.
Mrs I Robinson, Birtley, County Durham

FROM ME TO YOU

Captured on camera

Dead, nearly all dead or dying! I surveyed the garden again. No, not quite. For some strange reason one sole surviving pink head stood out among the long-brown hydrangea flowers.

I grabbed my camera and took a photograph, which I pinned on my notice board to remind me that, yes, summer is over but there is always next year to look forward to.

Frances Spiegel, Wembley, Middlesex

THIS WEEK THROUGH THE YEARS

- **10 September, 1933** British tennis player Fred Perry won the US Open tournament, the first Briton to win it for 30 years.
- **13 September, 1957** In London, Agatha Christie's The Mousetrap became Britain's longest-running play after its 1,998th performance.
- **14 September, 1962** The Distillers company agreed to pay £250,000 for research into damage done by the drug thalidomide.
- **14 September, 1974** Two giant pandas, Ching Ching and Chia Chia, a present from the People's Republic of China, arrived at London Zoo.

HEALTH CHECK

To dry or not to dry? That is the question... and the answer may change the habits of a lifetime

Hygienists recommend that it's safer to leave dishes to drain on a clean rack rather than dry them with a tea towel. The reason given is that tea towels, even if changed on a daily basis, harbour germs and microscopic particles of food that can be transferred to your clean cutlery and crockery. For best results, rinse your dishes and cutlery in clean, hot water before draining. The hot water will remove any lingering residues of food and the heat will mean that the dishes dry in just a couple of minutes, so you're saved the hassle of drying up.

RECIPE CORNER

Corn and Salmon Fritters

Ideal for a special-occasion breakfast or as a light lunch. You can make them ahead of time and reheat in a hot oven. Makes 10. Serves 4.

6 oz/150 g plain flour
3 teaspoons baking powder
3 eggs
6 fl oz/60 ml cold water
Salt and pepper
4 oz/ 100 g canned sweetcorn (drained)
1 small can salmon, drained and flaked
3 tablespoons chopped fresh mint or parsley
Oil for frying

1 Mix together flour, baking powder, egg and water. Season well. Mix in salmon, sweetcorn and fresh herbs, and chill in the fridge for 10 minutes.

2 Heat a spoonful of oil in a frying pan. Cook spoonfuls of the mixture, 2-3 at a time, turning to cook the other side as bubbles form in the mixture.

THOUGHT FOR THE WEEK

Forty is the old age of youth, fifty is the youth of old age.

Anon

THIS WEEK IN YOUR GARDEN

Now's the time to embark on garden projects and have a good clear up...

- Make a start on tidying up your borders.
- Start clearing away herbaceous plant debris to prevent pests and diseases bedding down for the winter.
- Buy or make a compost bin for the debris.
- Put wire mesh over ponds to stop falling leaves fouling the water.
- Remove dead grass and debris from the lawn which restricts air movement around the grass.

THIS WEEK THROUGH THE YEARS

- **16 September, 1984** Princess Diana left hospital 22 hours after giving birth to her second son, Prince Harry, on 15 September.
- **18 September, 1970** Rock star Jimi Hendrix died of a drugs overdose in London.
- **19 September, 1929** The Home Office announced that Britons were drinking 60 per cent less than they did in 1914 and that drunkenness was on the decrease.
- **22 September, 1955** ITV, the first alternative to the BBC for the British viewing public, went on air, and screened the first advert ever on UK television, for a brand of toothpaste.

FROM ME TO YOU

A tasty tipple

Some years ago friends of mine introduced me to the virtues of home brewing. I bought a tin of prepared mixture costing about £5 and sugar costing about 80p. For this small amount I could brew 40 pints of excellent beer at a cost of slightly less than 15p a pint.

True, the process included the use of a fermentation tub placed in a warm spot and a plastic beer barrel with a tap placed in a cool place after fermentation, which all took time and labour.

But the result was a delicious beer available at a moment's notice and especially appreciated when friends and relatives called round unexpectedly.

Memories of those delicious, cool pints still linger on my lips.

Lawrence Marson,
Bilborough, Nottingham

TIP TIME

Use a fish slice to pick up a finished jigsaw – it's much easier than using your hands.
Mrs T Pennell,
Southport

GO ON, SMILE!

Mistaken identity

Years ago my mum had bread delivered to her house by a man called Joe and everyone remarked how much he looked like Tommy Cooper. Many years later she was in a bar at Blackpool with my dad and suddenly my mum said: "That man over there looks just like Joe the baker." My dad replied: "It isn't Joe the baker – it's Tommy Cooper!"

Amanda Greenwood,
Walsall, West Midlands

HEALTH CHECK

Yoga for health

Exercise is very important for your health, and yoga, a system of Hindu philosophy and physical discipline, aids strength, suppleness, breathing, and is excellent for stress. Yoga is suitable at any age and is thought to be particularly beneficial for older people because it can help to retain mobility and relieve common health problems such as arthritis and poor circulation.

You should start by having lessons with a qualified teacher, although once you have mastered the techniques you will be able to practise at home. If you have a medical condition or injury, it's important to consult your GP first.

Lyn Standring from Stevenage in Hertfordshire, shares this photograph of her father practising for a race…

"This photograph was taken in the mid '30s. It's a picture of my father, Edward White, who worked at Covent Garden Market as a porter.

"As part of his job he usually carried three or four baskets of produce on his head. I remember that under his cap he always wore a protective pad, which was shaped like a doughnut and made by my mother from her old silk stockings.

"In this picture my father is practising for one of the races held each year at Herne Hill for the employees of Covent Garden. During the races, the baskets were empty, but they weren't very easy to balance – especially on a windy day. All the family would attend and it made a lovely day out, especially as my father often won his race.

"For weeks before a race, porters could be seen walking around Covent Garden all day practising for the big race."

RECIPE CORNER

Savoury Stuffed Tomatoes
Make sure you use ripe tomatoes to get the fullest flavour from this dish. Serves 4

4 large tomatoes
1 oz/25 g butter or margarine
2 rashers bacon, chopped into small pieces
1 onion, finely chopped
2 oz/50 g mushrooms, finely chopped
1 oz/25 g fresh breadcrumbs
1 tablespoons chopped parsley
1 egg yolk, beaten
Salt and pepper
Few drops Worcestershire sauce

1 Preheat oven to 190°C/375°F/gas mark 5.

Cut the stalk ends off the tomatoes and reserve to use as lids. Scoop out the seeds.

2 Melt the butter and fry the bacon and onion until bacon is cooked and the onions are soft. Add the mushrooms and cook for 2 minutes. Stir in the breadcrumbs, parsley and egg yolk. Season to taste

and add a few drops of Worcestershire sauce.

3 Fill the tomato shells with the mixture, replace the lids and place in an ovenproof dish. Bake for 25 minutes.

TIP TIME
When filling cannelloni, put the required filling into an icing bag without a nozzle and pipe into the cannelloni tubes.
H Wignell, Kettering, Northants

September 23-29

THOUGHT FOR THE WEEK

You will never be old
With a twinkle in your eye,
With the springtime in your heart
As you watch the winter fly.
You will never be old
While you have a smile to share,
While you wonder at mankind
And you find the time to care.
While there's magic in your world
And a special dream to hold,
While you still can laugh at life,
You will never be old.

Iris Hellelden

THIS WEEK THROUGH THE YEARS

- **23 September, 2000** Coxless four rower Steve Redgrave won his fifth consecutive Olympic gold medal.
- **24 September, 1998** The world's first-ever hand transplant was performed in Lyon, France, when the hand of a dead man was stitched to the wrist of 48-year-old Australian Clint Hallam.
- **26 September, 1958** West Side Story, a musical by Leonard Bernstein and Stephen Sondheim, based on the story of Romeo and Juliet, opened on New York's Broadway.
- **26 September, 1984** The perfectly preserved bodies of three English sailors were found – 139 years after they died on an expedition to find a route from the Atlantic to the Pacific.

THIS WEEK IN YOUR GARDEN

Plants to give your garden winter colour will be available from markets and nurseries at about this time...

- Some hardy annuals can be sown outside now for flowering next year.
- Reduce ventilation in the greenhouse as the temperature drops.
- Bring in pot plants that were put out for the summer.
- Sow winter lettuce.
- Growing bags can be used again after tomatoes have been harvested.
- For early flowering next year, sow sweet peas in seed and cuttings compost. Then keep them in cool, airy and bright conditions.

FROM ME TO YOU

Telephone hang-up
One thing guaranteed to annoy me is when people put the phone down without apologising when they've got the wrong number.

I'm usually busy doing household and garden tasks when the phone rings, and I hurry to wash and dry my hands only to lift the receiver and hear a distinct click.

How long would it take or cost to say just one word, 'sorry'. Yet another example of how good manners with some folk seem to have disappeared.

Elsie Voysey, Bristol

TIP TIME
To separate eggs, break into a saucer and place an eggcup over the yolk. Pour away the white, holding the eggcup in place.
Mrs J Pearce, Bognor Regis, West Sussex

HEALTH CHECK

A healthy appetite?
Although you should try not to gain too much weight, it's just as important not to become underweight either.

Sometimes, as people get older, they can suffer from a lack of appetite, which can sometimes be a side-effect of medication they are taking, or due to depression or a deficiency of zinc.

If you're off your food, try having small snacks throughout the day instead of three larger meals, and keep nibbles such as biscuits, nuts or fruit to hand in case you feel peckish.

You could also increase your zinc intake by eating enough foods such as cheese, lean red meat and tinned sardines to give your appetite the boost it might need.

Fascinating photos

Lily Simmonds from Milton Grove, London, remembers meeting her prince more than fifty years ago...

"I had a very unhappy childhood and could only dream of being rescued by a prince. And then, when I was 16, I met Nick. He pulled me up from the depths of despair and turned a blind eye to the dreadful poverty surrounding me.

"In 1950 we visited Savernake Forest near Marlborough in Wiltshire and Nick carved our names in a tree, while making a promise to be true to me forever. A year later we were married.

"At the time people tried to tell us we were weren't old enough and the song Too Young, by Nat King Cole, became our song. It talks about people being told they were too young to be in love and didn't understand what the word meant.

"But, as the song says, we were certain we weren't too young and knew that our love would last a lifetime.

"You'll be glad to know that this story has a happy ending. In September 2001, Nick and I celebrated our golden wedding anniversary. I often think back to that moment in Savnake Forest and wonder whether our names are still on the tree."

Recipe corner

Blackberry Clafoutis
Serve hot from the oven with a big dollop of cream or thick Greek yoghurt. Serves 6-8

5 oz/150 g plain flour
3 eggs
½ pint/275 ml milk
3 oz/75 g caster sugar, plus extra for dusting
1 teaspoon vanilla essence
1 oz/25 g butter
9 oz/250 g blackberries

1 Preheat the oven to 200°C/400°F/gas mark 6. Sift the flour into a bowl and make a well in the centre. Add the eggs and half the milk to the well, then stir with a wooden spoon from the centre, gradually drawing in the flour from the sides to make a thick batter. Next stir in the sugar, remaining milk and the vanilla essence.
2 Put the butter in a 3½ pint/ 2 litre ovenproof dish and place in the oven for 2-3 minutes until the butter is melted.
3 Pour in the batter, then sprinkle over the fruit. Bake for 30-40 minutes. Dust with sugar to serve.

Go on, smile!

In the frame
I couldn't help smiling when I saw in a lonely hearts column a request for 'a partner for an attractive window in her 60s'.
Mrs S Simkins,
Old Basing, Hampshire

Tip time
When opening a new box of scouring powder, only uncover half of the holes and it will last twice as long.
Joan Elliott, Crewe, Cheshire

THE LETTERS

By Thelma R Roberts

Margaret stood at the front door and waved Henry off to work. A quick wave in return was all she got in return. Her husband was late for the office and would probably get caught up with the mums doing the school run and congesting the roads.

She watched him scramble into the car and speed off down the gravel drive. He was always rushing. Overdoing it. Work was stressful and he wasn't sleeping properly.

"You'll make yourself ill," she'd warned him. But he ignored her pleas that he ought to slow down and take it easy.

In his hurry this morning he hadn't noticed the small key falling out of his pocket but Margaret heard the clink as it fell to the ground. She bent to pick it up and couldn't help but wonder what it opened.

Going back indoors her curiosity began to get the better of her. She made a fresh pot of tea, sat at the kitchen table and poured herself a cup. Stirring it slowly, she stared out of the window, trying to decide if it was the key that would open Henry's bureau.

He always kept it locked and she never questioned him about it. She had no reason to distrust him, he was a devoted and loving husband and she felt very lucky to have married him. The den was his domain – she rarely entered the room. A quick run over with the vacuum cleaner and a flick round with the duster once a week and that was that. She really wasn't interested in the work he brought home from the office. She was content to leave him to get on with it.

Rising from the chair she got on with her household chores. She toyed with the idea of trying the key in the bureau lock as she moved around in a slower than usual manner, struggling with her conscience. That would be dishonest, but if she was careful, there would be no need for him to ever know. She could throw the key back on to the gravel drive and he'd be none the wiser. Margaret made the bed and then tidied the bathroom. Crossing the landing she finally gave in to temptation and turned into the den.

Standing before the lumbering piece of furniture, a family heirloom, she began to feel overcome with guilt. With shaking hands she placed the key in the lock and turned. The drawer opened. She stared down at a fancy wooden box that was lying there. Where did that come from? She hadn't seen it before. Maybe it came with the bureau.

Lifting the lid she gasped, clasping her face with both hands. Letters. All written in Henry's neat, fluent handwriting. Lifting one of the neatly tied bundles, she stared at the bold print on the face of the envelope. Her own initials, MEJ, stared back. Margaret Ellen Jameson. A shiver ran down her spine. Dare she take out one of the neatly folded letters and read it? Why not? They were meant for her. There, she had done it. With trembling hands she opened the letter.

It would be dishonest, but if she was careful, there would be no need for him to know

Sitting down she began to read Henry's words of love for her. The happiness she had brought him, the child they had had together – all had added to the joy in his life. He treasured each and every day they spent together. He was, he confessed, a very happy man.

Margaret wiped away the single tear that trickled down her cheek as she folded the letters and placed them back exactly as she had found them. She was thrilled to have read them. She would never tell Henry that she'd discovered

She read Henry's words of love for her. The happiness she had brought him. The child they had had together. All had added to the joy in his life

beautiful letters he had written to her. She would treasure them more than ever now that he had gone. How she ached to have been able to speak to him in his last moments, to hold his hand for what little time he had left and to whisper how much she loved him. But it was too late. Too late…

The funeral was very well attended. Margaret wasn't at all surprised at the number of mourners who had come to pay their respects. Henry had been well liked in the community and at work. Appreciation for the years he spent as treasurer of the local football club was reflected by the number of players who were there. Margaret felt immensely proud. Yes, Henry was a good man. She was going to miss him terribly. After the cremation, she decided to have his ashes buried in the local churchyard. It would mean another service for the committal of his last remains but she wanted him as close to her as possible. She would then be able to visit his grave as often she felt the need to be near him.

After the service was over she became aware of people shaking her hand and offering her their condolences. Many of the faces were familiar to her, others were complete strangers. Turning to her son, she asked him if he knew any of them. Who was the woman standing under the tree by the gate as the cortege passed through? Why was she still there? Did she know Henry?

William was surprised to hear his mother didn't have a clue who she was. "Did Dad never introduce you? That's his secretary, or was his secretary. I'll do the honours now if you like. She never married, as far as anyone knows. But she has a beautiful daughter. Come on, meet Miss Mary Elizabeth Jackson. Strange coincidence that, Mum, her initials are MEJ. Exactly the same as yours."

them. It was safe with her, it was now her secret as well. But why was he keeping the letters from her? If only he could share his sentiments with her. He was a private man who had always found it difficult to express his emotions with her. Perhaps, she reflected, he could only open up when he put pen to paper.

The ringing of the phone brought her abruptly out of her daydream. Picking it up, she heard a kindly voice from the hospital telling her that Henry had collapsed in the office and had been taken to the intensive care unit.

Struggling to keep her sobbing under control, she immediately phoned their only son, William, with the news. Together they rushed to Henry's side, but they were too late. Henry had suffered a massive heart attack and passed away just minutes before they arrived.

Margaret was inconsolable with grief. Words, just words, that was all she was hearing. Empty words from people. How could anyone know how much Henry had loved her. Nobody knew of the

It's in the stars

Patrick Arundell looks to the heavens to predict what's in store for you this month

VIRGO
(24 August – 23 September)
Your attention to detail is legendary and you're also the most obliging of signs. But don't be fearful of shaking up your image if things have got staid. Your confidence will soar if you do.

LIBRA (24 September – 23 October)
If you are imaginative or artistic you can shine, especially in any solitary pursuits.

SCORPIO (24 October – 22 November)
People will be drawn to your personality from the 8th, which could mean new companions.

SAGITTARIUS (23 November – 21 December)
A big plan you've been working on might require revision, especially if it involves close association with others.

CAPRICORN (22 December – 20 January)
You can be very shrewd and this helps you to form strong links with influential people. Use your charms and people won't turn you down.

AQUARIUS (21 January – 19 February)
You've a tendency not to take people or situations at face value. This judgement serves you well, especially in money matters.

PISCES (20 February – 20 March)
Seeing another person's side of the story becomes as important as seeing your own. Be sure not to overtax your nervous system.

ARIES (21 March – 20 April)
Focus on making your life run more smoothly. Friends are eager to help, so take up all offers.

TAURUS (21 April – 21 May)
If you're still working, your fortunes continue to be positive. But this month will see your mind wander to the lighter things in life.

GEMINI (22 May – 21 June)
Socialising will bring pleasure this month. You'll enjoy some practical endeavours too.

CANCER (22 June – 23 July)
Your financial canniness has left you in good shape. Consider using it on your home.

LEO (24 July – 23 August)
You don't always find it easy to get projects started, but you feel very optimistic this month.

HOUSEWIFE'S CHOICE
Robert Opie takes a nostalgic peek at shopping-basket bygones

MARMITE

"Keeps you tuned up."

Marmite first sold in small earthenware pots from 1902. Made from yeast extract, it soon became an established brand, recognised for its nutritious properties. It was ideal for troops serving overseas as it helped prevent the outbreak of beri-beri and other deficiency diseases prevalent in places such as Mesopotamia during the First World War. By 1930, Marmite had moved into the now familiar glass jar with its distinctive shape. At the same time there was growing recognition and awareness of vitamins – the richest source of B group vitamins is brewer's yeast, the basic raw material of Marmite. In 1984 the jar lid was upgraded from metal to plastic, but the label still retains the same feel is did a hundred years ago.

NESCAFÉ

there's always time for NESCAFÉ

Traditionally, the art of coffee-making involved grinding freshly roasted coffee beans, but the search was on for an easier way to make coffee. By the 1870s, several manufacturers were selling ground coffee in tins, often as a mixture of chicory and coffee to make it cheaper. In 1938 Nestlé invented instant coffee following years of trials and after there had been a massive surplus of coffee in Brazil. Nescafé arrived in Britain during 1939 but was soon in short supply with wartime restrictions. It was, however, in the new instant age of the 1950s that Nescafé took off.

PUZZLE IT OUT!
Cryptic crosswords and tea-time teasers to keep your brain busy

Cryptic A full-blooded cryptic puzzle

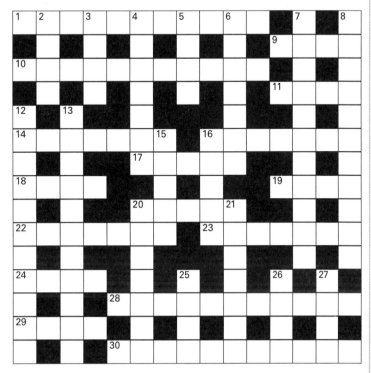

ACROSS
1 A regional game that brings notable families together (6,5)
9 It shows what one may get from a prime number (4)
10 Resistance leader whose aim was perfection! (7,4)
11 Hard spirit? (4)
14 Held to be placed inside a pipe (7)
16 Listen to only half the score, yet cheer (7)
17 Gloomy man called in to cure a sensitive organ (5)
18 Military weapon fastened in the middle (4)
19 Attractive tie? (4)
20 Evidently doesn't remain indifferent to scare off (5)
22 A flower – one round old ship (7)
23 A book-stand designed for 21 down (7)
24 It flies about in different directions (4)
28 By no means the whole of the matter, seemingly (3,1,3,2,2)
29 Mightily impressed, we put in a small announcement (4)
30 Time during which clerks are busy but professional skaters are not? (6,5)

DOWN
2 A classical author I'd nothing against originally (4)
3 A cardinal leading an old priest up a mighty river (4)
4 New deanery badly wanted (7)
5 It turns in pursuit of an opponent of reform (4)
6 A dog right for one employed to dig out (7)
7 Esoteric sign employed by executives (11)
8 A blow that is naturally sharp (7,4)
12 Angry violinist offering a definition of 10 across (11)
13 It shows what one can do with a car! (11)
15 'A ___ itself is but a shadow' (*Hamlet*) (5)
16 A girl left under a slight mist (5)
20 Succeed or fail as a bronco-buster? (4,3)
21 The tree whose lack customers bemoan! (7)
25 Levy put on one type of passenger vehicle (4)
26 Cut up over nothing, yet still game! (4)
27 Structure that offers visitors ripe sort of entertainment (4)

For solutions turn to Page 161

October 2002

MONDAY	TUESDAY	WEDNESDAY	THURSDAY
	1	2	3
7	8	9	10
14	15	16	17
21	22	23	24
28	29	30	31 Hallowe'en November YOURS on sale

...DAY	SATURDAY	SUNDAY
	5	6
	12	13
	19	20
	26	27 British Summer Time ends

Flower of the month
FOTHERGILLA
(Fothergilla major)

You don't have to go to exotic locations or search the lists of latest novelties to discover unfamiliar plants. Some plants which were introduced centuries ago are strangely neglected, appearing in few garden centres or gardens, yet have features that would seem to make them popular. Take fothergillas, for example, they have many good qualities and, named after Dr John Fothergill of Essex, they are not cursed with a name that is impossible to pronounce. They are native to south east USA and as there are only two species, it is not a confusing group of plants.

Fothergillas are related to the witch hazels and they have curious flowers, but this time they appear in spring, on the bare branches and they look like creamy bottlebrushes. The flowers are fragrant and quite showy and open in April. They are followed by the attractive leaves but it is in autumn that this tree excels when the foliage turns to scarlet, purple and gold making it one of the brightest plants in the garden, challenging and usually beating the Japanese maples for autumn colour.

This plant was first introduced in 1780 but was ignored even then and was not grown for a century until it was introduced again in 1902. It is not too difficult to grow, although it dislikes lime and heavy clay, but is a neat and attractive shrub that will enhance many gardens.

Born this month...
- Julie Andrews *(1 October, 1935)*
- James Herriot *(3 October, 1916)*
- Susan Sarandon *(4 October, 1946)*
- Kate Winslet *(5 October, 1975)*
- John Lennon *(9 October, 1940)*
- Luciano Pavarotti *(12 October, 1935)*
- **Roger Moore** *(14 October, 1927)*
- Rita Hayworth *(17 October, 1918)*
- John Cleese *(27 October, 1939)*
- Julia Roberts *(28 October, 1967)*

THOUGHT FOR THE WEEK

An old lady I once worked for always used to say: "The mystery of life is not a problem to be solved but a reality to be experienced." How true!

Maureen Carter,
Horsham, West Sussex

GO ON, SMILE!

Age before beauty
A stall on our local market carried a notice which read: 'Age-reducing cream'. I asked the stallholder if it really did work and he turned to his young, pretty assistant and said: "Give the lady a jar, Mother."

Mrs F Bourne,
Hall Green, Birmingham

THIS WEEK IN YOUR GARDEN

The garden is glowing with the vibrant autumnal colours of foliage, fruit and berries…

- Tulip bulbs can now be planted.
- Lift and divide old clumps of rhubarb.
- The soil is perfect for digging over empty areas but take it gently. Stop every few minutes for a breather.
- Dig garden compost and manure into the vegetable plot to encourage worms to break it up.
- Garlic produces a good crop when exposed to very cold weather, so plant cloves now.
- Start planting trees, shrubs and herbaceous plants before the soil cools off.

THIS WEEK THROUGH THE YEARS

- **1 October, 1962** British secret service agent James Bond, codenamed 007 and played by actor Sean Connery, made his first appearance in the film Dr No.
- **3 October, 1990** East and West Germany were finally reunited after 45 years of division.
- **5 October, 1998** The world's biggest chocolate bar, weighing 1.1 tonnes, was made by Cadbury in Birmingham.
- **6 October, 1927** The 'talkies' arrived in the cinema. The first film to feature live speech, The Jazz Singer, starring Al Jolson, amazed audiences – who stood up and cheered.

HEALTH CHECK

The alternative way!
The medical establishment is becoming more open-minded about the use of complementary therapies such as acupuncture, homeopathy or osteopathy. Some GPs will now even refer their patients to established practitioners. If you're thinking of embarking on a course of complementary therapy, here are a few pointers to bear in mind:

- Ask your GP for an opinion. He or she might be able to refer you to a practitioner – either private or NHS.
- Check a practitioner's credentials with the therapy's registering body.
- Ask in advance about the cost and length of the treatment – it might require several visits.
- Check whether medical insurance will cover the cost.
- Don't stop any conventional treatment you're having.
- Don't ignore side effects – report them to the practitioner and your GP.

FROM ME TO YOU

Make do and mend
Recently a neighbour in our retirement flats was waiting in the communal laundry for a dryer. Finally, one of the machines finished its programme and when my neighbour lifted out the person's washing a pair of man's socks fell to the floor.

Noticing that there were large holes in the toes, she thought, 'Oh dear! Some poor man on his own doesn't know how to darn his socks.'

Having a heart of gold, she took the socks home and neatly darned every hole. Some time later she returned the repaired socks to the laundry and left them on the worktop.

As far as she was concerned that was the end of the matter. But a few days later, when chatting to a neighbour, she was horrified to learn that the socks belonged to the woman's husband. Apparently he'd recognised them on the worktop, took them home and put them in his drawer. A couple of mornings later when he put them on he couldn't believe his eyes. "Come and look at these," he called to his wife. "Someone's mended the socks I was going to throw away." Somehow his old socks had got caught up with the washing.

J Beavan, Bognor Regis, West Sussex

Hazel Hollis from Boothville, Northampton, treasures this photograph, which brings back memories of the late singer David Whitfield...

"Here I am, more than 40 years ago, standing outside the Birmingham Hippodrome with the late, great singer, David Whitfield. I was a big fan, as were many of my friends, and we used to travel all over the country to see David's shows.

"I was thrilled to have this picture as a keepsake and David was quite happy to pose with me. It was typical of his kindness and he treated all his fans well. Just before this picture was taken he treated several of us to lunch at his hotel. We had spaghetti bolognese and he made us use only our forks to eat it, which seemed extremely sophisticated – we made such a mess!

"David then gave us a lift to the theatre in his massive American car. We had the top down and, as we drove along, he played his own recordings on tape. The city centre was crowded and everyone just stared at us."

RECIPE CORNER

Fancy Fruit Slice
This delicious sweet treat doesn't require any cooking.

4 oz/110 g butter
1/4 pint/150 ml condensed milk
1 packet (approx 9 oz/250 g) plain biscuits (digestives), crushed to crumbs
8 oz/200 g chopped dried apricots, pineapple, banana
4 oz/100 g desiccated coconut
2 tbsp lemon juice
For the icing:
2 oz/50 g butter, melted
3 tablespoons boiling water
1 tablespoon lemon juice
14 oz/350 g icing sugar

1 Melt butter and condensed milk and heat until boiling. Remove from heat. Stir in crushed biscuits, dried fruit, coconut and lemon juice. Press into a 12 x 9 in/ 30 x 24 cm baking tin and chill until set.
2 Combine all the icing ingredients. Ice the fruit slice, chill until set and then slice into bars.

TIP TIME
When making Yorkshire pudding, sprinkle a little pepper on the bottom of the tin before cooking and it'll stop the pudding sticking to it.
Mrs S Gosling, Braintree, Essex

THOUGHT FOR THE WEEK

Cut your own wood and it will warm you twice.

Anon

THIS WEEK IN YOUR GARDEN

Make the most of the late October sunshine by continuing the clear up you started last month...

- Rake up fallen leaves and pile them up to make rotted leaf-mould – it makes excellent mulch.
- Fish should fed less often as their activity level drops.
- Clean the greenhouse glass inside and out, scrub down benches with disinfectant and hose down.
- Keep collecting seedheads and bringing in the remaining harvest.
- Stock up on fleece and polythene to have ready as frost protection.

TIP TIME
Add a spoonful of porridge oats to a casserole – they will instantly thicken it and add extra flavour.
Miss G Brown, Loughborough, Leicestershire

GO ON, SMILE!

Graveyard shift
I saw this notice in a church magazine: "The old churchyard has been sadly neglected because there have been no burials for 25 years. We'd like to ask volunteers to remedy the situation."
Mrs F Bourne, Hall Green, Birmingham

TIP TIME
When putting away garden shears for winter, oil them, then slide them into the sleeve of an old jumper to prevent them going rusty.
Miss B Louth, Hull

HEALTH CHECK

Fight the flu!
If you haven't already, now's the time to see your GP about getting a flu jab. Studies have shown that the flu inoculation can reduce your risk of getting the illness by up to 75 per cent. And even if it doesn't protect you completely, the attack will be less severe. However, the jab is only effective against known strains of flu – it will have little impact against unexpected outbreaks. Flu jabs are available on the NHS to vulnerable groups, such as the elderly. Your best bet it to have the vaccine in autumn, before the start of the flu season, and repeat every year.

FROM ME TO YOU

Spitting sign
I recall a verse on the subject of spitting, which used to appear on the back of the driver's cabin on buses. It read: "In order to aid in the prevention of consumption, passengers are earnestly requested to abstain from the dangerous and objectionable habit of spitting."

What a shame that in today's world these notices just read: "Do not spit!"

Joan Crowe, Northwich, Cheshire

FASCINATING PHOTOS

A young Bert Wilkinson was caught red-handed by a press photographer when royalty paid a visit to the East End. His wife, Rose, from Wickford in Essex, tells the story…

"This is a photo of my husband Bert, taken when he was six years old in 1933, with the Queen Mother, who was then the Duchess of York. She was opening Frances Gray House – a new block of flats in Stepney. All the local children were given the day off school and lined up to wave Union Jacks at the roadside.

"Somehow, Bert managed to slip through the security cordon and up on to the balcony where the Duchess was appearing. When one of the Duchess's aides spotted Bert, he tried to move him away, but at that moment the Duchess looked over at him, smiled and waved at her aide to let him stay.

"It has lovely memories for us, especially of the lovely Queen Mother. The photo was printed in the evening newspaper. Imagine the surprise for my in-laws when they saw it the following day!"

RECIPE CORNER

Banana and Walnut Muffins
You can whip up these light and airy muffins in a flash. Makes 12.

4 oz/100 g butter, melted
1 cup sugar
2 eggs
½ teaspoon baking powder
½ up milk, warmed
1½ cups ripe mashed banana
1 teaspoon cinnamon
¼ cups chopped walnuts
2 cups self-raising flour

1　Preheat oven to 200°C/400°F/gas 6 and lightly butter 12 muffin tins.
2　Beat together butter, sugar and eggs. Dissolve baking powder in the milk and add to butter mix, along with banana, cinnamon and walnuts. Fold in flour and mix until just combined (don't overmix).
3　Spoon into tins and bake in oven for 15 minutes until risen and golden.

TIP TIME
Use a ceramic hob cleaner to clean glass shower doors. It quickly gets rid of watermarks and is not abrasive enough to scratch the glass.
Vivienne Jones, Tadworth, Surrey

THIS WEEK THROUGH THE YEARS

● **10 October, 1913** The last piece of rock between the Atlantic and Pacific oceans was blasted away, bringing the Panama Canal close to completion.
● **11 October, 1950** The first railway preservation society, the Talyllyn Railway Preservation Society, was formed.
● **11 October, 1982** The wreck of the Tudor ship, the Mary Rose, was raised from the seabed. The ship, which belonged to Henry VIII, sank in 1545.
● **13 October, 1988** The Turin Shroud, said to have been used to wrap the body of Christ, was declared a fake after extensive tests.

October 14-20

THOUGHT FOR THE WEEK

Age is all in your mind. The trick is to keep it from creeping down into your body.

Anon

THIS WEEK IN YOUR GARDEN

Garden pests are mostly on the decline but guard against mildew in the moist weather…

- Rake up fallen rose leaves to prevent blackspot spores entering the soil over winter. Burn them or bin them.
- Clear weeds which act as host to diseases and pests.
- Any tender plants which you want to over-winter must be potted up and put into the greenhouse.
- Move the herbs you potted in August inside now, to provide you with fresh shoots all winter.

FASCINATING PHOTOS

Margaret Berry from Cranbrook, Kent, recalls looking after patients in World War II…

"During the war I worked in the Voluntary Aid Detachment at Askham Grange, York. This picture was taken in 1940 when I was 24 I'm the first lady pictured on the left.

"We looked after soldiers and airmen and, for this photograph, the all dressed up in smart blue suits with white shirts and red ties.

"The staff wore their uniforms, which were always neat and tidy. I remember the headdress I had to wear. It was very neatly pleated at the back and had three pleats down each side, which were fastened with a tie-pin.

"I enjoyed working at Askham Grange. It was a really happy time for me, and all the staff got on well. However, I hear the Grange has now been turned into a ladies' prison!"

GO ON, SMILE!

Practical poacher

My brother-in-law said he'd make a poached egg. When my sister asked him if he knew how to poach an egg, he replied: "Yes, wait until it's dark and then creep up on it."

Joan Jarvis,
Culcheth, Warrington

> ### TIP TIME
> Cheese scones will look and taste better if you sprinkle the tops with grated cheese before cooking.
> *Z Sheppard,*
> *Stoke-on-Trent*

HEALTH CHECK

Work it out?

Many people look forward to retirement and see it as an opportunity to do all the things they've never had time to do.

Others feel imprisoned by it. They feel depressed and despondent and their health suffers. If you long to be back in a work environment, voluntary work is one option. There are plenty of charities in need of volunteers – or, if you're looking for part-time paid work, recent evidence shows that some companies are actively seeking older staff, seeing them as reliable and hard-working.

If this is not an option, remember the end of your working life doesn't mean the end of your social life – there are courses, social clubs and activities where you can make new friends and explore fresh interests. The library is a good starting point for finding out what's available in your area.

THIS WEEK THROUGH THE YEARS

- **14 October, 1990** Leonard Bernstein, US composer who wrote West Side Story, died.
- **16 October, 1978** John Paul II became the youngest Pope of the twentieth century.
- **16 October, 1987** England was battered by a hurricane with winds gusting up to 110mph.
- **17 October, 1925** Harry Carpenter, BBC sports commentator and presenter of Sportsnight, was born.

RECIPE CORNER

Caramelised Onion Frittata
Frittata is an Italian omelette, but it's thicker and more substantial and served in wedges. You can fill it with all kinds of ingredients – cooked leftover mushrooms, aubergines, potatoes and peppers are all good – but sticky, sweet caramelised onions are great. Serves 4.

1 lb/450 g onions, finely sliced
4 tablespoons olive oil
5 large eggs
4 oz/100 g grated Parmesan cheese
$1/2$ tsp paprika (optional)
Salt and pepper
Butter for frying

1 Put the onions in a frying pan with the olive oil and cook slowly over a low heat for about 20 minutes until the onions are dark brown and caramelised.
2 Break the eggs into a bowl and beat. Add onions to the mixture, with the cheese and paprika. Season.
3 Perheat the grill. Heat a generous knob of butter in a non-stick frying pan or large omelette pan and tip in the egg mixture. Turn the heat to its lowest setting and cook gently until the base is set but the top is still runny (about 15 minutes). Flash the pan under the grill to cook the top. Loosen with a palette knife and slide on to a warm plate.

FROM ME TO YOU

Plate project
J Goodyear from Dunstable, Bedfordshire, shares this simple idea that turned into a successful project…
"To keep us amused one afternoon, the over 60s club I go to asked us to make a table centrepiece by decorating a saucer with flowers, leaves and coloured paper. We were asked to bring six pence in pennies.

"The saucers were displayed on a table and it was clear the idea had fired the imaginations of our club members. All the decorations were beautiful and it got everyone chatting.

"Later we were asked to produce our six pence. We were told to put three pence by the saucer we liked the best, two by our second choice and one penny by our third choice. Once again it allowed our members to mingle and chat. We didn't have an overall winner but each plate designer seemed delighted with the few pence they had won."

THOUGHT FOR THE WEEK

Happiness is the one thing we can give without having.

Anon

FASCINATING PHOTOS

Claire Gould from Ely in Cambridgeshire, shares this photograph, which has been in her family for nearly eighty years…

"Here's a picture of my granddad's shop, Nethercott & Sons, in the early 1920s. It sold all types of vegetables and had cabbages and cauliflowers hanging outside to entice people in.

"The shop was in Willow Walk, Kentish Town, next door to a large fruit and grocery store. You can see my granddad, Ned Nethercott, standing outside the shop, towards the left of the photograph, with my dad, Ted, who was then a young lad.

"Nethercott & Sons was a real family business and later my father got his own grocer's shop in the High Street. Between 1940-45 my father was called away for the war and my mother had to take over running the shop."

THIS WEEK IN YOUR GARDEN

There's less time to work in the evenings now, so make the most of the hours of daylight…

- Continue mowing while the grass is still growing but set the blades fairly high.
- Prepare the ground for new fruit trees.
- Finish planting evergreens by the end of this month.
- Tubs can be planted up with bulbs for a spring colour display.
- Chrysanthemums must be lifted and stored.
- Sow broad beans outdoors in milder regions.

HEALTH CHECK

Sweet dreams!

Sigmund Freud, the father of psychoanalysis, believed that by interpreting dreams he could unlock the secrets of the unconscious mind and discover people's desires, drives and innermost thoughts. Others have argued that dreams are the result of a sort of gigantic filing system at work, whereby the brain processes the mass of information it receives during the day.

But the latest thinking suggests that dreams have less to do with psychological matters and more to do with our physical well-being.

Dreams, it is said, are simply a way to keep the unconscious mind entertained while the body gets on with the business of repair and recuperation. Without the stimulation of dreaming, so the argument goes, we would quickly become bored during sleep and wake before the body was fully recovered and ready to start a new day.

TIP TIME

I have found that using tea tree oil toothpaste and tea tree oil mouthwash helps prevent me getting mouth ulcers.
Cora Edwards, Machynlleth, Powys

THIS WEEK THROUGH THE YEARS

- **21 October, 1966** Tragedy hit the village of Aberfan in Wales when a slag heap from the local coal mine slipped and buried the village school.
- **21 October, 1996** Oscar-winning plasticine models Wallace and Gromit were reunited with their creator, Nick Park, after being left accidentally in a New York taxi.
- **22 October, 1955** Colour television was demonstrated for the first time in Britain by the BBC at London's Alexandra Palace.
- **26 October, 1965** The Beatles were made Members of the Order of the British Empire (MBEs) and were presented with their medals by the Queen at Buckingham Palace.

GO ON, SMILE!

What's in a name?

When I was a teenager, my father and his friend started their own roofing business. Not knowing what to call it, they decided to use their surnames, Fiddler and Leake.

Margaret Cann,
Stanmore, Middlesex

FROM ME TO YOURS

"I can't find it!"

Could anyone tell me why men are always so short-sighted when it comes to finding things? My husband was looking for a particular tie and I'd told him exactly where it was. "It isn't there," he moaned. Muttering, I went upstairs and found the tie exactly where I'd said it was.

And why is it that, although he has a drawer full of clean shirts, the only one that will do is the one that hasn't been ironed?

Olive Middleton, Bletchley, Milton Keynes

RECIPE CORNER

Ginger and orange slice

An irresistible combination of crisp shortcrust base and a gooey, fudgy topping. Makes approximately 20

4½ oz/125 g butter, plus extra for greasing tin
2 oz/50 g sugar
6½ oz/175 g plain flour
2 teaspoons ground ginger
1 teaspoon baking powder
Grated rind 1 orange

For the topping:
4 oz/100 g butter
6 oz/150 g icing sugar
3 tablespoons golden syrup
Juice half an orange
4 teaspoons ground ginger

1 Preheat oven to 180°C/350°F/gas mark 4 and grease a Swiss roll tin or shallow baking tin with a little butter.
2 Beat the remaining butter and sugar until creamy. Sift together the flour, baking powder, 2 teaspoons ground ginger and add to the butter and sugar mix with the orange rind. Mix to combine.
3 Spoon the mixture into a prepared tin and press into

sides of tin. Bake for approximately 20 minutes until golden brown.
4 While the base is cooking, place the topping ingredients in a bowl and heat gently until melted. Spread over still-hot base. Leave to cool slightly and cut into slices.

TIP TIME

After washing non-stick frying pans and tins, rub a little cooking oil over the surfaces to prolong their non-stick working life.
Ann Davies,
Milton-Keynes, Bucks

THOUGHT FOR THE WEEK

It's better to give than lend, and it costs about the same.
Philip Gibbs (1877-1962)
British author and journalist

THIS WEEK IN YOUR GARDEN

Send for fruit and vegetable seed catalogues now. Why not consider new varieties as well as old favourites?

- Leeks can be left in the ground and lifted through the winter.
- Make lily-of-the-valley beds. Choose a cool, shady place and plant the crowns separately, 3 in (7.5 cm) apart in rich soil.
- Weed and clean up those strawberry beds to reduce the risk of pests next year.
- Berry fruits such as blackberries should be pruned after harvest.

FASCINATING PHOTOS

This snapshot reminds Marjorie Lamb, from Broadstone in Dorset, of the father she waited over two years to meet...

"This photograph was taken in 1914 at the outbreak of war, when it was compulsory to billet soldiers if people had spare accommodation

"My mother and father housed four soldiers. My mother was just 21 at the time and she also had her hands full looking after a new baby – my older sister, Doreen. I often think of her and how hard she must have worked. The soldiers were Royal Lancashire Fusiliers and I believe they were all later killed in action.

"My father served with the Warwickshire Regiment and was later taken prisoner. My mother was told he was 'missing, presumed killed in action', and she was even sent her widow's application form.

"Then suddenly, out of the blue, a postcard arrived from my father who was in a prison camp, saying he was alive and well. Imagine the joy we felt.

"I was born two years after this photograph was taken and I finally met my dad when I was two-and-a-half years old."

GO ON, SMILE!

A light read
The lady standing before me in the library queue complained to the librarian: "I was looking forward to reading this novel because I saw a picture of a beautiful girl in a large hat on the cover. But when I turned to the back, I read, 'A tale of lechery and treachery'."

With that, the lady handed the book back to the librarian and turned on her heel in disgust. "Quite right too," the librarian sighed, "we can get all that at home."

Miss S Betts,
Kingsbury, London

FROM ME TO YOURS

Smoke screen
I wonder how many people have had the honour of having their name on a war-time smoke machine.

When I was 16, I returned home from college to find an ugly boiler-like contraption at the end of the road.

"Hello love, what's your name?" The military man in charge shouted to me. I told him and with due ceremony he rubbed out an existing name on the machine to chalk mine boldly across the side.

I was flattered until, passing the same spot later, I found another female name had been superimposed on mine.

Later that night the thick smoke designed to hide the town from the bombers woke me and I got my parents out of bed thinking the house was on fire – until we remembered the machine at the end of the road.

I don't know what it did for the good of the country but it certainly made a mark in my young life.

Thelma Pennell,
Southport, Lancashire

THIS WEEK THROUGH THE YEARS

- **31 October, 1935** The British Government announced that it intended to raise the school leaving age from 14 to 15.
- **31 October, 1984** Indira Gandhi, prime minister of India, was assassinated by two of her bodyguards in her own home.
- **1 November, 1962** The Russians launched their first rocket towards Mars.
- **2 November, 1982** Channel 4 went on air, showing the first episode of Brookside as well as the first edition of the gameshow Countdown.

HEALTH CHECK

Caffeine alert!

Caffeine is a substance found in coffee and cola drinks, and also, to a lesser extent, in chocolate and tea. It can cause you to feel agitated and irritable, and consuming too much of it can prevent your body from absorbing vitamins and minerals properly. Caffeine is also a diuretic (it makes you urinate), which can lead to dehydration if you are only having caffeinated drinks. If you are drinking a lot of coffee and tea – more than six cups a day – and are finding it hard to cut down, you could try decaffeinated versions. Try to find brands that use natural filtration processes to do this – the caffeine is often removed using chemicals which can be harmful.

RECIPE CORNER

Chicken in Sherry

Quick, creamy and full of flavour. Serves 2.

2 boneless chicken breasts
2 oz/50 g butter
Flour for coating
1 cup dry sherry
4 tablespoons double cream
Few sprigs fresh tarragon, chopped (optional)
Salt and pepper

1 Put the chicken between two sheets clingfilm and bat with a rolling pin until about ¼ in/½ cm thick.

2 Melt butter in a pan. Dust the chicken with flour on both sides and lay in the sizzling pan. Cook for 2-3 minutes on each side until golden brown. Remove from the pan and keep warm.

3 Pour away most of the butter, turn up the heat and pour in the sherry and toss in the tarragon. As the mixture bubbles, scrape any sediment off the base of the pan. When the sherry has reduced by half, stir in the cream and season. Return the chicken to the pan and cook for a further minute or two until chicken is cooked through.

SONGSHEET STARS

Eric Taylor provides a fascinating glimpse of the music hall artistes of yesteryear, pictured on the front covers of Victorian sheet music

D uring the early 19th century, tavern landlords would hire song and dance acts to draw in customers, attempting to keep order by banging a gavel. The audience, fired with enthusiasm and alcohol, heckled and joined in with the performers.

Before long, this entertainment, known as music hall, caught on and peaked in the 1880s when venues were packed to the rafters.

During this time, the music hall stars who made the songs famous were drawn by artists such as Henry Maguire, Alfred Concanen and H G Banks, the portraits produced as colour lithograph prints on songsheets, which had a great impact on their sales.

The wonderful quality of the lithographs made sure that many songs survived long after the music and words had passed out of favour and stars had long been forgotten.

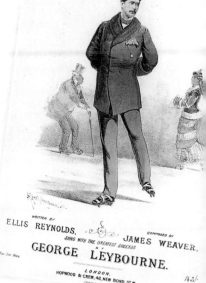

GEORGE LEYBOURNE (1842-1884)

Champagne Charlie insisted on being brought to the theatre in a carriage drawn by four white horses

George Leybourne, born in 1842, was the original Champagne Charlie. He made his music hall debut in 1865 and was one of the most impressive men to appear on the music hall stage. So impressive that Moët and Chandon subsidised his performances with a retainer and free champagne for the audiences.

When he first appeared at the Canterbury Arms, he was paid a record £30 a week and insisted on being brought to the theatre in a carriage drawn by four white horses. He remained top of the bill both at the Canterbury and Oxford halls for 20 years.

Though Champagne Charlie was his biggest hit, he made popular a song which is also remembered today, The Man On The Flying Trapeze.

He wore suits of puce, violet or green, a top hat and a coat with a large fur collar and, like many music hall artistes, lived furiously, drank heavily and died early.

The Belle of the Rink shows Leybourne's enthusiasm for using topical material, seen in the picture as a craze for roller skating, but the Belle is relegated to the background so that the star can take pride of place.

● The lithographer, Alfred Concanen, was the leading illustrator of British popular music and songsheets. He was a colourful personality and would have made his reputation as an artist in other areas were it not for his death in 1886.

HARRY LISTON (1843-1929)

Harry Liston was known as the Star Comique (comedy star). He was born in Manchester and his first stage appearance in 1863 was at the Scotia Theatre, Glasgow, then at the Metropole and Alhambra theatres in London in 1865.

A likeable young man in a top hat, white tie and tails, he was an elegant and graceful dancer. Liston traded on Leybourne's idiosyncrasies and would arrive at the theatre in a small carriage drawn by four white donkeys.

● The lithograph for London Lions was produced by Henry Maguire the younger, whose speciality was full-length portraits of music hall artistes.

JENNY HILL (1850-1896)

She had a hard life, with failed marriages and was only 46 when she died

Jenny Hill was a witty, bright-eyed girl who was known as The Vital Spark and famous for her dancing. She made her debut at the Dr Johnson Concert Room in London. Her career was influenced by Maurice de Frece, who booked her into the Oxford and Canterbury halls. Impresario John Hollingshead thought her 'one of the greatest female geniuses who ever appeared on the music hall stage'. Jenny left the halls to pursue a career as an actress. She had a hard life with failed marriages and was only 46 when she died.

● The illustrator is William Spalding who worked with Thomas Packer, an influential lithographer who trained many of the leading music illustrators.

VESTA TILLEY (1864-1952)

Vesta Tilley's real name was Matilda Alice Powles and she was the second of 13 children. Her father was comedian Harry Ball and, as a child, Vesta would watch him from the wings. Seeing the possibilities, Harry wrote her some male character songs and dressed her up in boy's clothes to work the Midland music halls. She was billed as Tilley Ball, the Pocket Sims Reeves and later as The Great Little Tilley.

She made her London debut in 1878 at The Royal, Holborn, and during the First World War, Vesta sang recruiting songs such as Jolly Good Luck To The Girl Who Loves A Soldier, dressed in uniform. She appeared in the first Royal Command Performance in 1912, singing Algy, The Piccadilly Johnnie. Her career spanned 50 years, appearing in military or male dress and always a picture of elegance.

Other well-known songs included I'm Following In Father's Footsteps, Naughty Boy and After The Ball.

Vesta married Walter de Frece, who came from a distinguished theatrical family and who was knighted for wartime services. She died in 1952, aged 88.

● The song Sisters has Vesta singing as a 'brother'. The lithograph is by H G Banks, who often used vignettes surrounding the subject to add humour. He worked chiefly for music publishers Francis, Day & Hunter.

IT'S IN THE STARS

Patrick Arundell looks to the heavens to predict what's in store for you this month

LIBRA
(24 September – 23 October)
Money matters need your attention from the 10th. If you're travelling or starting a course, expect limitations and a few setbacks, but don't be put-off.

SCORPIO (24 October – 22 November)
Although Venus attracts admirers to you, you should take care to use its energy wisely. You may need to put others first.

SAGITTARIUS (23 November – 21 December)
Friendships shine brightly this month, but someone could still try to restrict you.

CAPRICORN (22 December – 20 January)
At last, people will start to acknowledge your talents and recognise your achievements.

AQUARIUS (21 January – 19 February)
You can be a complicated person at times! October will find you either seeking out new ground, or sticking rigidly to what you know.

PISCES (20 February – 20 March)
Superficial issues are of little concern to you. Deeper matters can fascinate you. Property issues may also feature at this time.

ARIES (21 March – 20 April)
A long-term investment or finances to do with a partner could disappoint. This could cause tensions but your diplomacy skills will help.

TAURUS (21 April – 21 May)
Relationships need working at. It might be a good idea to cut down on spending.

GEMINI (May 22nd – 21 June)
The most romantic and playful sides of life are enhanced at the start of the month.

CANCER (22 June – 23 July)
A nagging doubt or an old personal wound may finally need confronting.

LEO (24 July – 23 August)
If you're still working, you might feel you deserve better terms. Fortunately you are able to express yourself clearly.

VIRGO (24 August – 23 September)
You might find it hard to read other people's moods effectively, so family discussions need tact and care.

HOUSEWIFE'S CHOICE

Robert Opie takes a nostalgic peek at shopping-basket bygones

COLGATE

Colgate Dental Cream first appeared in America during 1873, where it was originally sold in jars. At that time few people cleaned their teeth. A toothpaste 'for cleaning and preserving the teeth and refreshing the breath' was considered revolutionary. Quick to spot a growing trend, Colgate repackaged its dental cream in 1896 into a tin tube and boxed in a bronze carton. In 1908 it  arrived in Britain, the same year an ingenious rectangular tube opening was introduced – it enabled the paste to come out like a ribbon and lie flat on the toothbrush. It was in 1965 that one of the most memorable TV advertising campaigns began for Colgate's 'Ring of Confidence'.

HARPIC

Originally developed as a laboratory cleanser in the early 1920s, Harpic was registered in 1924. The inventor, Harry Pickup, a London heating and sanitary engineer, had used his name to devise the brand. In 1932 he sold his company to Reckitt & Sons who promoted Harpic with the ditty, 'A little Harpic every night, keeps your lavatory clean and bright'. An image of a knight on horseback – the health  crusader – was added to the tin. The main purpose of Harpic was to get 'WC bowls white and clean and free from germs'.

PUZZLE IT OUT!

Cryptic crosswords and tea-time teasers to keep your brain busy

Double-cross

Fill in the answers to the clues (*below left*) in the grid alongside, then transfer each letter to the corresponding numbered square in the lower grid to make a quotation. Reading down column 'A' will give the name of the author.

1 To rock (4); huge sea mammal (5)
2 Song of praise (4); grain plant (5)
3 Deadly pale (5); a tenth of a dollar (4)
4 London's botanical gem (3,7)
5 Organ of vision (3); genteel, delicate (6)
6 Perspiration (5); female servant (4)
7 Investigation (5); helpful clue (4)
8 Resound (4); tame rabbit's home (5)
9 Greece's capital (6); bow wood (3)
10 Recall (8)
11 All over the place (10)

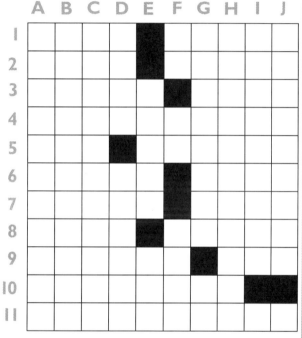

For solutions turn to Page 161

November 2002

MONDAY	TUESDAY	WEDNESDAY	THURSDAY
4	5 Guy Fawkes Night	6	7
11 YOURS Christmas Special on sale	12	13	14
18	19	20	21
25	26	27	28

Born this month...

- Vivien Leigh (5 November, 1913)
- Sally Field (6 November, 1946)
- **Richard Burton** (10 November, 1925)
- **Grace Kelly** (12 November, 1929)
- The Prince of Wales (14 November, 1948)
- Petula Clark (15 November, 1932)
- Goldie Hawn (21 November, 1945)
- Winston Churchill (30 November, 1874)

IDAY	SATURDAY	SUNDAY
	2	3
All Saints Day		
	9	10
		Remembrance Sunday
	16	17
	23	24
	30	
	St Andrew's Day December YOURS on sale	

Flower of the month

SCHIZOSTYLIS

The starry, delicate flowers of schizostylis would be welcome at any time of year but they are especially precious in autumn, the natural flowering time for this enchanting perennial plant.

In its native South Africa this relative of the gladiolus grows beside streams, where it never stands in stagnant water but its roots never dry out. And that gives a clue as to the kinds of conditions it prefers in gardens. Although never considered a pond plant, it flourishes best in moist soil.

Because of its country of origin and its love of sun, it is often planted in rather dry sites where it will survive and flower in autumn but never to its full potential. In moist rich soil, it rapidly spreads into broad clumps of narrow, grassy foliage. Its spears of flowers can start as early as September and continue through to December, decorating the garden and providing welcome cut flowers to brighten the dull months at the end of the year.

The common kind has bright flowers of dazzling red, but there are also various kinds in all shades of pink. These are just as effective in the garden, combining especially well with many of the shades of Michaelmas daisies which bloom at the same time.

149

THOUGHT FOR THE WEEK

If at first you don't succeed, try, try again. Then quit. No use being a damn fool about it.

WC Fields

THIS WEEK IN YOUR GARDEN

There should still be rich autumn colour to gladden the eye as you work…

- Continue to sweep up the leaves. Wet leaves on paths can be a safety hazard.
- Finish digging if you can – the earlier the autumn ground can be roughly turned over, the better.
- Pruning most bush and standard roses can start as soon as all the leaves have fallen.
- Lift and store dahlia tubers as soon as possible.
- Drain off hosepipes, wind them up and store in a cool, dry place.

GO ON, SMILE!

Wallflower

One year when all my garden plants had caught the frost, I saw one alive among the dead. I said to my friend: "This one's living." "No," my friend replied, "It's just taking longer to die than the others."

Mrs C Cooper, Barnsley, South Yorkshire

HEALTH CHECK

Cold comfort

A cold, with sneezing, a blocked nose and body-temperature changes is a viral infection. You're more likely to get a cold if your immune system is weakened – perhaps because you're tired, stressed or recuperating from an illness.

The cold weather makes us all more vulnerable too, probably because we spend

more time cooped-up together indoors. Boosting your diet with foods rich in vitamin C (such as oranges and tomatoes) and zinc (liver, eggs, seafood) is thought to help ward off a cold. But if you do succumb, the best advice is to ask your pharmacist to recommend a cold remedy, drink plenty of fluids and rest.

To help clear congestion, put a few drops of thyme and eucalyptus oils into a bowl of steaming water, and inhale deeply. There's little point in asking your GP for antibiotics, as they are ineffective against the common cold, but don't hesitate to see your GP if your common cold takes a turn for the worse.

RECIPE CORNER

Mulled wine

On bonfire night, fill your Thermos flask with this tasty tipple. It will keep out the chill as you watch the fireworks with your grandchildren!

½ pint/300 ml water
4 oz/100 g sugar
4 cloves
1 cinnamon stick
2 lemons, thinly sliced
1 bottle red wine

1 Boil the water, sugar and spices together. Add the lemon slices and leave to 'infuse' for 10 minutes.

2 Add the wine and reheat (but don't boil). Strain and serve while still hot.

FROM ME TO YOU

A memorable minute

One Remembrance Day I felt even more sadness than usual. I was in a large store when a message was given out over the loud speaker telling shoppers that at 11 o'clock we could join in the minute silence with the store staff.

I stopped in my tracks and pondered about sadness, loss of lives and the heroes who had given their lives our freedom. My silent gratitude was for those who fought for their country. But I was among so few.

Shoppers continued filling their baskets and chatting while children rushed up and down the aisles making a noise. I was not born until after the war but I shall never forget what was done for me.

I felt a great sadness that a minute was too much for many to give up when lives had been sacrificed for us.

Sylvia Monk, Attleborough, Norfolk

FASCINATING PHOTOS

Beryl Fenton from Hove, Sussex, remembers the time she took part in a radio competition…

"This is a photo of me and three other contestants who were finalists in a competition, sponsored by a home perm company, which featured on Radio Luxembourg in the '50s. I am pictured standing second from the left.

"Richard Attenborough asked us questions and we also had to guess the identity of a mystery voice. The winner was crowned Princess For A Day and was granted one special wish. The winner (pictured right) said she wanted to take her husband out to make up for him having been a Prisoner Of War.

"The show was taped in a London theatre for airing the following Sunday. There was no audience but we had a fascinating day."

THIS WEEK THROUGH THE YEARS

- **4 November, 1980** Movie actor Ronald Reagan was elected president of the United States of America.
- **4 November, 1995** The Israeli prime minister, Yitzhak Rabin, was assassinated by a Palestinian law student, minutes after addressing a peace rally in Tel Aviv.
- **8 November, 1996** In the US, a one-hour-old baby, Cheyenne Pyle, became the youngest patient ever to have a heart transplant.
- **10 November, 1989** The Berlin Wall, which divided the city for 28 years, was opened.

THOUGHT FOR THE WEEK

My favourite saying is: 'Always remember that you are the master of the unspoken word. Once said, those words can never be recalled and you will become their slave.'

Maureen Fullerton, Malmesbury, Wilts

THIS WEEK IN YOUR GARDEN

What you do in the garden now will save a lot of time and effort when the busy days of spring arrive…

- If you're planning a bonfire, check the heap for toads and hedgehogs hibernating. If you can, leave the creatures in peace.
- Check and repair fences, trellis and sheds while plant growth is reduced.
- Check on stored fruit and throw away any that show signs of rot.
- Sharpen up lawn edges and repair worn patches. Turf can be laid now.

FROM ME TO YOU

Wrapped up for winter

When I was a young child at primary school the winters were freezing. I would be sent to school wrapped up in several layers of clothing, including a pair of my Dad's thick socks inside my Wellington boots to keep my feet warm.

The only form of heating in the classrooms was a coke stove in the corner. And our headmistress used to make us run around an annexe building, then clap and shake our hands before going into class.

These days the children only need a thin layer of clothing as most are ferried to school in warm cars, before sitting in centrally heated classrooms all day. I know we were colder but I'm sure we were much healthier.

Rosemary Medland, Letchworth, Hertfordshire

HEALTH CHECK

Are we too clean for our own good?

Doctors are convinced that our squeaky-clean lives are making us ill! It seems we're becoming so obsessed with fighting dirt – bathing daily, washing clothes after a few hours' wear and sanitising our homes with anti-bacterial wipes and sprays – that our immune systems are becoming 'lazy' through lack of activity. This leaves the body vulnerable to attack when infection strikes. So next time you get a bit grubby working in the garden or develop a sniffle after playing with your grandchildren, think of it as a good way of giving your immune system a much-needed 'tune up'. It might keep you healthier in the long run!

TIP TIME

To keep winter boots in shape, put a plastic lemonade bottle down each leg when you're not wearing them.
Miss Jones, Stoke-on-Trent, Staffs

THIS WEEK THROUGH THE YEARS

- **11 November, 1918** The First World War, also known as the Great War, ended. More than ten million lives had been lost.
- **11 November, 1925** The first full-length play written for radio, The White Chateau by Reginald Berkeley, was broadcast by the BBC.
- **14 November, 1973** Princess Anne married Captain Mark Phillips at Westminster Abbey.
- **17 November, 1995** Today, Britain's first national colour tabloid newspaper, closed down.

TIP TIME

When you give any clothes to a charity shop, put a slip of paper with the size on it in the pocket, or pin it to a dress or shirt – it makes it a lot easier for people when they are browsing in the shop.
Mrs Griffiths, Stourport-on-Severn, Worcestershire

RECIPE CORNER

Stilton and Mustard Steaks
Creamy Stilton melts over tender steak – pop it under the grill and it's ready in a flash. Serves 2.

2 sirloin steaks
2 oz/50 g Stilton cheese, crumbled
1 oz/25 g butter or margarine, softened
1 oz/25 g walnuts, finely chopped
1 teaspoon English mustard
Salt and pepper

1 Heat grill to medium-high.

Mix together the cheese, butter and walnuts. Season the steaks with pepper, spread both sides with the mustard and grill for 4 minutes on each side or until cooked to your liking.

2 Remove from grill and press the mixture over the steaks

then return to the grill for a minute or so until cheese is browned and bubbling.

THOUGHT FOR THE WEEK

The only place where success comes before work is in a dictionary.

Vidal Sassoon,
British hairstylist

THIS WEEK IN YOUR GARDEN

Rainfall will increase this month, so protect the ground you've worked on with plastic sheeting...

● Lag outdoor pipes and taps to prevent them freezing.
● Heating is now essential to keep your greenhouse frost free. Consider investing in some insulation to keep costs down.
● If you see lily bulbs for sale, you'll have better quality flowers next year if you buy and plant them now.
● Re-write plant labels while you still know which are which. Mark where new bulbs are planted.

RECIPE CORNER

Chicken and mushroom bake

Poaching the chicken keeps it moist and tender and provides a flavoursome stock for the sauce. Serves 4

4 chicken breasts, skinned
1 bay leaf
1 carrot, peeled and sliced
1 onion, peeled and sliced
Rind and juice 1 lemon
Salt and pepper
6 oz/175 g button mushrooms, wiped and sliced
1 oz/25 g butter
1 oz/25 g flour
pinch nutmeg (optional)
4 oz/125 g Cheddar cheese
2 tablespoons fresh breadcrumbs

1   Put the chicken in a large pan with the bay leaf, carrot, onion, lemon rind and salt and pepper. Cover with cold water. Bring to boil, reduce heat and simmer gently until chicken is thoroughly cooked (15-20 minutes). While chicken cooks, sauté mushrooms in half the butter. Remove meat from stock and keep warm. Boil stock until reduced to ½ pint /275 ml. Strain and set aside.
2   Melt remaining butter in pan and add flour. Stir over the heat for a minute or two and then slowly add flour, stirring continuously until thickened. Remove from heat, add lemon juice, nutmeg and three-quarters of the cheese. Stir and season to taste.
3   Arrange chicken and mushrooms in baking dish. Add sauce then sprinkle on breadcrumbs and rest of cheese. Grill until cheese melts and breadcrumbs turn golden brown.

FROM ME TO YOU

A beltless bargain

Colin Middleton, from Leeds recalls an amusing incident...
We were coming to the end of our annual jumble sale and were all very tired, so we decided to sell as much as possible at any price rather than re-packing items and storing them.

A lady was holding up a nice dress for some time and it was clear that she was interested in buying it. After carefully examining the garment she asked how much it was and I said: "Seeing as it's you and we are all tired, you can have it for one penny." She looked at it again, then said: "I would but it hasn't got a belt!"

FASCINATING PHOTOS

Olive Jennings from Retford in Nottinghamshire, tells the story of a trip to a photographer's studio by her family...

"During the early 1930s, a photographer rented a studio in our small market town.

"My mother thought it would be lovely to have a family portrait taken. Our big day came and, with great excitement, we prepared to set off for our appointment at the studio. But at the last minute we discovered that my young brother, Tom, was missing. A desperate local search revealed no sign of him, but eventually a scruffy and black-kneed little boy strolled in.

"There was no time to chastise him. My mum gave him a good scrub down before we started the mile-and-a-half walk to the studio in our adjoining village.

"The finished photograph is lovely and a fitting tribute to a devoted and hardworking mother. I'm the one standing up holding my two-year-old sister, Peggy, and Tom's sat next to us, looking suitably sheepish."

THIS WEEK THROUGH THE YEARS

- **18 November, 1928** The first cartoon with sound, Steamboat Willie, was released. It featured a new character called Mickey Mouse.
- **18 November, 1991** Terry Waite was released from captivity nearly five years after being taken hostage by Shiite Muslims.
- **22 November, 1963** John F Kennedy, president of the United States, was assasinated in Dallas, Texas, by Lee Harvey Oswald.
- **22 November, 1946** The Biro pen, an invention by a Hungarian journalist, Ladislao Biro, first went on sale.

HEALTH CHECK
Stay strong in your sixties
At this time in our lives, we have more time to ourselves, so spend some of it looking after yourself! Research has shown that people of 60, 70 and 80 who walked 30 minutes a day, five days a week, spent half as many days a year nursing a cold as their inactive peers. Here are a few tips to help you stay in tip-top condition:
1 Never spend a day without taking exercise.
2 Keep your mind active with games, books, puzzles and quizzes.
3 Keep supple with stretching or other gentle exercise.
4 Do something you enjoy every day.

GO ON, SMILE!
Cagey advert
I had to smile at the following advert in a local paper: "For sale – large birdcage suitable for one or two parrots on legs in good condition."
Mrs J Smith, Cambridge

TIP TIME
Charity shops are a good source of buttons. You can often find unusual designs on cheap clothes, which are worth buying for the buttons alone.
Jane Barrett, Norwich, Norfolk

THOUGHT FOR THE WEEK

Experience is not what happens to a man. It is what a man does with what has happened to him.

Anon

THIS WEEK IN YOUR GARDEN

If your garden is host to squirrels, put up a feeder which distracts them from taking food you put out for the birds…

- Clean out old nesting boxes which can harbour parasites.
- Rabbits do an enormous amount of damage. Put guards around young trees.
- Insulate pots left out for the winter.
- Inspect potted bulbs regularly and water a little if necessary.
- Take perennial root cuttings from now until late winter.

FROM ME TO YOU

The Christmas present

Mrs E Kenzie, from All Stretton in Shropshire, shares her story about a visit to see Santa Claus in his grotto…

During the run-up to Christmas, my granddaughter had a holiday job as Santa's helper in a large shopping store.

A small girl appeared in tears and her mother explained that the girl was crying because she'd just lost her little handbag, which was decorated with a teddy motif. And, although they'd searched, they couldn't find it.

When the little girl came out of Santa's grotto and unwrapped her present it was a similar handbag to the one she'd lost. The little girl was overjoyed.

FASCINATING PHOTOS

A Neilands, from Ducklington in Oxfordshire, treasures memories of the day she was set a special challenge…

"I share my birthday with Winston Churchill (November 30) and, like him, I was also born on the Blenheim estate, where my father worked as a tenant farmer. Some 11 years ago, the local Rotary club offered Jim'll Fix It-type prizes and I was a lucky winner.

"I am a keen flower arranger, and it had always been my dearest wish to make a display for the magnificent entrance hall of Blenheim Palace. I was thrilled when the Duke of Marlborough agreed.

"When the day arrived, I picked a few flowers from my garden and then collected the rest from the florist. The display was to have a pink and mauve theme and feature carnations, gladioli and lilies. When I arrived at 9am, I was told that the Duke wanted me to make an arrangement in a huge silver bowl. I was mortified – I had only planned to make a small display. But undeterred I got to work. It was quite tricky – the table was very high and I had to make an arrangement that could be viewed from all angles. And to make matters worse, I was also working against the clock, as the first visitors to the Palace were due in an hour!

"I finished in the nick of time, just as the staff opened the door to the first tourists of the day."

GO ON, SMILE!

Words of warning

After I'd given my eight-year-old daughter a dose of children's cough medicine, I noticed these words on the box, 'May cause drowsiness. Do not drive and avoid alcohol'. I see I'll have to keep my young daughter away from cars and pubs when she's ill!

June Arnold, High Heaton, Newcastle-upon-Tyne

HEALTH CHECK

Winter warmers

It's vital to keep warm in winter to avoid the risk of hypothermia. The symptoms of hypothermia include drowsiness and lowered breathing and heart rate. Try to ensure your home is kept at a temperature of not less than 18°C and have plenty of warm clothes and blankets to hand for when it gets really chilly.

One of the best ways to keep warm is to wear a hat – 20 per cent of body heat is lost through the head – and make sure you eat hot, nutritious meals and have warm drinks several times a day.

RECIPE CORNER

Peach and Apricot Crunch

Serve hot or cold with a good dollop of custard or crème fraîche. There's enough here for four.

1 large tin (1 lb/450 g) peach halves in syrup
1 large tin (1 lb/450 g) apricot halves in syrup
4 oz/100 g butter or margarine
Pinch salt
1 teaspoon ground cinnamon
½ teaspoon grated nutmeg

THIS WEEK THROUGH THE YEARS

- **29 November, 1978** In Guyana, the mass suicide of an American religious cult living in a commune called Jonestown was discovered. They had killed themselves to prove their loyalty to their leader, the Reverend Jim Jones.
- **30 November, 1900** Oscar Wilde, the novelist and playwright who wrote The Importance of Being Earnest and was famously convicted of homosexual offences in 1895, died in Paris.
- **1 December, 1989** Pakistan's Benazir Bhutto became the first woman prime minister of an Islamic country.
- **1 December, 1990** The first stage in the building of the Channel Tunnel was completed with the breakthrough of the service tunnel.

½ teaspoon ground ginger
6 tablespoons clear honey
6 large slices bread, toasted, crusts removed and cut into ½ in/1 cm cubes
2 oz/40 g cornflakes

1 Preheat oven to 180°C/350°F/gas mark 4. Drain and reserve syrup. Halve peach and apricots. In a large pan, mix ¼ pt (150 ml) of the reserved syrup with the butter, nutmeg, cinnamon, salt, ginger and honey and heat gently until butter is melted.

2 Add the bread, peaches, apricots and cornflakes to the syrup and toss all the ingredients together lightly. Spoon the mixture into an ovenproof dish and bake for 30 minutes.

WHAT?
AT YOUR AGE...

By Ysobel Purkis

The sun shone out from a clear blue sky, slowly thawing the overnight frost. Today should have been her wedding day. It would have been perfect. She lay awake looking out of the window, watching the birds in the trees outside as she had done for years, letting the events of the past year march past in her mind, thinking of him – George.

They had not known each other for a lifetime, although for Jean it had always felt that way. From the moment George had made contact again she had felt happy and relaxed with him. He had phoned on that dreary, rain-soaked day, just when she had been at her lowest ebb.

It wasn't long after the funeral and for the first

He had phoned on that cold, miserable day, just when she had been at her lowest ebb

time in more than 50 years she had been on her own. No John, no children, no one asking what was for supper. It was just her and she hadn't liked it one bit. And then the telephone had rung and it had been George, offering his condolences and saying that, although he knew it was early days, perhaps she would like to come out with him for a drive one day, or a trip to the cinema or...?

Gradually, their friendship had blossomed and, although Jean felt silly admitting it, when she heard his car pull into the drive her heart gave a little lurch. You silly old woman, she had scolded herself – you're nearly 70, not 17!

She'd been 17 when she'd married John all those years ago. They were madly in love and fit to take on the world. They were penniless but happy and although it had been a struggle to make ends meet at first, they'd made a good life together. Their four children, two boys and two girls, were married now with children of their own. They led busy lives, which meant the phone calls were usually hurried affairs, and the weekends spent with any family were few and far between. It wasn't their fault but Jean was beginning to feel very lonely indeed.

Then George's phone call had come out of the blue. This time it was so much easier to be happy – there were no money worries, no mortgage to fret about, no tired children to put to bed; just each other to talk to and care for and, as it had happened, to fall in love with. George had asked her to marry him quite early on in their relationship but she had put him off, worried about the reaction of her children.

Her son said that his father would turn in his grave and suggested George was a money-grabber

Her eldest son, Jim, had been very unhappy, said that his father would turn in his grave and suggested George was a money-grabber. She remembered the conversation vividly. He'd phoned her, not long after she had started seeing George. She hadn't told him straight away but he was surprised to hear her telling him that she couldn't stop to chat as she was going out.

"Who's the lucky fella, then?" He'd chuckled down the phone.

She took a deep breath: "Well, now that you ask, he's not actually a boyfriend..." she giggled – oh heavens, this wasn't the right approach, she thought, but now that she'd started...

Nervously, she continued: "Do you remember George, George Sims? He was married to Joanna. Your father and I used to play bridge with them sometimes."

"Yes," Jim said, vaguely. "Well, he called me, not long after Dad died. He's a widower now, and he just phoned to offer his sympathy and, well, we chatted and then we went out for tea and well... it's gone on like that."

"Like what?" asked Jim, to Jean's mind he was being deliberately exasperating.

"Oh, for goodness sake, Jim. We're friends. We go to the cinema, to dinner – to wherever people go." She could hear her voice beginning to rise.

"Ma, you do know what you're doing? Don't..."

Jean interrupted sharply: "Know what I'm doing? I should hope that I do, Jim, I've been making my own decisions for quite some time

now, you know. Don't be so cheeky."

"Sorry, Ma. It's just that, considering Dad left you quite well off, I was just concerned how this George chap was placed – concerning his own funds as it were."

"Funds!" Jean didn't want to fall out with her eldest son. He'd loved his father very much and she knew that out of all her children, Jim would take it badly if he thought someone was trying to take his father's place. Taking a deep breath, she began: "Jim, darling, I know what you're trying to say, but you'll just have to trust me. George is a lovely man – you'll see, when you meet him."

"Okay, Ma. I only want what's best for you, you know that. And if you think that it's what dad would have wanted..."

That was a bit below the belt, Jean had thought, but she let it go. They had said goodbye and after Jean had put down the receiver, she suddenly realised what she had said. She had told her eldest son just what a lovely man George was. The words had tripped off her off her tongue, because it was true. He was lovely and wonderful and she finally admitted to herself that she was falling in love with him.

After that, it was easy. They decided there was no time to waste. The date was fixed, the church booked, the reception venue chosen, the photographer hired. Then George had collapsed.

Seeing him in that white hospital bed had terrified her. Surely God wouldn't be so cruel. He couldn't take George away now. She touched George's face with her fingertips. Day and night she had sat there, holding his hand, talking to him, until one night he had responded and had squeezed her hand back. She had smiled into his eyes and he into hers.

Their elaborate plans went out of the window. They decided to bring the date forward. The hospital chaplain had been wonderful and so had the two nurses who acted as their witnesses; they had made it so special, even bringing in a bottle of champagne to toast the happy couple.

She smiled, remembering it all now. She got out of bed and went over to the window and looked out at the lovely sunny day. Today, George was coming home from the hospital at last. Today their future as Mr and Mrs George Sims was just beginning.

It's in the stars

Patrick Arundell looks to the heavens to predict what's in store for you this month

SCORPIO (24 October – 22 November)
Your intensity means you don't take life lightly, yet you stick at things until they come good. This month take a firmer grip on your life. Financial matters are crucial.

SAGITTARIUS (23 November – 21 December)
A current tie or past memories are making you sad. Look forward to energy levels rising.

CAPRICORN (22 December – 20 January)
One friendship could develop into something deeper. Money matters begin to stabilise at last.

AQUARIUS (21 January – 19 February)
If you help others you will be appreciated. You might want more responsibilities too.

PISCES (20 February – 20 March)
You want to break out of a restricting situation. This is admirable, but make sure you have reasonable expectations or you'll be frustrated.

ARIES (21 March – 20 April)
Improving your life skills will take dedication. Don't be put off by minor setbacks!

TAURUS (21 April – 21 May)
The importance of relationships becomes clear and is key to your happiness.

GEMINI (22 May – 21 June)
Saturn's presence in your sign is oppressive and energy is low. Cut out any non-essentials.

CANCER (22 June – 23 July)
People find you quite a strong opponent. Be conciliatory but don't neglect your objectives.

LEO (24 July – 23 August)
Make your home special this month. Otherwise, you'll spend more time with your family.

VIRGO (24 August – 23 September)
This is an exciting period for communications. But don't promise more than you can manage.

LIBRA (24 September – 23 October)
Librans like good things in life and now is the time to spend your money enjoying yourself.

Housewife's choice

Robert Opie takes a nostalgic peek at shopping-basket bygones

BRYLCREEM

Brylcreem was launched in 1928 by the County Chemical Company for use by hairdressers. It was a mixture of brilliantine and cream, and proved so popular that in the 1930s it went on sale to the public in glass jars and metal tubes with the promise: 'Imports a splendid gloss to the hair. Fixes it in any desired position.' Advertisements even linked it to athletic prowess. During the Second World War RAF pilots were nicknamed the 'Brylcreem Boys'. When the cricketer Denis Compton (who also played for Arsenal) was signed up to promote Brylcreem in 1946, sales soared. In 1954 a new, squatter glass tub proved especially popular.

COLMAN'S MUSTARD

The firm of J & J Colman of Norwich was founded in 1823 to make mustard. Around 1850 Colman began to experiment with packing mustard in tins and bottles for retail sale and by 1855 the Bull's Head trademark was established. In 1880 two promotional ideas came into being to boost the Christmas trade – the issue of decorated mustard tins and the publication of illustrated booklets for children. In 1886 the first oval mustard tins went on sale at 1d each, a shape that continued until around 1975.

PUZZLE IT OUT!
Cryptic crosswords and tea-time teasers to keep your brain busy

Solutions

Alphabet ends

```
█ S C O O T █ █ █ S L A V
M █ R █ U █ F █ S █ A █ A
O █ A █ T █ E L A S T I C
U █ M █ D █ Z █ M █ E █ U
L A P D O G █ █ P E R D U
D █ O █ █ I █ L █ █ █ M
█ I N F R E Q U E N C Y █
M █ █ █ E █ █ █ █ O █ S
A D L I B █ █ S A L A M I
R █ U █ U █ R █ W █ S █ O
R A T A F I A █ A █ T █ U
O █ E █ F █ J █ S █ A █ X
W A S P █ █ █ C H A L K █
```

Splashing out
Shirley, Church, expensive hairdo, Wednesday, Mae, North, new dress, Thursday, Judy, Bouquet, meal out, Friday.

Entertainment

```
█ V E R T I G O █ A R C H I E
A █ D █ R █ E █ R █ O █ A █ M
P I D G E O N █ O S B O R N E
E █ I █ A █ E █ O █ E █ M █ R
M E E T S █ V A M P █ P O L A
A █ █ █ U █ I █ █ █ █ █ N █ L
N E W O R L E A N S █ L I N D
█ U █ E █ V █ O █ P █ C █
M A T T █ G E O R G E R A F T
I █ H █ █ █ T █ T █ █ █ U
T R E E █ A R C H █ E L M E R
C █ R █ T █ O █ W █ R █ A █ N
H E I G H T S █ E L S T R E E
U █ N █ A █ E █ S █ O █ I █ R
M I G H T Y █ S T I N K E R █
```

Code-cracker

```
C H I R O P O D Y █ P █ S
█ A █ A █ A █ I █ J I L T
P L U M P N E S S █ S █ E
█ F █ P █ I █ C █ S T Y E
C █ N █ S C O O T █ A █ L
O B E S E █ D █ R O C K Y
N █ G █ V O D K A █ H █ A
Q U O T E █ L █ W H I R R
U █ T █ R O Y A L █ O █ D
E P I C █ X █ Z █ T █ A
R █ A █ L I Q U O R I C E
O N T O █ D █ R █ I █ H
R █ E █ D E V E L O P E R
```

Letter set

```
P E P █ C L E A N
R A I S E █ A L E
O R E █ R █ S I X
W █ R E T R E A T
█ W █ R A Y █ S █
M A R R I E D █ C
A G O █ N █ E E L
C O D █ L L A M A
E N E M Y █ R U M
```

Royal quiz
1 Princess Beatrice
2 Highgrove 3 Peter Philips
4 Stanley Baldwin 5 Clarence House
6 Captain Tim Lawrence 7 Philip Arthur George 8 The Duke of Kent
9 Corfu 10 Caernarfon
11 Patti Palmer-Tomkinson
12 Glamis 13 The Duke of Gloucester 14 1900
15 Viscount Linley.

Cryptograms
1 I think she must have been very strictly brought up, she's so desperately anxious to do the wrong thing correctly. (Saki)

2 There is only one thing in the world worse than being talked about, and that is not being talked about. (Oscar Wilde)

Skeleton

```
T E N T A T I V E █ R O C
A V E R █ N █ L E A V E
P A T I O █ V I E █ D E N
█ D █ T U B A █ C H A N T
S E V E N █ D E T E R █ I
A █ A █ C H E W █ I █ █ P
S E T T E E █ E U R O P E
S █ A █ E A R N █ W █ D
E █ S T A L L █ D A N C E
N A T A L █ W E E D █ L
A G E █ T E A █ R A N E E
C U R S E █ Y █ G O A L
H E N █ R A S P B E R R Y
```

Pyramid

```
        I
      A S P
    A L L O W
  S T E E P E N
```

Cryptic

```
C O U N T Y M A T C H █ S █ C
█ V █ I █ E █ N █ O █ M E N U
W I L L I A M T E L L █ C █ T
█ D █ E █ R █ I █ L █ G R I T
C █ S █ N █ I █ E █ I
R E P U T E D █ H E A R T E N
O █ E █ D R E A R █ A █ G
S T E N █ E █ Z █ D R A W
S █ D █ C A R E S █ I █ I
B L O S S O M █ L E C T E R N
O █ M █ M █ R █ S █ D
W R E N █ E █ T █ V █ P █ P
M █ T █ N O T A B I T O F I T
A W E D █ F █ X █ C █ L █ E
N █ R █ O F F I C E H O U R S
```

Word-count
Eon, hem, hen, hey, hoe, hoy, men, mon, moo, ohm, oho, one, yen, yon, homy, hone, hymn, mono, moon, neon, none, noon, omen, homey, honey, hooey, hymen, money, moony, no-one. The nine-letter word is honeymoon.

Double-cross
1 Sway; whale 2 Hymn; wheat 3 Ashen; dime 4 Kew Gardens 5 Eye; dainty 6 Sweat; maid 7 Probe; hint 8 Echo; hutch 9 Athens; yew 10 Remember 11 Everywhere.

Men are April when they woo, December when they wed: maids are May when they are maids, but the sky changes when they are wives. (Shakespeare)

December 2002

MONDAY	TUESDAY	WEDNESDAY	THURSDAY
2	3	4	5
9	10	11	12
16	17	18	19
23	24 Christmas Eve	25 Christmas Day Public Holiday	26 Boxing Day Public Holiday
30	31 January YOURS on sale		

IDAY	SATURDAY	SUNDAY
		1 Advent Sunday
	7	8
	14	15
	21	22
	28	29

Flower of the month

WINTER-FLOWERING HEATHERS

Ground-cover plants have a reputation as the ideal garden panacea, smothering unwanted plants, looking colourful and saving effort, and they seem to be almost indestructible. But the reality is often less impressive. Some establish slowly, others are almost as invasive as weeds and others are as visually exciting as covering the ground with black polythene!

Heathers have long been regarded as superior ground-cover plants with their colourful foliage and flowers. They do not spread too wide and they will tolerate poor, acid soil. But they hate the shade of trees – remember these are plants from open moors so they're used to wide open spaces. And unfortunately they generally prefer acid soil conditions and dislike alkaline soils.

The good news is that the most useful group of heathers, those that bloom in winter, will grow happily in alkaline soil and that means we can all benefit from their cheerful flowers in shades of pink, white and deep ruby red. Planted 16in (40cm) apart, they mix well with conifers and other evergreens, and they can be planted in containers with winter-flowering pansies.

These heathers are also essential for autumn and winter baskets, mixed with ivies and spring bulbs.

Born this month...

Woody Allen *(1 December, 1935)*
Maria Callas *(2 December, 1923)*
Kenneth Branagh *(10 December, 1960)*
Frank Sinatra *(12 December, 1915)*
Jane Fonda *(21 December, 1937)*
Ava Gardner *(24 December, 1922)*
Humphrey Bogart *(25 December, 1899)*
Maggie Smith *(28 December, 1934)*
Anthony Hopkins *(31 December, 1937)*

THOUGHT FOR THE WEEK

Things may come to those who wait, but only the things left behind by those who hustle.

Abraham Lincoln

THIS WEEK IN YOUR GARDEN

December can be an exceptionally cold month but it's a real joy to be out in the garden in the fresh air on sunny, frosty days...

- Start pruning apple and pear trees now to encourage strong growth.
- Depending on the weather, give the lawn its last mow.
- Bring in Christmas bulbs for flowering.
- If you want use holly for Christmas decorations, net part of the tree to prevent the birds eating all of the berries.

THIS WEEK THROUGH THE YEARS

- **2 December, 1982** The first operation to implant an artificial heart in a human being successfully took place.
- **3 December, 1984** 103-year-old Harry Stevens of the US became the world's oldest bridegroom when he married his 84-year-old fiancée, Thelma Lucas.
- **4 December, 1991** Terry Anderson from the US was released from captivity after being held hostage by Hezbollah terrorists for more than six years.
- **8 December, 1984** More than 2,000 people were killed in an industrial disaster at a chemical factory in the Indian city of Bhopal.

GO ON, SMILE!

Money trouble
I went to see my brother and his wife and found her in a bad mood. My brother explained: "She's just had plastic surgery – I cut up her credit cards."

Mrs C Primrose, Manningtree, Essex

TIP TIME
A shoebox and flannels make an excellent bed for dolls when small children visit.
Barbara Duncan, Morley, Leeds

HEALTH CHECK

Put your best foot forward
Look after your feet and they'll be comfortable and free of problems. Wear well-fitting shoes that offer support, avoid sitting with your legs crossed and exercise to boost your circulation. Once a week, treat yourself to a pedicure:

- Soak your feet in warm water for 5 minutes and then scrub them with a pumice stone to get rid of hard skin.
- Dry them thoroughly with a towel to prevent any fungal infection.
- Trim your toenails using nail scissors or clippers. Cut straight across to avoid in-growing toenails. You can file them with an emery board if you want them to look neater.
- Rub in foot lotion and wear cotton socks for a couple of hours to help the lotion become absorbed.
- Regular visits to the chiropodist are a good idea for treating athlete's foot, verrucas, bunions and corns.

FROM ME TO YOU

I wish it could be Christmas every day
From childhood I have always loved Christmas and I am always the first to put up my tree. I am always sad when all the beautiful decorations have to come down after the celebrations. So every year I always leave a little piece of the trimmings in a corner of my ceiling so I can look up and see it at any time of the year. The sight of it there in spring, summer and autumn cheers me up because it's a reminder that Christmas will come around again and I'll soon be able to put up all those decorations that I love so much.

All through the year, my little piece of trimming will be fluttering away bravely until Christmas comes again.

Mrs M Shattock, Knowle, Bristol

RECIPE CORNER

Spiced Red Cabbage
A deliciously sweet-and-sour treatment for a traditional winter vegetable. Serves 3 to 4.

1 tablespoon sunflower oil
2 rindless bacon rashers, diced
2 oz/50 g light soft brown sugar
1 onion, chopped
4 fl oz/125 ml red wine

Red cabbage, weighing about 1 lb/450 g, shredded
1 small cooking apple, peeled cored and diced
2 tablespoon red wine vinegar
2 oz/50 g prunes, chopped
¼ tsp ground cinnamon
Pinch of nutmeg
Salt and pepper

1 Heat oil in a large pan and fry the bacon for about 5 minutes until crisp and browned. Stir in half the sugar and cook for 1-2 minutes, stirring constantly. Add the onion, cabbage and apple and cook for about 5 minutes.
2 Add the wine and half the vinegar, then the prunes, cinnamon, nutmeg and salt and pepper to taste. Cover and cook over a low heat

for 30 minutes. If there's too much liquid, boil until it evaporates. Stir in the rest of the vinegar and sugar, heat through and serve.

THOUGHT FOR THE WEEK

Definition of a fir: Tree which keeps its leaves all-year-round, except during Christmas.
Mike Barfield

TIP TIME

Keep a safety pin handy in the kitchen to pierce the 'flat' end of an egg before boiling – it will prevent it from cracking
Mrs Y Jackson, Thirsk, North Yorkshire

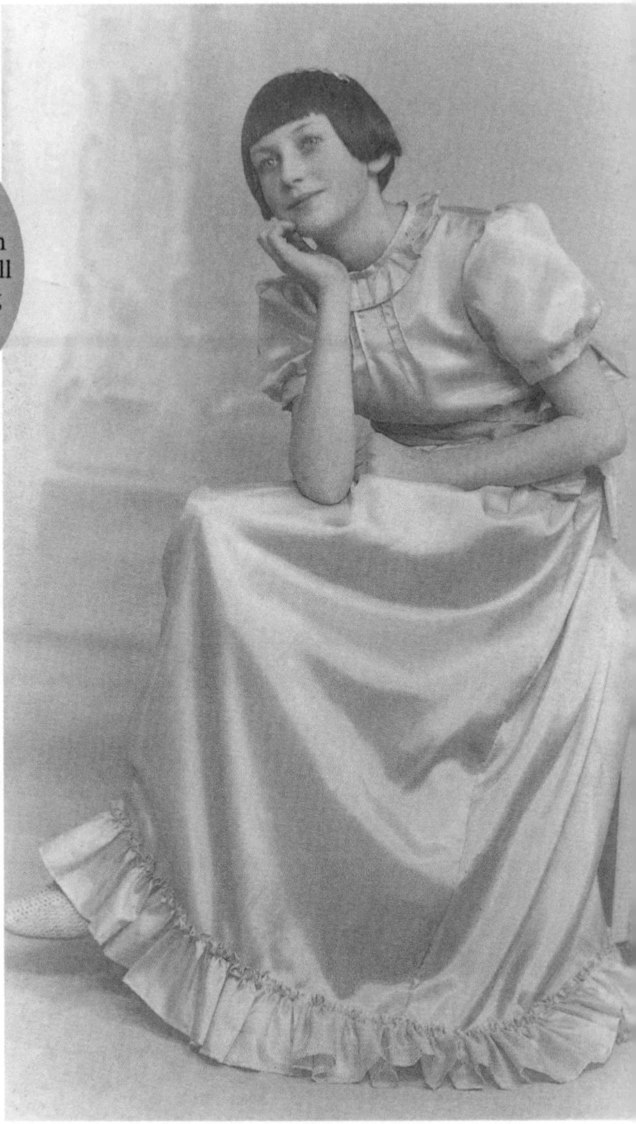

FROM ME TO YOU

Festive fun

Margaret E Griffiths, from Scarborough in North Yorkshire, wrote this poem to celebrate the many meanings of Christmas:

What does Christmas mean to you?
To some it's time to booze.
Have parties, games and lots to eat,
Then full... sit down and snooze.

For others, it's a fantasy time,
When Santa pays a call.
Riding through the starlit sky,
Bringing gifts for one and all.

For some it is a family time,
When loved ones get together.
Exchanging gifts and bringing love,
A love that lasts forever.

Others find it very lonely,
Alone with little to eat.
No friends to send a gift or card,
But not wishing to admit defeat.

Others remember its true meaning,
The birth of a child is voiced.
Christians celebrate all over the world,
Jesus's name is rejoiced.

The time to wish happiness and good will,
To friends both near and far.
Sharing joys of the past and future hopes,
And to be thankful for who we are.

If we can do this, on this special day,
Then why can't we do it forever?
On Christmas day, tomorrow and always,
Keep the true spirit of Christmas, forever.

TIP TIME

Turn ordinary mince pies into luxury ones by grating a little marzipan on top of the filling before putting on the pastry lid and baking.
Mrs R Evans, Sturry, Kent

GO ON, SMILE!

Trouser trouble

I was in a crowded lift when suddenly in the silence, a young lady said quite loudly to her male friend: "Did you get your trousers back?" – presumably they had been at the cleaners.
Mr P Smith, Crawley, West Sussex

Fascinating photos

Mrs M T Strickland, from Aylsham, remembers how a party dress made her feel at home during a traumatic time…

"In 1936 the Spanish Civil War broke out and the English community that lived and worked in Madrid was suddenly alerted to the danger from the forces rioting everywhere. Women and children were hastily herded on to trains for San Sebastian on the north coast where a ship was waiting to take us to Liverpool. We slept nose to tail, all lying out on the open decks.

"It was an unsettling time but everyone was so kind to us and keen to make us feel at home. For a time I was quartered with a family in Cheshire. The landlady was an excellent dressmaker and she made me a long, beautiful dress on her hand sewing machine to wear to a party.

"It was a full-skirted shiny, aquamarine taffeta, which rustled as I walked. It had a deep frill round the hem, which matched the little pie-frill round the neck, big puffed sleeves and a wide rose-pink sash. I was nine years old at the time and felt like a princess."

This week through the years

- **9 December, 1960** The first episode of the soap opera Coronation Street was shown on British TV.
- **10 December, 1903** Marie Curie was awarded the Nobel Prize for Physics in recognition of her work investigating radioactivity, making her the first woman to win this award.
- **10 December, 1979** Mother Teresa was awarded the Nobel Peace Prize for her work with the poor people of India.
- **11 December, 1936** Edward VIII abdicated the British throne to marry American divorcée Wallis Simpson.

This week in your garden

Take time to plan new ideas for the garden and drop hints as to what you'd like to receive for Christmas…

- A cold frame is invaluable and if you're handy at DIY, why not make one?
- Spray fruit trees and bushes with a tar oil winter wash to reduce pests and diseases.
- Tidy greenhouse plants, removing yellow leaves and fading flowers.
- Hoe off weeds when the weather is mild.
- Paint fences and other timber with preservative, making sure it's not harmful to plants.

Health check

Sleep on it!

It's a fact that as you grow older, you need less sleep. Studies have shown that older people take longer to get to sleep and wake earlier in the morning. But on the plus side, they tend to wake up more alert and feel more refreshed. The reasons aren't fully understood but researchers think it's because, as the years advance, the body uses up less energy on a daily basis and therefore needs less time to recuperate at night. And quick catnaps during the day make the need to become effectively unconscious for eight hours at a stretch less necessary.

Recipe corner

Quick Christmas Cake

Mrs M Smith from Swindon recommends her delicious fruit cake which can be mixed in a pan. It's an ideal Christmas cake – and there's no need to make it months in advance!

1 lb/450 g mixed fruit or sultanas
4 oz/110 g butter
1 cup sugar
2 eggs, beaten
2 cups self-raising flour

1. Grease and line an 8in cake tin. Preheat the oven to 180°C/350°F/gas mark 4.
2. Put the fruit, butter and sugar in a large saucepan. Heat, stirring constantly, until the butter and sugar have dissolved. Allow to cool for 30 minutes
3. Stir in the eggs and fold in the flour, mixing well to combine thoroughly. Spoon mixture into cake tin and bake in oven for $1^{1}/2$ hours, or until a skewer inserted in the centre comes out clean.

THOUGHT FOR THE WEEK

I have often thought, says Sir Roger, it happens very well that Christmas should fall out in the middle of winter.

Joseph Addison (1672-1719)
English essayist and politician

THIS WEEK IN YOUR GARDEN

Winter digging can continue and you could well have a robin for company at this time of year…

- Make sure you regularly put food out for the birds. You'll keep them happy – and resident in your garden.
- Keep off the lawn if it's frosted or wet, to avoid damaging it.
- If you grow pelargoniums from seed, sow them now.
- To prevent your pond from freezing over completely, float a ball on the surface.
- Put your feet up in front of the fire and plan your dream garden.

FROM ME TO YOU

Sounds of the season

Just before Christmas in 1945, when I was about ten, a group of carol singers came to our house.

Mum said: "Just listen. Isn't that lovely." She sent me to the door and their collector said: "Would you like to help the carol singers?" I quickly replied: "No sorry. I can't come out. Mum's just filled the bath." I didn't know they were collecting money.

Now when I go to the door, I have the money ready and can't help but have a smile on my face.

Brenda Green, Gainsborough, Lincolnshire

HEALTH CHECK

Stress busters

Anything that makes you tense, angry, frustrated or unhappy can cause stress. One person's stress may be another's pleasure – racing drivers and marathon runners seem to thrive on physical challenges. A certain amount of stress is good for us – facing problems and overcoming them stops us from getting bored – but too much affects our health and well-being. We can defend against stress by keeping a healthy body and mind:

TIP TIME

Chocolate mousse with added chocolate chips makes a delicious filling for a chocolate sponge cake – and it makes a welcome change from Christmas cake, too!
M Smith, Bettws, Newtown

- Make sure you get enough sleep each night.
- Try to stay at the ideal weight for your height.
- Take regular exercise – keeping active is a great stress-reliever.
- Learn techniques to help you relax. A popular method is to sit quietly, take deep breaths, clear your mind and concentrate on the sound of your breathing.
- Tackle your problems by devising a plan to cope with them.

THIS WEEK THROUGH THE YEARS

- **17 December, 1973** The Conservative government, led by Edward Heath, announced the start of the three-day working week because of limited fuel supplies due to industrial disputes.
- **21 December, 1937** Walt Disney's feature-length cartoon, Snow White and the Seven Dwarfs, was released.
- **21 December, 1965** Plans for a Road Safety Bill included introducing legal alcohol limits and random breath testing.
- **22 December, 1989** A Pan Am passenger jet exploded over the Scottish town of Lockerbie on 22 December, killing all those on board as well as at least 11 people on the ground.

GO ON, SMILE!

Old boot

A friend remarked on how nice my boots looked and I replied without thinking: "Yes, but they're on their last legs".

Mrs J McLarty, Wallasey, Wirral

Recipe corner

Cheese and Olive Puffs

These light bites are simple to make but look oh-so impressive – they're perfect to take to a party or for when people drop by for a pre-Christmas drink. They're delicious with a strong blue cheese such as Roquefort or Stilton, but any kind of cheese will do – use whatever's in the fridge to save a special trip out. Makes 18.

¼ pt/150 ml milk and water mixed (half and half)
2 oz/50 g butter
3 oz/75 g plain flour, sifted
Pinch of salt
2 large eggs
2 oz/50 g cheese, diced
2 oz/50 g pitted black olives, chopped

1 Preheat oven to 200°C/400°F/gas mark 6 and grease a baking sheet. Put the liquid and butter in a pan. Heat until the butter melts and then bring to the boil. Remove from the heat and tip in the flour and salt.

2 Beat until the mixture forms a stiff paste and lifts away from the sides of the pan. Cool for 5-10 minutes and then beat in the eggs one at a time until the mixture is smooth and glossy. Stir in the cheese and olives.

3 Drop spoonfuls of the mixture on to the prepared tray and bake in the top half of the oven for 10-12 minutes.

4 Switch off the oven, open the door slightly and leave the puffs in the oven for a further 3-5 minutes.
Serve hot or cold.

Fascinating photos

Olive Monkcom from Bexhill-On-Sea, East Sussex, remembers being the belle of the ball nearly 50 years ago…

"In 1953 my husband, Harry, and I were youth hostel wardens working in Keswick, Cumberland. During the winter, when there were fewer holidaymakers and hikers, we used to take part in old time dancing to fill the long, dark evenings.

Our dancing tutor decided that the last meeting of the winter session would be a grand ball to celebrate the coronation of young Queen Elizabeth II earlier in the year. And to make it more of an occasion she decided that everyone should come in period costume.

In 1953 money was in short supply for most of the members, so we had to make do and improvise. I spent hours at my hand-sewing machine, after searching the stalls in Keswick market for suitable, cheap material.

The ball was a glittering occasion in our small market town and the press wrote about it the next day. For the first, and only, time in my life I was the belle of the ball."

TIP TIME
If heavy shopping bags cut through your hands, place a piece of garden hose, split lengthways, underneath the handles to protect your fingers.
Mrs M Ward, Lexden, Colchester

THOUGHT FOR THE WEEK

At Christmas play and make good cheer,
For Christmas comes but once a year.

Thomas Tusser (1520-1580)
English agricultural writer

THIS WEEK IN YOUR GARDEN

A very Happy Christmas to gardeners everywhere…

- Wind can loosen tall rose bushes, allowing ice to form at the base. Prune them down by half.
- Cut a few shoots from winter jasmine, put them in water indoors and you should soon have scented flowers.
- Keep Christmas poinsettias healthy by keeping them in even heat away from draughts. Make sure you mist the leaves regularly.
- Check that anything under glass has adequate ventilation.
- Give yourself a few days off – after all, it is Christmas!

FASCINATING PHOTOS

Violet Hawley from Bognor Regis, West Sussex, enjoyed being part of an amateur dramatic group when she was 22…

"Fifty years ago I was a telephonist and joined a concert party made up of mostly telephone and Post Office workers.

"We had great fun entertaining all over London and our favourite venue was the old people's home in Balls Pond Road. We had to use steps at the side of the stage to change on and the curtains were so full of dust I thought my hay fever would stop me being able to sing my solo piece.

"This picture was taken in 1949 at a dress rehearsal. The girls are wearing black bra tops and pants with short pink skirts and the boys are wearing top hats and tails. We copied the ideas for the costumes from a Follies programme in London. I'm the one on the far left."

FROM ME TO YOU

A Merry Christmas
Last year, I had to spend Christmas Day on my own. And I sat and counted my blessings:

- I had a roof over my head – I was not homeless.
- I was warm and comfortable – I was not penniless.
- I was not suffering because of flooding – I live on a hill.
- I had a radio, television and my dear cat for company – I was not lonely.
- It was a beautiful sunny day – it was raining elsewhere.
- I had four telephone calls from friends, wishing me a Merry Christmas.

In all, I had a lovely day!

Freda Guest, Stourbridge,
West Midlands

TIP TIME

Save the trays from gift boxes of chocolates and use them in the freezer to make ice cubes.

Jocelyn Fairbrother,
Boston, Lincs

HEALTH CHECK

Eat, drink and be merry!
Plates piled with turkey and stuffing; sherry, wine, a beer in the evening, Christmas cake, mince pies, chocolates, Turkish delight, nuts, figs and dates. We can indulge ourselves once a year but after the presents have been opened and the turkey picked over, it's time to get your coat on!

However great the temptation to doze in front of the fire, while there's still daylight left, get out for a stroll. It needn't be very far but the fresh air will do you a power of good. You'll meet little ones trying out new bikes and you'll be able to wish your neighbours Happy Christmas!

THIS WEEK THROUGH THE YEARS

- **25 December, 1914** British and German soldiers facing each other in the trenches briefly suspended hostilities and played football together to celebrate Christmas.
- **25 December, 1977** The Morecambe and Wise Christmas Show, famously featuring newscaster Angela Rippon in a spectacular high-kicking dance routine, was screened.
- **30 December, 1942** Frank Sinatra made his singing debut at New York's Paramount Theatre.
- **30 December, 1975** International Women's Year ended with the introduction of the Sex Discrimination Act and the Equal Pay Act.

RECIPE CORNER

Not turkey again!

If you were catering for friends or family over the festive season, come Boxing Day, you're probably wondering why on earth you bought such a huge turkey! Here are a few ideas on how to make the most of those leftovers:

● Cream a little Stilton (or any blue cheese) with a little butter to soften. Add a few chopped walnuts if you have any. Spread the cheese mix on thick slices of turkey breast and grill until bubbling. Split a French baguette or soft roll and fill with the turkey, crisp lettuce and mayonnaise.

● Cut thick slices of turkey breast and place on a grill rack. Cover with a dollop of pesto and slices of your favourite melting cheese. Grill until the cheese

bubbles and browns. Serve with salad.

● For the ultimate turkey sandwich, fill brown bread spread with mayonnaise with leftover turkey and grated apple mixed with a little cranberry sauce and a few chopped walnuts. It makes a delicious filling.

● The leftover brown meat works well in a creamy curry – don't go to the trouble of making your own curry paste, shop-bought ones are excellent. Serve with a yoghurt.

● Once you're down to the carcass, use it as the base for a delicious soup. Break up the carcass and place it in a large pot with a chopped carrot, quartered onion, chopped celery stalk, sliced leek, a pinch of dried herbs and generous seasoning. Pour on enough water to cover, bring to simmering point, skim and cook for 2 hours. Strain. Sweat onion and leek in turkey dripping and add to stock with chopped carrots and swede. Simmer until vegetables are soft before puréeing.

GO ON, SMILE!

Driving dilemma

A friend of mine was driving through Oxfordshire recently when suddenly her car ground to a halt beside a grassy verge. After the initial panic she calmed down, reached for her mobile phone and called the emergency services.

"Whereabouts are you?" inquired the AA man. "I have no idea," she replied. Suddenly, she noticed a large sign by the side of the road about 50 yards away. She asked the AA man to hold the line, got out of her car, read the sign hurriedly and dashed back to her car.

"Hello! I'm at a place called Loose Chippings," she replied.
Ruby Debnam, Ilford, Essex

IT'S IN THE STARS

Patrick Arundell looks to the heavens to predict what's in store for you this month

SAGITTARIUS (23 November – 21 December)
Your ability to link well with others enhances friendships and any group projects you're involved with. Something you've long worked towards can now pay off.

CAPRICORN (22 December – 20 January)
You are reluctant to join in the Christmas spirit, but by the end of the month you'll end up as the life and soul of the party.

AQUARIUS (21 January – 19 February)
Your independent nature reigns until the final run-up to Christmas, after which spending time with loved ones is essential.

PISCES (20 February – 20 March)
The spotlight will fall on you this month. Enjoy the moment.

ARIES (21 March – 20 April)
The passionate side of your nature needs to be harnessed. Be diplomatic.

TAURUS (21 April – 21 May)
Attention to detail is required. Look after the small things and the bigger picture will take care of itself.

GEMINI (22 May – 21 June)
A smooth relationship is essential but this will require give and take, especially financial.

CANCER (22 June – 23 July)
Although a health, diet or fitness matter might require attention, you'll have the drive to get this sorted out.

LEO (24 July – 23 August)
The more gregarious side of your nature comes through in time for Christmas, but someone may feel you're too frivolous.

VIRGO (24 August – 23 September)
Time spent with family and friends at home provides an oasis from outside pressures.

LIBRA (24 September – 23 October)
If anyone expects too much from you, stand your ground and you'll gain their respect.

SCORPIO (24 October – 22 November)
Be open-minded and flexible and you could be in a position to gain financially.

HOUSEWIFE'S CHOICE

Robert Opie takes a nostalgic peek at shopping-basket bygones

MILK TRAY

Cadburys created a new assortment of chocolates in 1914 to be sold loose from the tray, simply called Tray Chocolates. The following year a Milk Tray was introduced. Chocolates sold in boxes were comparatively expensive, but when both milk and plain Tray Chocolates were sold in their own boxes from 1916, the additional cost of the box was kept to a minimum, which increased the potential market. Chocolate was still a luxury, while toffee was a more affordable sweet. In order to emphasise the fact that Milk Tray was reasonably priced, each pack had the slogan 'the box for the pocket' upon it.

OVALTINE

First marketed as Ovomaltine in 1904, this concentrated extraction from malt, milk and eggs, flavoured with cocoa, was created by Dr George Wander, a Swiss chemist. The British company was formed in 1909 and a factory was built at Kings Langley, Buckinghamshire, four years later. In 1935, the League of Ovaltineys was born, broadcasting on Radio Luxembourg on Sunday evenings. It became a national institution that every child aspired to join – reading the comic, singing the song, learning the secret sign and wearing the badges. By the end of the decade there were five million club members.

SILENT NIGHT

Avis Randall tells us of the history of her favourite Christmas carol and the memories it evokes for her

Christmas is here again and churches and school assembly halls will ring with the words and music of Silent Night, the best-loved Christmas carol of all time.

Silent Night was written in December 1818 by a parish priest, Father Joseph Mohr, in the tiny village of Oberndorf, 15 miles north of Salzburg in Austria and first performed at St Nikolaus Church. Father Mohr was convinced that his preparations for the festive season were ruined when, on Christmas Eve, he discovered that mice had gnawed through the church organ's bellows. Without an organ there would be no music and without music, there could be no service.

That night, unable to sleep, he glanced out of his bedroom window at the peaceful village and the snow-covered rooftops bathed in moonlight. Suddenly, in the quiet night, the words came to him, 'All is calm, All is bright.'

Through the night, he wrote the words to a carol that could be sung without organ music. The next day he showed them to his organist, Franz Gruber, and together they set the words to a tune that could be sung with only a guitar accompaniment. It was a great success and its popularity grew. By the end of the 19th century, the Christmas carol was known around the world – translated into more than 50 languages.

The first time the carol's beauty registered with me was in December 1946. I was at a Christmas service at my village church in north Somerset and we were joined by a group of German prisoners of war.

Our vicar made a point of welcoming them and asked us all to do the same. Many of the congregation rejected this invitation to greet our former enemies and silently but resolutely declined to extend a hand of friendship; the old soldiers, the widows and those who'd fought the Germans in the First World War on the bloody battlefields of the Somme and Passchendaele. They had seen too much and suffered too much to be softened by the sentimentality of Christmas – though it was a peaceful one with war at an end.

We younger ones accepted the presence of the young Germans and harboured no grudge. It was a break from the usual routine and in any case, none of the lads looked like the monsters which wartime posters had led us to believe they were. School lectures had warned us of German spies, (who often went about in pairs, we'd heard, sometimes dressed as nuns).

The vicar invited the Germans to sing a carol in their own tongue. They chose Silent Night – Stille Nacht. I doubt it softened the hearts of those who hated the Germans. We discovered the young lads were as glad as us that the war was over and they'd soon be returning to their homeland to see their loved ones again.

There was another memorable occasion when this beautiful carol made a great impact on me. It was 1965 and my son was in his first year at a boys' grammar school in Bristol and my friend and I went to their Christmas service. We found ourselves seats near the front, all the better to see our boys – 11-year-old shrimps!

The carol was announced – Silent Night – to be sung by a first-year pupil. I listened to the little boy's sweet voice trilling out into the large school hall and my eyes filled with tears. Tears, remembering that special Christmas two decades before when German prisoners sang it. And tears of pride because, to my total surprise, the angelic child with the soaring voice was my own little boy – my firstborn son, Nicholas.

In 1914 German soldiers began singing Silent Night in the trenches during the Christmas period. British troops heard the voices, joined in, and for a while the fighting ceased.

In my lifetime, too, there was a memorable evening when I felt as one with those German boys who away from their homes, were united by the peaceful, holy sound of Silent Night.